ANIMAL ALTERITY
Science Fiction and the Question of the Animal

Liverpool Science Fiction Texts and Studies

Editor David Seed, *University of Liverpool*

Editorial Board
Mark Bould, *University of the West of England*
Veronica Hollinger, *Trent University*
Rob Latham, *University of California*
Roger Luckhurst, *Birkbeck College, University of London*
Patrick Parrinder, *University of Reading*
Andy Sawyer, *University of Liverpool*

Recent titles in the series

ANIMAL ALTERITY

Science Fiction and
the Question of the Animal

SHERRYL VINT

LIVERPOOL UNIVERSITY PRESS

First published 2010 by
Liverpool University Press
4 Cambridge Street
Liverpool
L69 7ZU

This paperback edition published 2014.

British Library Cataloguing-in-Publication data
A British Library CIP record is available

ISBN 978-1-84631-815-3 limp

Typeset by Carnegie Book Production, Lancaster
Printed and bound by CPI Group (UK) Ltd, Croydon CR0 4YY

For Richard and Jane,
whose support got me through a difficult time

Contents

Acknowledgements

Research is a collaborative process and I owe many thanks to those who have supported me and challenged me to become a better scholar as I worked on this book. I thank my colleagues in the Department of English at Brock University, especially my chair, Neta Gordon, for creating a supportive and active research culture that enables work like this to get done. I also thank my co-editors of the journal *Extrapolation* – Andrew M. Butler, Michael Levy, Javier A. Martinez and Lisa Yaszek – with whom astute critical exchanges have sharpened my critical skills. I owe thanks also to the members of my theory reading group, Catherine Chaput and David Fancy, who never failed to challenge me to think more critically and respond more fully. I owe most thanks to my frequent collaborator, Mark Bould, whose insights and stylish flair have enlivened my work.

As I worked on this project, I benefitted from the opportunity to exchange ideas with a number of colleagues and comrades in the fields of science fiction studies and human–animal studies. The networks of conferences and email exchanges that support both fields of study have enriched my intellectual experience. An exhaustive list of those from whom I have learned would double the length of this manuscript; yet certain people deserve special mention for the support and friendship they have extended, along with their scholarly expertise. Within the science fiction studies community, I have particularly benefitted from exchanges with Istvan Csicsery-Ronay, Jr, Neil Easterbrook, Carl Freedman, Joan Gordon, Veronica Hollinger, Darren Jorgensen, Rob Latham, Roger Luckhurst, Farah Mendelsohn, Helen Merrick, China Miéville and Joe Sutliff Sanders. Within the field of animal studies, thanks are due to Phillip Armstrong, Erica Fudge, Carol Gigliotti, Susan McHugh and Annie Potts.

Enormous thanks are due to Lorna Toolis and her staff at the Merrill Collection of Science Fiction at the Toronto Public Library. Their generous efforts on my behalf allowed me to include many works from early pulp sf within my analysis and enriched the project greatly.

On a more personal level, I thank my parents, whose air miles funded the travel necessary for research during the early stages of this project. I thank Terence Fowler for helping me rediscover my motivation when I thought I had lost it. Many of those already mentioned have also provided friendship and 'life support' (and you know who you are); additionally, thanks are due under this category to Ann Howey, Richard Nemesvari, Jane Strickler and Karys van de Pitte.

Finally, I thank the editorial team at Liverpool University Press for their enthusiastic support of this project, and the press's anonymous readers for helpful comments on the manuscript. I would also like to thank Lisa LaFramboise for indexing extraordinaire and other feats of editorial genius.

Of course, although my work was strengthened by my exchanges with all of these people, any errors or oversights that remain are mine alone.

The research for writing this book was supported by a grant from the Social Sciences and Humanities Research Council of Canada. I thank them for their generous support. Parts of Chapter 5 were published in a different form in 'Species and Species Being: Alienated Subjectivity and the Commodification of Animals' as part of the collection *Red Planets: Marxists on Science Fiction and Fantasy*, published by Pluto Press. I thank them for permission to reprint this material.

Introduction

Animal Alterity: Science Fiction and Human–Animal Studies

The project of bringing together science fiction[1] (sf) and research in the emerging field of human–animal studies (HAS) might at first seem counterintuitive; indeed, when I spoke of my interest in researching animals in sf, a number of colleagues assured me that there probably were not that many. Although this book, by providing an overview of the many ways in which animals are present in sf, shows the degree to which such a conclusion is wrong, it is nonetheless not an unreasonable one for many readers of the genre to have reached. One does not tend to think of animals as *belonging* in sf for a number of reasons related both to the genre and to the assumptions that we make about animals and their place in Western cultural life. Animals, once central to human quotidian life, have steadily disappeared from human experience with the rise of modernity, whose processes of industrialisation, urbanisation and commodification have affected animal lives as much as human ones. Twenty-first-century society is no less dependent upon animal products than was the seventeenth (although many of the specific products may have changed, such as the replacement of animals used for transportation or the rise of animals used for biomedical research); yet a crucial difference between our use of animals and that of earlier cultural moments is that the use of animals in contemporary society is increasingly invisible: they are hidden away in laboratories and factory farms; slaughtered at mass disassembly plants and transformed into sanitised packages of meat; visible in mediated forms on Animal Planet or National Geographic television, but purged from city geographies. It is then not surprising that readers do not intuitively associate sf, 'the literature of technologically saturated societies' (Luckhurst 3), with the presence of animals.

Yet there are many reasons to connect sf and HAS. Both are interested in foundational questions about the nature of human existence and sociality. Both are concerned with the construction of alterity and what it means for subjects to be thus positioned as outsiders. Both take seriously the question of what it means to communicate with a being whose embodied, communicative, emotional and cultural life – perhaps even physical environment – is radically different from our own. One of the premises of this study, then, is that sf and HAS have much to offer one another: sf has a long history of thinking about alterity, subjectivity and the limits of the human which is precisely the terrain explored by much HAS, while HAS offers new and innovative ways to think about sf's own engagement with such issues, situating it within a material history in which we have always-already been living with 'alien' beings. Additionally, sf's interest in thinking through the social consequences of developments in science and technology intersects usefully with key questions being worked out in HAS in an era of genetic transformation of animal species into 'products' more suitable for human consumption, 'factories' to produce useful chemicals or 'models' to study disease. A central concern of HAS – and of this text – is the extent of our ethical duty to non-humans with whom we share the planet, and both HAS and sf have much to say on this topic. Finally, in the past thirty years our discursive and material relationships with animals have changed radically, resulting in, on the one hand, what Derrida has called '*unprecedented* proportions of ... subjection of the animal' (*The Animal* 25), and on the other increasing knowledge of animal cognition, communication skill and tool use, all of which reveal the tenuous nature of the firm and singular boundary between human and animal existence.[2]

Sf contains many animals and a plethora of perspectives on the nature of animal existence, and is an excellent tool for thinking through the implications of these cultural changes. The texts explored in the following chapters have no single perspective on the question of animals and their place in our social world, but rather demonstrate the range of ways humans have thought about this issue, sometimes challenging conventional wisdom and advocating a position of sympathy for the animal, and at other times embodying cultural anxieties about potential erosion of the human–animal boundary, a line which has been used to secure notions of human subjectivity since at least Plato. Sometimes the animals seem incidental to a text and their presence offers us a window on their ubiquity in laboratory life, such as the farcical 'The Feline Light and Power Company Is Organized', by Jacque Morgan, which depicts an attempt to produce cheap power through the static electricity generated by 'a plurality of cats' (320) trapped in a room. Similarly 'The Hungry Guinea Pig', by Miles J. Breur, is more interested in the details of the massive military assault necessary to destroy a giant guinea pig that has escaped from the pineal gland research lab than it is in the animal's experience, even though the guinea pig is described as causing destruction through panic and fright, not malice. W. Alexander's 'The Dog's Sixth Sense' does not even include the entire animal in the story, but instead focuses on the detective who becomes telepathic when he is given dog's rather than pig's eyes in his transplant surgery because he gains with the dog's eyes its ability to read human thoughts. Although this story is premised on the observation that dogs seem better attuned to human communication than do pigs (which might lead one to knowledge of dogs' cognitive skills), the story is not interested in exploring the ethics of sacrificing such creatures for their organs (the intelligence of pigs, the usual donors, is even further removed from the story's view).

More often, though, sf stories include animals because they are interested in what animals experience and in how our social relations with them might be transformed. Clare Winger Harris's 'The Miracle of the Lily' (1928), for example, ironically draws attention to the world we make through an ethic of 'man' as 'master of the world with apparently none to dispute his right' (49); domination is taken to such an extreme in a war against insects for control of crops that humans destroy 'every living bit of greenery, so that in all the world there was no food for the insect pests' (49). Often stories explore the perspective of reversing the human–animal hierarchy, such as F. Pragnell's 'The Essence of Life' (1933). Humans are taken to visit a cat-eyed Jovian society by its pets, human-like beings who do not resent their subservient status but rather love their masters, who 'are very humane and gentle, and have made poverty and want unknown amongst us' (443). The visitors offer 'armies and guns' to help the human-like pets escape subservience, which is rejected as 'obscene and traitorous' and as evidence that the Masters were right that on Earth 'we shall find a race of men, lustful for power for its own sake, always ready to quarrel for the sake of quarreling' (443). The humans are there, it transpires, to be interviewed so that the Jovians might decide whether humans should be exterminated for the safety of the solar system, or whether 'by careful selective breeding and developing, and above all, by the help of the Essence of Life, they might develop into quite unobjectionable and even pleasant creatures, like the domesticated men of Jupiter' (443). At times writers are even more directly polemical in their use of sf premises to question the treatment of actual animals in contemporary society. In an afterword to *Slave Ship* (1957), a novel about military use of animals to run unshielded nuclear weapons vehicles, Frederick Pohl draws his readers' attention to existing research on animal language, then rejects the idea that humans can be defined as exclusive tool users or exclusive language users; instead, he suggests, 'Perhaps there is room for a third definition of Man, not much better than the other two, but very likely not much worse: 'Man, the snobbish animal … who clings to evolution's ladder one rung higher than the brutes beneath and saws away, saws away at the ladder beneath in an attempt to sever the connections between himself and the soulless, speechless, brainless Beast … that does not, in fact, exist' (147, ellipses in original).

Grant Morrison's *We3* (2005) similarly explores the potential for sf to query the ethics of using animals within military applications, embedding his tale of cyborg, weaponised animals within larger discourses of the human–animal boundary which structure twenty-first-century life. A graphic novel of three chapters, *We3* begins each with a 'missing pet' poster of one of its animal protagonists: the dog Bandit who becomes 1; the cat, Tinker, or 2; and the rabbit, Pirate, later 3. These posters draw our attention to the widely disparate ways animals are integrated into human society. The posters show the animals in middle-class, domestic comfort, part of the home and family. The text indicates that these are individualised animals, named, known and loved by their owners: Bandit is 'friendly and approachable', Tinker's individual markings are described in detail in text whose i's are dotted with hearts, and Pirate 'likes lettuce and carrots'. These posters are in stark contrast to the rest of the text in which we see the animals on their last mission, encased within armour and able to talk via implants in their heads. They are to be decommissioned, that is, killed, as their model is now obsolete. A sympathetic trainer enables their escape from the lab, and much of the rest of the book is about their attempts to find home which they define as 'RUN NO MORE'. The contrast between pet animals (part of human social networks) and numbered lab animals (instrumentalised and turned into things) is made all the more poignant by 1's continual anxiety about whether he is 'GUD DOG' and especially by his evident desire to help the humans he encounters, even though they are trying to kill him. In the end, he reclaims his name and sheds the armour, concluding that it 'IS COAT NOT "BANDIT"' that is bad. While Pirate is killed, Bandit and Tinker, purged of their cyborg enhancements, find a metaphorical home with a homeless man who recognises that they are not dangerous but merely outcasts like him. This draws our attention to the relationship between ways of marginalising and exploiting animals and the ways in which the discourse of species is used to animalise and marginalise some humans.

As Morrison's tale makes clear, one of the things sf can do is convey some sense of the animal's experience, in this case through the *novum* of technology which enables the animal to talk. Morrison's use of all caps, phonetic spelling and numerals (for example, 2 for the word 'to' as well as for Tinker's new name) visually conveys animals' liminal category in human culture: they are similar but not identical to us, caught up within human language and other semiotic systems but not native speakers, precariously positioned along the axis of the binary pair nature/culture. And yet literary representations of animals are precisely that, *representations*, filtered through human consciousness and language. Must such representations be rejected, then, as necessarily false or at the very least limited, able to tell us only what we think of animal life and nothing about actual animal experience?

J.M. Coetzee explores the issue of animal experience and literary representation in *The Lives of Animals* (1999), the printed version of his Tanner Lectures on Human Values, and further in *Elizabeth Costello* (2003). In the Tanner Lectures, Coetzee constructs a story around the character of Elizabeth Costello, a novelist also called upon to give public lectures; the bulk of the text comprises the two lectures she delivers on animal rights, one called 'The Philosophers and the Animals' and the other 'The Poets and the Animals'; the expanded novel, *Elizabeth Costello*, includes this material and further background to Costello's life and her struggles to understand the role of literature in ethical and intellectual life. Whether or not literature can convey some truth of animal existence, and in so doing enable its readers to perceive them as fellow beings and thereby to heal the instrumentalised and damaging relationship that Western culture has with animal life, is one of Costello's central concerns. Coetzee's own investments are more difficult to ascertain as Costello's viewpoint is both expounded and challenged throughout the text, but at root they are interested in the same issue: the power of literature to shape subjectivity and all that flows from it. Costello refers to this as our capacity for sympathetic imagination.

Costello argues that the tradition of philosophy has failed to enquire about animal life and instead has used animals as a foil against which to define the distinct features of the human, a position very similar to that taken by Derrida in his posthumously published *The Animal That Therefore I Am* (2008). Derrida, too, divides human conceptions of the animal into two camps: philosophers 'who have no doubt seen, observed, analyzed, reflected on the animal, but who have never been *seen seen* by the animal' and thus 'have taken no account of the fact that what they call "animal" could *look at* them, and *address* them from down there, from a wholly other origin' (13); and the poets 'who admit to taking upon themselves the address that an animal addresses to them', but whose engagement with questions of animal–human relations is never from the point of view of 'theoretical, philosophical, or juridical man, or even as citizen' (14). Derrida's point, ultimately, is that the entire discourse of philosophy and ethics must be reconceived if one conceptualises the animal – as poetry does – as another subject who looks upon and addresses the human; such thinking, he says, is 'what philosophy has, essentially, had to deprive itself of' (7).

Combining the poetic with the philosophical or juridical, then, will enable us to recognise the degree to which our entire philosophical tradition of subjectivity has been premised upon the separation of human from animal. Sf, more than any other literature, can defy this separation because its generic premises enable us to imagine the animal quite literally looking at and addressing us from a non-anthropocentric perspective, as in *We3*'s talking animals or the cat-like aliens of 'The Essence of Life'. Further, the ideal that sf should in some way reflect both the content of current scientific knowledge and the scientific technique of logical extrapolation – although of course never rigorously enforced in the genre – means that the genre's imaginings of animal being are inclined to incorporate knowledge gained from ethology (the scientific study of animal behaviour) and thus to approximate what we know of animals' experiences of their worlds. Such an impulse is present even in early sf written before the development of such holistic methods of studying animal behaviour.

For example, Edward Rementer's 'The Space Bender' posits a society of intelligent beings evolved from cats rather than from primates, and speculates on the different cultural world that might emerge under such conditions. Careful to avoid anthropocentric hubris, the story's protagonist concludes,

> I could not decide if our system or theirs was better. The callous selfishness of King Tabi in regard to the welfare of his people was truly appalling, but, as he, himself, pithily remarked, is our paternalism altruistic or does it largely gratify a simian desire to poke our noses into some other fellow's business? (847)[3]

Thus sf offers a wider scope than does most literature for enabling animal agency to become part of the quotidian world, as well as space to attempt to grasp animals as beings in their own right rather than as beings defined through their place in human cultural systems. In addition to this specific concern with science, sf's long history of exploring questions of alterity and particularly of the boundary between human and other sentient beings – frequently explored through robot or AI characters – further positions it as uniquely suited to interrogating the human–animal boundary.

Why is it important that such ideas are explored through sf as a literature? Elizabeth Costello insists that it is only through the capacities cultivated by literature that we become able to be seen by the animal, to engage with it as a fellow being. She rejects the perspective of 'behaviourists' who limit understanding to 'a process of creating abstract models and then testing those models against reality. What nonsense. We understand by immersing ourselves and our intelligence in complexity' (Coetzee 108). Thus only the worldbuilding of fiction, something at which sf excels, is adequate for conveying the fullness of life before it has been contained within the reductive categories we use as shorthand to constrain the complexity of the world into units that can be grasped by rational thought. It is never entirely clear the degree to which Coetzee endorses Costello's position, but at the very least we can conclude that the question of whether literature enables us imaginatively to inhabit the animal's perspective is one that compels us to re-examine literary realism more broadly. This understanding of literature is similar to Derrida's suggestions that his entire work has been about the question of the animal's place in philosophical systems and notions of human subjectivity, that it 'was destined in advance, and quite deliberately, to cross the frontiers of anthropocentrism, the limits of a language confined to human words and discourse' (*The Animal* 104). Derrida sees this as not necessarily a question of giving speech back to animals but 'of acceding to a thinking, however fabulous and chimerical it might be, that thinks the absence of the name and of the word otherwise and as something other than a privation' (*The Animal* 48). Costello, writing in a more passionate idiom, puts it thus: 'If I do not convince you, that is because my words, here, lack the power to bring home to you the wholeness, the unabstracted, unintellectual nature, of that animal being. That is why I urge you to read the poets who return the living, electric being to language' (Coetzee 111).

Erica Fudge points out that 'a humanist arrogance lurks dangerously nearby' (*Pets* 46) the argument that human imaginative power is unlimited and might effectively capture an animal's perspective. In *Elizabeth Costello,* Coetzee positions this issue of the poet's access to animal experience within a broader series of deliberations which impel us toward the conclusion that, however imperfect, literature's ability to convey the experience of the animal being is no more or less problematic than any literary representation. Costello gains fame as a novelist for a book written from the perspective of Molly Bloom, one that counters the canonical representation of this woman's perspective as conveyed by a male writer. As one reader tells Costello, reading this book made her realise 'that Molly didn't have to be limited in the way Joyce had made her to be, that she could equally well be an intelligent woman with an interest in music and a circle of friends of her own and a daughter with whom she shared confidences' (14). One might suggest that Costello was able to offer something of Molly's perspective that Joyce could not because, as a woman, she shares an embodied experience with Molly, unlike Joyce. While there is a degree of insight conveyed by this fact, at the same time Coetzee is careful to remind us that this is not the whole story either, first by a series of exchanges Costello has with an African writer which reveals the problems of becoming the voice of his 'people' for a white audience, and second through Costello's insistence that 'If I can think my way into the existence of a being who has never existed, then I can think my way into the existence of a bat or a chimpanzee or an oyster, any being with whom I share the substrate of life' (80). The embodied, vulnerable being that we share with animals is emphasised elsewhere by Costello and, it would seem, also by Coetzee, reminding us that humans, too, are animals, despite a long philosophical tradition, mostly strongly associated with Descartes and Heidegger (in different ways), that insists upon a separate kind of being for human subjects.[4]

Part of rethinking the human–animal boundary, then, is recognising the embodied nature of human existence, that *Homo sapiens* is a creature of the same biological origin as the plethora of species we label 'animal' and that we have greater or lesser degrees of kinship and common experience with them. Equally important, however, is recognising that the beings we call 'animals' are also inevitably caught up in human social systems and the language we use to create and give meaning to the world. On both a material level – what habitat remains, whether they spend their lives in captivity or 'wild', and if 'captive' whether as laboratory tools or pampered pets – and a discursive one – whether they are companions or pests, fellow beings or packaged meat, 'noble' sign of a threatened wilderness or 'foreign' species invading a human-designated boundary of indigenous locale – animal lives are complexly interrelated with human culture. How we think about animals affects how we live with them, and how we live with them determines who they are, socially and biologically. Thus, in thinking about the ability of literature to convey new insight into animal being and potentially to reconfigure human–animal social relations, we must 'acknowledge the limitations of our own perspective, but simultaneously accept that what we can achieve with those limitations is important and worthwhile' (Fudge *Animal* 159). In so doing, it is essential that we remain cognisant of the fact that 'our perception is based upon our limitations' and animal lives 'exceed our abilities to think about them' (Fudge *Animal* 160). In examining sf representations of animals, then, my focus will be twofold: on the one hand, such representations can provide insight into the way the discourse of species informs other ideologies at work, often opening the texts up to new meanings not evident when they are read without the insights of HAS; on the other, some sf texts themselves perform the work of HAS, striving to gesture beyond normative conceptions of animal and human being and thereby to glimpse, however imperfectly, something of their lives beyond the potentialities currently available to them in Western social relations.

Both Elizabeth Costello and Derrida are also interested in common vulnerability as one of the ways that humans and animals share embodied being. For Derrida, this critique is part of his deconstruction of the Cartesian *cogito* as model for human subjectivity, in a move in which Descartes abstract[s] from the 'I am' his own living body, which, in a way, he objectivizes as a machine or corpse (these are his words); so much so that his 'I am' can apprehend and present itself only from the perspective of this potential cadaverization, that is to say, from the perspective of an 'I am mortal,' or 'already dead,' or 'destined to die,' indeed 'toward death'. (*The Animal* 72)

Similarly, Costello argues,

The knowledge we have is not abstract – 'all human beings are mortal, I am a human being, therefore I am mortal' – but embodied. For a moment we *are* that knowledge. We live the impossible: we live beyond our death, look back on it, yet look back as only a dead self can. (Coetzee 77)

Thinking about alterity, ethics and literature through the perspective of HAS, then, has wider implications than merely a new way of thinking about animal being – although this too is an important site of ethical intervention for many working in the field. Thinking about our relationships with animals – social, conceptual, material – equally forces us to rethink our understanding of what it means to be human and the social world that we make based on such conceptions. In reconnecting with animals, we are also reconnecting with our embodied being, what might be thought of as our animal nature: this new way of conceptualising human subjectivity and our relation with the rest of the living world thus has important affinities with scholarship on posthumanism.

In an essay that has become central to the discipline of HAS, 'Why Look at Animals?', John Berger argues that industrial capitalism has radically transformed human's relationship with the natural world. When animals and humans look at one another, Berger suggests, it is across a gap of non-comprehension and thus when 'man' is *being seen* by the animal, he is being seen as his surroundings are seen by him'; that is, humans recognise that animals have a point of view regarding us, just as we see them as part of our surroundings. In pre-industrial times, Berger argues, humans acknowledged the mutuality of this gaze, grasping animals as both familiar and distinct, as having 'a power … comparable with human power but never coinciding with it' (3). As animals were gradually removed from our day-to-day experience through urbanisation, industrialism and other changes to the landscape wrought by capitalism which has eroded animal habitats and populations, we no longer encounter animals as fellow creatures who return our gaze. Instead, we see them in spaces that emphasise the radical disproportion in human–animal social relations: spaces such as zoos where animals are compelled to be visible in circumstances in which everything that would enable them to appear as fellow beings with their own perspective on the world and on us – freedom of movement, the opportunity to interact with other species, the habitat which is part of their lifeworld – has been stripped away. In such circumstances, humans are compelled to be like the philosophers critiqued by Derrida, able to look at the animal but not to be seen by it. Thus Berger concludes that the zoo is not a site of human–animal interaction, but rather 'a monument to the impossibility of such encounters' (19).

For Berger, capitalism has irredeemably isolated man, who can no longer share an exchange of mutual looks with other species, whom he has marginalised or destroyed. Derrida begins his own reflections on philosophy and animals with an attempt to return to this site of exchange, reflecting upon the look of his cat, which he is careful to stress is *'this* irreplaceable living being' and not 'the exemplar of a species called "cat," even less so of an "animal" genus or kingdom' (*The Animal* 9). To understand being from the point of view of mutual exchange of gazes, Derrida insists, one must take as axiomatic that the cat is fully as individuated, as much both part of her species and a being of 'unsubstitutable singularity' (9) as is Derrida himself. He acknowledges that the cat 'has its point of view regarding me. The point of view of the absolute other, and nothing will have ever given me more food for thinking through this absolute alterity' (11) than encounters which enable him not only to see his cat, but also to see himself being seen by the cat. Such encounters facilitate an ability to see 'the abyssal limit of the human: the inhuman or the ahuman, the ends of man, that is to say, the bordercrossing from which vantage man dares to announce himself to himself, thereby calling himself by the name that he believes he gives himself' (12). In other words, thinking through the concept of 'the animal' as well as through our relationships with material animals is indispensable for grasping what it means to be human, first because the concept 'animal' has always been the ground for production of 'the human', and second because in examining the real, material, complex existences of other species – as well as our own – we can also begin to see the ends of a certain historical concept of the human, as Foucault described in *The Order of Things*. But Derrida's critique is more radical yet, for he also incorporates knowledge of the observed capacities of animals instead of relying solely on philosophical abstractions, and comes to the conclusion that not only are humans not alone in possessing the capacities thereby deemed 'proper' to humankind, but in fact for the most part humans do not achieve the qualities they ascribe to themselves with the name 'human'.

Derrida uses the human–animal boundary to ask questions about subjectivity that are very similar to those raised by critics such as N. Katherine Hayles under the rubric of posthumanism. Just as Hayles found in sf a tool for thinking through questions of embodiment, subjectivity and ethics in concrete ways, so too might HAS turn to sf to explore the issues raised by Berger and Derrida. In sf we can once again find ourselves confronted by the gaze of 'absolute alterity', an other who looks back at us from its own point of view and often one whom we must acknowledge as having power comparable if not identical to our own. The dialectic between similarity and difference that humans experience as we come face-to-face with animals is part of what Berger feels has been lost with industrial capitalism which has transformed them from fellow subjects into objects of consumption. This process has dramatically intensified in the past twenty-five years with genetic manipulation producing patented living beings that from one point of view cannot be regarded as other than objects. Animals modified for medical research, for pharming production, to survive the extremely restrictive conditions of factory farming without injury or for use in xenotransplantation research are patented creations of human culture that would not exist in nature and often cannot survive outside the artificially controlled conditions for which they are made.

Animals in sf can return to us a face-to-face encounter with another being whom we regard as a fellow subject. For example, Roger Zelazny's *Eye of Cat* (1982) is told in part from the point of view of a telepathic, polymorphic being called Cat. Cat has been imprisoned in a zoo by animal-trapper William Blackhorse Singer, who supplies the exotic zoos of this future with animals from many planets. Like most of the sf I will discuss, Zelazny's novel uses the tropes of sf in ways that simultaneously draw attention to our social relations with the 'real' aliens with whom we share this planet (i.e., other species) and at the same time betrays in other ways some of the as-yet-unexamined assumptions about species and other difference that inform the human–animal boundary. The novel sets up a problematic equation, for example, between Cat as the last of his species (his planet has been destroyed since his capture) and Singer as the last Navajo, an authentic practitioner of the old ways who has made it into the twenty-first century through a combination of longevity treatments and the time-dilation effects of FTL travel. This parallel reinforces a colonialist history of seeing native peoples, like animals, as insufficiently possessing the land which then justifies its appropriation and also their treatment as less-than-fully-human subjects. Yet at the same time Zelazny interweaves traditional Navajo tales within his futuristic text, showing a respect for Navajo cultural traditions in the resemblance he demonstrates between them and sf as two ways of explaining the world through story. The Navajo tales also reveal the quite different way in which human–animal relations are conceptualised within native traditions, a mutual respect that resembles the ideal Berger describes.[5] Further, *Eye of Cat* both offers

Cat as an exception to the normalised incarceration of animals in zoos – Singer apologises and offers reparations once he works out that Cat is sentient and thus not 'really' an animal – yet at the same times challenges our ability to know and judge sentience and thus to 'correctly' make decisions about which beings might 'ethically' be put in zoos. Further, news clips inserted in the text gesture toward a world in which significant changes have restructured the human–animal boundary in this future: dolphins are settling a lawsuit with a canning firm, and a composition by a humpback whale will premiere at the New York Philharmonic, but whooping crane populations will be culled. *Eye of Cat* complicates and makes multiple what we now take to be a simple binary division between all humans and all animals. Finally, the novel makes an effort to convey that Cat's consciousness is sentient but different from our own through sections of text expressing Cat's point of view that are fragmented streams of consciousness without clear word divisions, similar to ee cummings' poetry.

Eye of Cat successfully captures the dialectic of the human–animal relation that Berger feels has been lost with the rise of industrial capitalism that doomed humans to isolation in the universe. The emergence of sf during this same period might thus be understood as at least in part a desire to re-establish a world shared with other beings. Animals thus 'haunt'[6] sf, always there in the shadows behind the alien or the android with whom we fantasise exchange. Another spectre, anthropomorphism, also lingers about HAS and sf. Precisely how like or unlike us are animals, and what barriers does this pose to our ability to have an exchange across the border of alterity? This question has troubled animal-rights activists and defenders of anthropocentrism alike, and is one of the most contentious in the field of HAS. Although anthropocentrism has consistently been vilified since the rise of a culture of science, it nonetheless has proven impossible to stamp out, from the plethora of humanised animals in children's literature, to a consumer culture of pet ownership which interpellates them into such human practices as birthday celebrations and babysitting, and even to research such as Sue Savage-Rumbaugh's work on communication in primates that is attempting to establish a shared human-bonobo culture. As Derrida's interrogation of philosophy further points out, at issue in discussions of anthropocentrism is not merely whether or not it is acceptable to attribute some 'human' characteristic – such as consciousness or language or emotion – to animals, but rather the more far-reaching question of the validity of the grounds upon which humans attribute certain capacities to themselves. Daston and Mitman credit the waning of anthropomorphic understandings of the world to the rise of the modern culture of science,[7] but further point out that 'despite the official ban on anthropomorphism in science, thinking with animals permeated practice in the field and the lab' (8).

Thus, the 'fallacy' of anthropomorphism is an alibi for human behaviour. We construct animals as radically unlike ourselves in order to justify our behaviour toward them: they do not feel pain but merely respond to stimuli as do automatons, says Descartes; they do not experience personal attachment and thus do not suffer when separated from their young, says the dairy industry; they have no capacity for consciousness and hence cannot experience boredom, say the factory farm and research industries. The challenge, then, is to pay attention to the actual lives of animals, to observe carefully the times at which it is appropriate to attribute to them motivations for behaviour that are similar to our motivations for similar behaviour, and times when their differences of embodiment, sensory organs and other capacities make such attributions unlikely.[8] Although there is a risk of what Frans de Waal has called anthropodenial in our refusal to see the ways in which fellow primates and fellow mammals in particular are similar to humans, at the same time we need to be careful that in the rush to embrace similarity we do not erase specificity.

If literature in general, and sf in particular, are to offer us something of the animal's experience and thus enable us to recover an encounter of mutual exchange of gazes, we must be attuned to resisting the two fallacies of too inclusive an anthropomorphism and too constant an anthropodenial. Beyond the rationale that anthropodenial provides for our continued exploitation of animals, resistance to anthropomorphism is also motivated by a concern about the historical ways in which the discourse of species has been used similarly to exploit other humans animalised through this discourse, the two most significant historical examples being American enslavement of those of African descent and German extermination of Jews and others. Just as we must avoid extremes of both anthropomorphism and anthropodenial in trying to work through the place of animals in our ethical and social milieu, so too must we be sensitive to specificity in thinking through the similar, but not identical, exploitation of animalised humans and animals themselves. Often the desire to include animals within the circle of those to whom we owe an ethical duty is seen as a way of humanising these animals, which seems then to imply a shadow double of animalising some humans, particularly given that we live in a world in which many humans continue to be exploited and denigrated by others.[9]

Thomas Nagel's essay 'What Is It Like to Be a Bat' (1974) has become a touchstone in HAS considerations of this problem. In contrast to Coetzee, who suggests that the literary imagination would enable us to capture something of an other's experience, Nagel cautions us to remember the difference between 'what it would be like for *me* to behave as a bat behaves' (439) and what it would be like really to *be* in the way that a bat has being because, although bats have something in common with us, they are also differently embodied, have a different range of activity and a different sensory apparatus, which means that an encounter with them is essentially one with 'a fundamentally *alien* form of life' (438). Nagel further stresses the serendipitous correspondence between the sf imagination and the sort of problematic he is developing by observing that 'in contemplating the bats we are in much the same position that intelligent bats or Martians would occupy if they tried to form a conception of what it was like to be us' (440). The challenge of how to understand the alien, how to convey experience from a non-anthropocentric view, is similarly faced by sf. In *Archaeologies of the Future* (2005), Fredric Jameson connects this struggle to the difficulty of conceiving utopian possibility without allowing it to collapse into a necessarily reductive programme: how to achieve the delicate balance of enough familiarity such that the alien can be comprehensible to the human readers, but yet still incorporate enough alterity in the text such that the alien also pushes us to conceive of the world and ourselves otherwise. Even in sf's failure, then, to fully characterise the alien without reference to the human – a kind of anthropocentrism – Jameson finds a trace of hope, asking, 'What, then, if the alien body were little more than a distorted expression of Utopian possibilities? If its otherness were unknowable because it signified a radical otherness latent in human history and human praxis, rather than the not-I of a physical nature?' (118).

There are parallels to literary representations of animals, all the more so when these representations are within the genre of sf and thus the limits of current human–animal relations can be transcended by imagining the world otherwise, a utopian desire for a world as it might appear had we not founded our subjectivity on the ideal of a radical separation of human from animal, and thus inherited many of the dualisms that structure Western thought: culture over nature, man over woman, coloniser over colonised, capital over labour. Nagel's insistence on the difference between *behaving* as a bat and *experiencing being* as one seems, on one level, to re-establish a radical separation between humans and animals – or at the very least a separation between the specific nature of being among all individual species. At the same time, however, he takes as axiomatic that at least some animals, like humans, do have conscious experience and thus can experience a mental state of being, a connection between human and animal denied by much of the philosophical tradition. Further, as Erica Fudge points out, Nagel 'challenges humanist assumptions about the power of humans to construct and know the world ... we can see that there are animals – many of them living in our homes – who share our world and who escape our understanding' (*Pets* 46), thus moving us closer toward the mutual exchange of gazes which Berger suggests once constructed less damaging human–animal social relations and prevented humans from feeling isolated as a species.

I want to suggest that sf literature is a particularly productive site for exercising Costello's sympathetic imagination, striving to put ourselves in the place of the animal other and experience the world from an estranged point of view. Ralph Acampora advocates what he calls symphysis (common understanding based on shared embodied experience) – rather than sympathy (common understanding based on shared feelings) – as the basis for beginning to understand what it is like to be another species. He argues,

> to gain ontological access to the varied life-modes of different animals, one must enter environments not wholly of human making. This means beginning without making the assumption that there is just one world, permitting the possibility of other *Umwelten* – foreign, yet potentially familiar, forms of worldhood. Indeed, starting out this way may itself contribute to the revelation (or even constitution) of other animal worlds. (*Corporal Compassion* 12)

In contrast to Nagel, Acampora argues there is no need for thought experiments in being another species: 'it will suffice "merely" to arrive at some comprehension of what it means to *be-with* other individuals of different yet related species, because the experience of "being-with" gives us all the mileage we need for tracking cross-species community' (*Corporal Compassion* 27).

This technique will no doubt seem very familiar to readers of sf. Much of the energy of the genre comes from the idea of 'foreign, yet potentially familiar' worlds, from working through in detail how the world might be otherwise if some condition were changed. Examples include changing one's gender at will, as in the works of John Varley; humanity retreating from the material realm to civilisations within digital networks, as in Greg Egan's *Diaspora*; or having all necessary yet unfulfilling work done by non-sentient drones, as in Iain M. Banks's *Culture* series, or by genetically modified animal serfs, as in Cordwainer Smith's *Underpeople* stories. It is important, for two reasons, to look at the specificity of sf worldbuilding whose estranged perspective is that of an animal. First, animals have been the other of human identity at least since there has been recorded human history, and perhaps even before as is suggested by the animal subjects of the Lascaux cave paintings. Thus, remembering the specificity of this history of human–animal relations broadens our sense of sf's particular confrontation with alterity when this alterity is represented by an animal, connecting its motifs with a certain symbol of human history.[10] Second, it is important to remember that any alien animals or aliens who have animal-like qualities are both aliens *and* animals: we are currently in a time of ecological crisis and sf's animal representations are one of the places where we struggle to think our way through it. There is now general agreement[11] that we are living through a mass-extinction event, brought about by climate change (itself the result of human activity), the destruction of habitat by human industry and urbanisation and the continued slaughter of animals for sport or food (a human practice that began causing animal extinctions as early as the period when Cro-Magnon replaced Neanderthal,[12] and has accelerated rapidly since 1500).[13] To understand how sf engages the history of animals in human social and intellectual life, and more importantly how recent sf intervenes in the ongoing struggle to reconfigure human subjectivity, often in ways that transform our destructive relationship with the rest of the natural world, it is important to remember that the alien and futuristic animals in sf draw on this historical and material context. If our readings of such texts forget or minimise their animal being – transforming them into analogues of robots or images of technoscience or 'just' aliens who might share some features with animals – then we foreclose the texts' radically other utopian impulses. If we understand sf from the post-WWII period to have been haunted by the spectre of our own extinction through nuclear annihilation, we can similarly see late twentieth and early twenty-first-century sf as shadowed by the impending threat of even more animal extinctions and perhaps the collapse of our entire ecosystem.

From this perspective, we might understand our relationship with other species as an expression of the current governance model of biopolitics, which Foucault has characterised as a change in the power of sovereignty: the old right to 'take life or let live' is now complemented and at the same time transformed by the new power 'to make live and to let die' (*Society* 241). This formulation is useful for understanding human sovereignty over other species on the planet: some we make live in zoos or factory farms or specially breed as laboratory tools and designer pets; others we let die through habitat erosion, euthanasia of unwanted domestic animals or the exclusion of rodents from the US Animal Welfare legislation (in order to control costs for pharmaceutical companies). Knowledge about animals which takes them only as objects might be understood in Foucault's terms as a disciplinary norm that is used to reinforce the species boundary through a policing of what is 'proper' to humankind alone and the construction of institutions and practices that work not only to reinforce this boundary but further to prevent us from gaining any knowledge of the animal as subject, knowledge which might challenge our investment in this norm. HAS, then, might be understood as a subjugated knowledge that revisits and interrogates this split, which has implications not only for our ability to see animals as subjects but further for our ways of conceptualising what it means to be human once this ground of species difference has been destabilised. Akira Lippit points out:

> it is interesting to note that the invention of the idea of humanity, its appearance in the human sciences, was accompanied by an intensive investigation of the animal in those very sciences. At precisely the moment when the bond between humanity and animal came to be seen as broken, humanity became a subject and the animal its reflection. (19)

Interrogating the species boundary thus has important implications for ethics, not restricted to the question of our ethical duty to other species; rather it relates more broadly to the philosophical foundations of ethical discourse as a whole, as well as to the political implications of biopolitics, which thinkers such as Foucault, Agamben, and Hardt and Negri have defined as a shift from governing humans as legal or civil subjects toward governing the biological life of the species. One of the premises of this book is that resistance to the biopolitical regime of neo-liberal capitalism requires acknowledging the degree to which species difference has been foundational in structuring the liberal institutions that one might wish to contest. In this way, looking at HAS and sf is a continuation of my earlier work on posthumanism and its critique of disembodied metaphysics of subjectivity. A necessary supplement, in Derrida's sense, to this project of returning to a sense of embodied subjectivity connected to the material world is an understanding of humans as merely one species among many with whom we are in obligatory, symbiotic, complex, contradictory and confusing exchange. This is a pressing political question of our times, for as Rosi Braidotti observes in *Transpositions*:

> What 'returns' with the return of Life and of 'real bodies' at the end of postmodernism, under the impact of advanced technologies, is not only the others of the classical subject of modernity: woman/ native/nature. What returns now is the 'other' of the living body in its humanistic definition: the other face of *bios*, that is to say *zoe*, the generative vitality of non- or pre-human or animal life. Accordingly, we are witnessing a proliferation of discourses that take 'Life' as a subject and not as the object of social and discursive practices. (37)

Foucault understands these shifts to create a specifically new form of war within the twentieth century, one which is 'the splitting of a single race into a superrace and a subrace' rather than an understanding of racial difference and war as 'a clash between two distinct races', one of which 'came from elsewhere' (*Society* 61). Now, the discourse of power becomes

> the discourse of a battle that has to be waged not between races, but by a race that is portrayed as the one true race, the race that holds power and is entitled to define the norm, and against those who deviate from that norm, against whose who pose a threat to biological heritage. (*Society* 61)

In *The Open*, Agamben traces this split to the species boundary between man and animal, suggesting that religious visions of everlasting peace imply not only harmony among humans but also between humans and other species. Thus, the first biological split within the species is that of humans from their animal being, leading Agamben to conclude that 'man ... can be human only to the degree that he transcends and transforms the anthropophorous [man-producing] animal which supports him, and only because, through the action of negation, he is capable of mastering and eventually destroying his own animality' (12). Agamben is here following the work of Heidegger, who insists upon separating the Being of humans, the *Dasein*, from the being of other species, who live but do not have being 'as such'. Heidegger defines humans as world-having in that their Being is both part of the world and apart from it: humans 'have' the world in the way of standing apart from it, able to abstractly conceptualise it rather than be captivated by materiality. Animals, in his view, are poor-in-world in that they are living and motile, able to react to their environment, but not able to conceive of themselves as set apart, separate from the world. A crucial part of Heidegger's distinction is the relationship to technology, which he describes as an 'unconcealing' of nature: animals, in their captivated and limited relationship to the world are closed off from the realm of technology.

Technology, however, is something that humans must master. It is a way of encountering the world as a possibility of tools and resources, a way of bringing forth, but at the same time technology is a way of revealing the world that shapes our understanding and limits our possibilities. Technology makes nature into a standing-reserve, and given their inability to access the realm of technology, animals become part of this standing reserve. Heidegger argues that 'instrumentality is considered to be the fundamental characteristic of technology' (12), and modern technology poses a particular problem for Heidegger as it is 'an ordered revealing' that 'gathers man into ordering' (19). He refers to the 'essence' of modern technology as 'Enframing' and argues that it 'starts man upon the way of that revealing through which the real everywhere, more or less distinctly, becomes standing-reserve' (24), a process so ubiquitous that humans are susceptible to being compelled to see the world in this way, thereby losing the world 'as such' and being reduced to a captivated and limited relation to the world, that is, to animal being: 'he comes to the very brink of a precipitous fall; that is, he comes to the point where he himself will have to be taken as standing-reserve' (27). Thus Enframing 'conceals that revealing which, in the sense of *poiçsis*, lets what presences come forth into appearance', that is, it 'not only conceals a former way of revealing, bringing-forth, but it conceals revealing itself' (27). Heidegger is thus continually concerned with finding ways of retaining the human's separation from animal being, in order to preserve what he sees as uniquely valuable about human Being, spirit and freedom.

Yet as Agamben makes clear, the task of separating human life from all other life is not easily achieved. As Judith Butler has suggested in another context regarding the 'naturalness' of gender identity, the anxious and constant reiteration of 'normal' performance betrays the lack of ontological grounding for difference. It must be continually reiterated to exist. Similarly, Agamben suggests that the difficulty in trying to separate anatomical or biological life (*zoe*) from consciousness or human life (*bios*) is that humans possess both; the gap between human and animal is always already internal to human existence. Thus, the real question of humanism is not to think of humans as a conjunction of body and soul; instead we need to 'think of man as what results from the incongruity of these two elements, and investigate not the metaphysical mystery of conjunction, but rather the practical and political mystery of separation' (Agamben *The Open* 16). Humanism thus becomes an 'anthropological machine' (29) that attempts to define what is 'proper' to humans, which proves precarious work since humans are neither properly divine nor fully animal, suspended between celestial and terrestrial states and forever at risk of degenerating into animal being. The discourse of speciesism in science, philosophy and culture is an expression of this machine's continual work to distinguish human from animal. Yet because this division between human and animal is always-already internal to humanity, there is constant risk. From the animal welfare perspective, we might be concerned about the ethical exclusion of at-least some animal species from the domain of ethics; one of Derrida's key arguments in his writing on this topic is the philosophical bankruptcy of the term 'animal' to refer to a plethora of non-human species, the differences among which are often greater than the difference between humans and some species in this category. He argues that rather than defining a single boundary between human and animal, 'it is rather a matter of taking into account a multiplicity of heterogeneous structures and limits: among nonhumans, and separate from nonhumans, there is an immense multiplicity of other living things that cannot in any way be homogenized, except by means of violence and wilful ignorance' (*The Animal* 48).

Yet there is a further risk, pertinent even to those who have no concern for animal welfare. As both Foucault and Agamben make clear, the human–animal division is both external and *internal* to human being, and thus the anthropological machine's work of including and excluding can – and has – put some *Homo sapiens* in the category 'animal'; that is, the category of those who can be killed but not murdered because their lives and deaths are not included within the scope of our ethical discourse. Agamben argues that 'In our culture, the decisive political conflict, which governs every other conflict, is that between the animality and the humanity of man. That is to say, in its origin Western politics is also biopolitics' (*The Open* 80). In addition to these questions of ethics, an important aspect of biopolitics is the degree to which life becomes managed as a calculation, a governance of people that sees them in terms of the statistical norms decided for the population, as Foucault makes clear in *Security, Territory and Population*. In *The Birth of Biopolitics*, Foucault elaborates this analysis and connects its particular mode of governance to neo-liberalism, which involves a shift toward competition as the primary image through which we understand social relations. Neo-liberalism involves a shift, also, in the object of governance such that price stability – rather than other aims such as full employment – becomes the goal, and further 'the idea as not, given the state of things, how can we find the economic system that will be able to take account of the basic facts ... [but rather] how can we modify these facts, this framework so that the market economy can come into play?' (*Birth* 141). In the realm of technoculture and biopolitics, one of the ways such a world has been materialised is through what Melinda Cooper calls the biotech revolution, 'the result of a whole series of legislative and regulatory measures designed to relocate economic production at the genetic, microbial, and cellular level, so that life becomes, literally, annexed within capitalist processes of accumulation' (19). This shift means the extraction of surplus value is enacted on bodies on the biological level, resulting in the massive suffering of animals in locations such as factory farms, where they are reduced to machinic components of an industrial productive system whose ethos admits only efficiency as a value. From the point of view of Heidegger's argument concerning technology, however, we must also recognise that humans – conceived of as the population, the object of governance – have similarly become a standing-reserve of surplus value from the perspective of neo-liberalism.

Resisting such fates for humans and for animals requires a reconcep-tualisation of subjectivity, and what Rosi Braidotti calls 'future-oriented perspectives, which do not deny the traumas of the past but transform them into possibilities for the present. It is not the heavenly future which we aim, but rather a more sustainable one, situated here and now' (268). Matthew Calarco argues that HAS's project of tracing the genealogy of the human–animal boundary across institutions, practices and discourses enables us to understand this distinction more fully in its various, contingent and specific manifestations, and also 'help to uncover alternative ways of conceiving of human beings and animals that have been ignored, covered over, and distorted by dominant discourses' (140–141). This book participates in such a project, exploring what Teresa de Lauretis identified as sf's capacity to be 'potentially creative of new forms of social imagination, creative in the sense of mapping out areas where cultural change *could* take place, of envisioning a different order of relationships between people and between people and things, a different conceptualization of social existence, inclusive of physical and material existence' (161). Each of the chapters explores the tension between, on the one hand, the gravitational pull of the sedimented weight of the species boundary and its attendant metaphysical and ethical boundary, which shapes the ways in which animals can and do appear in sf; and, on the other, the potentially subversive and new ways of conceiving species interrelations made possible by the genre's creative extrapolations, its ability to provide us with a future-oriented perspective that we might also achieve in the here and now. I have selected texts from across the spectrum of sf from early scientific romances and pulp magazine stories through golden-age novels to twenty-first-century works. Some of my examples are by authors who are well established within the sf tradition such as Frederik Pohl and Ursula K. Le Guin; others are authors from the early pulps who have since largely disappeared from academic considerations of the genre, but whose appearance in venues such as *Amazing Stories* signals the importance of animal themes to the emerging genre; and finally some texts, such as those by Karel Čapek and Kirsten Bakis, represent the more literary tradition within the genre and often find an audience outside its boundaries. Throughout I have organised my analysis of these works in terms of their thematic concerns, comparing and contrasting various ways animals serve to answer some of sf's questions about alterity, subjectivity and visions of another world. Thus texts from different historical and national contexts mingle in each chapter, serving to illustrate the richness of sf's engagement with the question of the animal.

Chapter 1 considers texts that foreground the problems of consumption as one of the demarcations of the human–animal boundary. The anxiety that accompanies visions of humans consumed by other beings speaks to the disquiet that haunts our relationship to animals as food. Further, these texts reveal the deep connection between the ethics of eating another and the metaphysics of subjectivity based on exclusion of the animal, which has significant consequences for our conception of the human as well.

Chapter 2 focuses on the difficulty of defining sentience in a non-human being, offering a model of becoming-other in the image of becoming-animal that promises to transcend the isolation of the human subject as defined through the human–animal boundary. The recognition of sentience in animal others thus promises a transformation of human subjectivity that simultaneously enables a revolution in intersubjectivity, ultimately changing the relation of self/world. The experience of becoming-animal offers a glimpse of the utopian desire that Jameson suggests animates our imagining of alien bodies.

Chapter 3 turns to the question of language as one of the key criteria that has been used to differentiate human from animal being. Texts that narrate animal language and the experience of the world as perceived through this different semiotic filter, like the images of animal sentience, propose other ways of experiencing the world and thus work toward the sustainable-but-otherwise future that Braidotti desires. Sf's power to allow the animal to speak enables a powerful fantasy of communication with an alien other that might be realised in our material world.

Chapter 4 reflects on the various ways that discourses about gender and discourses about animality intersect, overlap and challenge one another. The parallel oppressions of women and animals suggest many sites for allied intervention and resistance to a biopolitical regime that constructs both as producers of surplus value. Sf animals in many of these texts offer a counter discourse of animal being that resists the hegemonic construction of 'animal' by dominant anthropocentric discourse in a manner similar to feminist responses to patriarchy.

Chapter 5 similar explores the parallels between colonial discourse and the representations of animals. At root, both colonial racism and speciesism share a desire to accumulate wealth at the expense of excluded – because dehumanised – others, and thus struggles over resources and the status of labour unite them. Animals in sf texts who emerge as colonised others and exploited labour classes serve to dramatise the damaged relationship between humanity and the rest of the world that is the product of such discourses, and some offer visions of another way to structure our social relations.

Chapter 6 evaluates the uses of animal aliens in sf texts, considering them productive sites for thinking through sf's relationship with alterity and its desire to imagine a world of different subjects and different social relations. At times, alien animals serve only to reinforce a discourse of human exceptionalism, but other texts speak to a continuing desire to connect with another being whose subjectivity is unlike our own. In their staging of various ways that humans and animal aliens negotiate an ability to share the world – or refuse or fail to do so – these texts offer insight into the struggles we face in the twenty-first century as we come to recognise that humanity is part of a biosphere and in many ways dependent upon the existence of other beings.

Chapter 7 looks to the other common trope of incorporating animals into sf, reversing the position of humans and animals such that humans are treated by alien beings in ways similar to how we treat animals. Such texts resemble those discussed in the previous chapter in that they offer visions of how we might reconfigure our relationship with other species in the complex multispecies world in which we live but from which we have separated ourselves. Like texts discussed in earlier chapters, these reversal tales emphasise that transforming the relationship between humans and animals requires reconceptualising what it means to be human, striving for an animal-oriented posthumanism.

Chapter 8 centres on the human-made animals that populate much of sf and increasingly parts of our material world as well. This chapter most fully explores the roots of sf as a genre linked to the rising culture of science and its values of technical rationality. The animals in laboratories and the spaces of biological manipulation that serve as the settings for such tales draw our attention to the links between the human–animal boundary and the biopolitical ethics of rational calculation that also informs the biopolitical governance of people as populations.

Finally, my conclusion looks to sf texts that offer lines of flight out of this configuration of human subjectivity based on the denial of the animal, and out of the damaged and damaging relationships to the world and other beings that it produces. I argue that closely considering the animals in sf offers promising ways in which we might reconceptualise human subjectivity, trying for a posthuman identity that addresses the pressing ecological problems of the twenty-first century. The conjunction of animals and sf produces other possible futures and envisions one of the longings that animates so much of the genre, a vision of communicating with a non-human species.

1. Always-Already Meat:
The Human–Animal Boundary and Ethics

Carol Emshwiller's 'Sanctuary' (2007) opens with the phrase, 'just like Russian thistle and starlings, they took over' (59), placing us in a world that might be science-fictional – is it aliens who have taken over? – but which might equally as plausibly be merely that of contemporary reality, in which invasion metaphors are regularly used to describe the spread of species from areas where human culture designates them as 'indigenous' to areas where they are designated as foreigners taking over.[1] Yet these invaders seem to be unobtrusive; 'they must have thought', the narrator tell us 'we wouldn't notice them at all – ever – or, if we did we wouldn't care' (59). Seemingly aware that they are seeking life in space already claimed by others, these creatures 'were staying out of our way, and were careful not to take anything we might be using, and didn't live in places we might want to live in … they must have thought: Why would we care whether they were here or not?' (59, ellipses in original).

Such careful occupation of the planet, it would seem, presages a story about multispecies co-operation and harmony, a tale quite other than that of colonial conquest familiar from history. And Emshwiller does deliver on this promise of an estranged tale of invasion, albeit in a way that startles the reader's sensibilities and does not fulfil the utopian hope of this opening. One day the narrator has an encounter with a being who seeks him out and attempts to communicate with him, but the narrator refuses to allow this encounter to become a mutual exchange between sentient beings. He 'didn't want to' perceive what was being communicated to him, but instead uses the encounter to trick and capture the being who is 'gullible' (59) enough to take his gestures of friendship at face value. The narrator then proceeds to boil the creature, although later he discovers 'they taste a lot better fried' (59). The story ends with the narrator reflecting on his good fortune that this new food source 'came along just when global warming got really bad and most types of cows and sheep weren't doing so well' (60). This short tale highlights one of the most important sites of the human–animal encounter: consumption. Emshwiller uses the shocking punchline of her story to compel readers to question the ways in which we regard other species, indicting humans for their refusal to see, in Derrida's terms, that they are being seen by the other.

The story stresses this parallel when the narrator notes, after describing the creature's capture, that 'I once caught a squirrel that way' (59) and later comments that 'no matter how much they wave, gesticulate, shake their heads no, try to escape ... even so, by now lots of us are in this business' (60, ellipses in original). Such a description might also apply to our contemporary meat industry: despite research that increasingly confirms the cognitive and emotional capacities of animals – and the very evident illustration that, whatever of these capacities they might possess, they prefer not to go to slaughter – profit is more important and cannot be jeopardised. Even more crucially, Emshwiller makes her readers uncomfortable with this scenario by collapsing the different between carnivorism and cannibalism: the crucial point is not only that these species seem able to engage in social exchange with humans (as can many animal species) or that they use gestures and vocalisations to communicate (as can many animal species): they also look human, but smaller, with 'eyes ... larger than is comfortable to look at', 'overdeveloped' thighs that enable their fast running and the ability to 'jump four or five times their height' (59). Most people may be comfortable with the notion of eating meat, even if they prefer not to think of it as something that originates in a living being. But it is something else to imagine eating beings who come to humans and ask for our help. The communication was initiated because a number of the creatures had become trapped in an old cistern and one went to ask for human help; when the narrator discovers those who are trapped, 'they looked as if they thought I'd help them' (60). Although we might protest that there is clearly a difference between consuming such human-appearing creatures and consuming animals, such an argument grants too much to common appearance. Tiffin, for example, notes how much pigs resemble humans: they share our food preferences, they are intelligent problem-solvers, they respond emotionally to stress with symptoms such as weight loss or gain and they behave aberrantly when confined ('Pigs'); yet given their radically different morphology, most people have little trouble consuming pigs, a discrepancy that is precisely Emshwiller's point.

Our contemporary culture is characterised by an enormous 'gulf between the material basis by which our civilization feeds itself, and the system of meaning through which it understands its relationship to the rest of nature' (Benton and Redfearn 48). Meat consumption is a huge part of this tension.[2] It is not a coincidence, for example, that global warming is mentioned in Emshwiller's story, nor that the lack of meat animals in this future is linked to climate change, for the increasing cultivation of land to feed meat animals is one of the contributors to climate change, and also a factor in world food shortages.[3] Worldwide meat consumption 'has quadrupled over the last five decades to reach an all-time high of 20 billion farmed mammals per year, an increase of 60 percent since 1961' (DeMello 77), a shift that directly correlates to the increase of factory-farming methods.[4] The ethical dilemma of who eats whom has always been central to human–animal interaction. Harriet Ritvo's study of Victorian attitudes toward animals notes that consumption of other species was an important part of the performance of Empire and human dominion over the natural world. Hunting, for example, served the purposes of both food production and directly displaying such dominion, and although those killed were far in excess of what might be consumed (and very often were not species one would think to consume, such as rhinoceros or elephant), at the same time the consumption of exotic flesh became an important marker of class at elite social affairs (237–240). Further, she explains, tigers became vilified because their willingness to prey upon humans was regarded as 'the ultimate rebellion, the radical reversal of roles between master and servant' (29). Brigette Resl notes that such presumption of hierarchy and division is a particularly modern way of conceiving of the relation between humans and other species:

> In many medieval texts, however, *animal* was used in its strictest Latin sense to refer to all breathing, moving, living beings, that is, to human and nonhuman animals alike. In this language system no single word was available that corresponded to our modern animal in referring to all nonhuman animals. (3)

Our contemporary sense of the human–animal boundary, then, is one that arose only in the Early Modern period in conjunction with other important cultural changes, such as the shift toward a capitalist economy that increasingly regards the world as resource, and toward a rationalised conception of the universe that turns everything into object for the human subject. The estranging perspective of sf can enable us to think through the human–animal boundary and its relationship to diet from a non-anthropocentric point of view. As the narrator of Wells's *The War of the Worlds* (1896) notes, although he finds the Martian's consumption of human blood 'from a still living animal' (125) horrifying, 'we should remember how repulsive our carnivorous habits would seem to an intelligent rabbit' (126).[5] Such a reconsideration need not lead to 'the universal recognition of a single, comprehensive order of Nature or Being' (Herrnstein Smith 166); rather, as Derrida has suggested, interrogating the human–animal boundary requires recognising that what has been taken to be a single division should instead be recognised as 'more than one internally divided line' (*The Animal* 30), an 'increasingly rich and operative appreciation of our irreducibly multiple and variable, complexly valenced, infinitely reconfigurable relations with other animals, including each other' (Herrnstein Smith 166–167).

Part of this process involves recognising what other ideological struggles are at stake in the policing of the human–animal boundary. Agamben argues that the split within humans between *bios* (the civic life of the citizen) and *zoe* (what he calls the 'bare life' of biological existence) is what makes possible classes of *Homo sapiens* who are not treated as nor regarded as 'human' because 'human' becomes a category which is more than just biological taxonomy, an argument similar to Foucault's regarding the new construction of racism enabled by biopolitics. In *Homo Sacer*, Agamben argues that concentration camps enable us to see the undistorted operation of the biopower as the foundation of Western political life as it is here that we see enacted most fully and materially the full separation of the bare life of *Homo sapiens* from their life/status as humans. Thus, Agamben suggests, instead of asking how such atrocities could be committed against human beings, we should instead 'investigate carefully the juridical procedures and deployments of power by which human beings could be so completely deprived of their rights and prerogatives that no act committed against them could appear any longer as a crime' (171). Previously I have argued something similar about the human–animal boundary in John W. Campbell's *Who Goes There?* (1938), suggesting that the thing's ability to take over (that is, consume and become) the humans functions as an alibi for their desire to enact violence against one another.[6] The gender dynamics of the story make clear that assertions of the superiority of 'humanity' simultaneously function as assertions of the superiority of masculinity and scientific rationality, thus betraying the degree to which the very category human is premised on the exclusion of both animals and women from fully attaining this status.

Who Goes There? is also concerned with issues of consumption and fear of being consumed. The thing's ingestion/incorporation of humans such that their former fellows *cannot tell the difference* raises anxiety – and thus provokes violence – in two ways. First, the thing's fluid movement between human and animal being, at one point becoming-husky and at another becoming-man, suggests a point of view from which there is no firm and inviolable line between 'what calls *itself* man and what *he* calls the animal' (Derrida *The Animal* 30), the absence of which would require us to rethink our metaphysics and ethics (neither of which seem to be endeavours the story might endorse). Second, the story's subplot about murder draws our attention to the centrality of killing in establishing the human–animal boundary, and simultaneously to the tenuous nature of this important division between those who might be killed with impunity and those whose death must be deemed murder. When one of the team is discovered with his throat cut, this initially seems to be a case of murder since it is presumed he was killed because his expression of anxiety through endless singing had become too annoying. Closer examination, however, reveals that the murdered man was already changed by the thing, hence not a man, hence not murder-able. Ironically, then, the one team member about whom the others have no suspicion – the most fully 'human' of those on the station – is the one willing to murder his fellow human, because had he been changed by the thing he would not seek the death of another aspect of himself in the other human body.

The story does not dwell on such moments of discomfort in the way that 'Sanctuary' asks us to dwell on our consumption of other living beings, but nonetheless *Who Goes There?* does require an effort of disavowal for the reader not to acknowledge the complex issues of species interrelations towards which it gestures. The story, like our carnivorous and capitalist culture, requires that we do not question the premise that animals are always-already meat – that certain others can fall outside the bounds of our ethical duty for self-evident reasons and hence reasons that we do not need to interrogate. 'Sanctuary' invites us to consider the validity of the human–animal boundary and the institutions and practices it supports; *Who Goes There?* reveals such issues as sites of anxiety and ambivalence in our culture, but simultaneously attempts to contain the rupture they threaten. Yet both stories create a space in which we might think more complexly about issues of inter- as well as intra-species relations, and perhaps thereby create a more sustainable and equitable world. Haraway argues that such transformation is not about figuring out to whom 'Thou shalt not kill' applies

> so that 'other' killing can go on as usual and reach unprecedented historical proportions. The problem is to learn to live responsibly within the multiplicitous necessity and labor of killing, so as to be in the open, in quest of the capacity to respond in relentless historical, nonteleological, multispecies contingency. (*When Species Meet* 80)

This is not an innocent dream of all species living in harmony, but instead a more complex politics of how to live as omnivores among herbivores and carnivores, in relations of mutual consumption and mutual dependency, but without reducing some species to objects that can be ruthlessly exploited without ethical dilemma.

Cary Wolfe argues that

as long as this humanist and speciesist *structure* of subjectivization remains intact, and as long as it is institutionally taken for granted that it is all right to systematically exploit and kill nonhuman animals simply because of their species, then the humanist discourse of species will always be available for us by some humans against other humans as well, to countenance violence against the social other of *whatever* species – or gender, or race, or class, or sexual difference. (*Animal Rites* 8)

The gendered characterisation at work in *Who Goes There?* demonstrates this slippage in action. Max Horkheimer and Theodor Adorno, in an appendix to *Dialectic of Enlightenment* entitled 'Man and Animal', draw a connection between the 'idea of man in European history' and the exclusion of the animal, and point out that the disenchantment of the world they associate with the dominance of reason above all else becomes the justification for mass violence against animals and animalised humans, such as the Jews in Germany, creating a culture in which 'respect for animals is regarded no longer as sentimental but as a betrayal of progress' (254). In *Minima Moralia* Adorno locates the origin of violence itself in the human–animal encounter, suggesting that 'the possibility of pogroms is decided in the moment when the gaze of a fatally wounded animal falls on a human being' who then defiantly repels this gaze with the mantra 'after all, it's only an animal' (105). A similar logic is at work in the refusal of the narrator of 'Sanctuary' to recognise the creatures' very obviously human features, both morphological and behavioural.

Agamben insists that the human is '*the animal that must recognize itself as human to be human*' (*Open* 26), a formulation he takes from Linnaeus's refusal to set out criteria of the human in his classificatory system, substituting the imperative 'know thyself'. Yet as Adorno's comments on violence and the history of the human–animal boundary make clear, this recognition must be social and collective. Erica Fudge notes in her study of animals in Early Modern England that 'being human is not a given, it is achieved' (*Perceiving* 10); signs of successful achievement of human status come only when one is treated with the special status accorded to human subjects in our culture, but as Adorno points out 'those in power perceive as human only their own reflected image, instead of reflecting back the human as precisely what is different. Murder is thus the repeated attempt, by yet greater madness, to distort the madness of such false perception into reason' (105). It is by such 'mad reason' and false perception that Jews were defined as animals and hence exploited in similar ways: as labour power, as experimental subjects, as raw material for the manufacture of other projects, as disposable life.[7] For Adorno violence always involves a delusional economy: the statement 'it's only an animal' transforms other beings into things whose suffering makes no ethical claim upon us. Akira Lippit argues that

> Adorno's insight reveals that the animal as such is never a mere animal, its gaze exceeds the 'thingness' of a nonhuman being and penetrates the human species – which is to say that the 'it's only an animal' utterance fails, in the first instance, to perform the immunity from guilt that the metaphor promises to the perpetrator of violence. Thus the series of pathic projections [by which those in power perceive as human only their own reflected image] that leads inevitably to the pogrom begins with the collapse of the metaphor, with the failure of the figure to prevent a fundamentally ethical exchange: an irrevocable contact between human and nonhuman being. (169)

The violent denouement of *Who Goes There?* is an example of such a dynamic. Yet the collapse of metaphor need not lead only to pathic projection and violence, as is suggested by the equally bloody but more thought-provoking ending to 'Sanctuary'. Thus a collapse of metaphor provokes violence on the part of those who wish to fortify the species boundary, but can equally serve to open a space in which metaphysics and ethics might be reconfigured. Philip K. Dick's *Do Androids Dream of Electric Sheep?* (1968) uses the tropes of sf to offer a more complex meditation upon the nature of ethical exchanges between human and non-human being. In the novel, the reverence for now all-but-extinct animals is matched in intensity by the utter indifference to the fate of humanoid androids who are illegal on Earth and thus hunted and killed. The gaze of such androids has the potential to 'penetrate the human species', particularly protagonist Deckard who comes to feel compassion for his targets, catalysed by an encounter with Rachel, an android who is not initially aware, it seems, that she is not human (at least one of the variants of Ridley Scott's 1982 film adaptation, *Blade Runner*, goes even further in suggesting that Deckard is himself an android but does not know this). As Lippit suggests, the metaphor that makes some subjects 'only an android' and others fully human fails for Deckard, but this failure makes it all the more imperative that he finish his contract and kill the remaining androids, because he seems to believe that doing so will restore the order of his universe and enable him to escape the discomfort of the ethical exchange.

The novel's religion of Mercerism is about both compassion for animals and resistance to 'kipple', the novel's term for debris resultant from a process of degeneration by which the world seems to be turning to dust, and a metaphor for the intellectual and spiritual emptiness of this future. Mercerism's resistance to kipple and to the 'killers' of animal and other life on the planet (which is contaminated by nuclear pollution and abandoned by most of the human population) offers an ideal of a new relationship with the world, one that is not based on dominating nature, which emerges from a sense of self as shared by others instead of isolated and finite. The novel reveals the fractures of the discourse of Mercerism as well, whose metaphor of empathic fusion collapses as thoroughly as does the metaphor 'it's only an animal', used to justify violence. The killing of androids is required, so says the 'mad reason' of this society, because their inability to experience the fusion of Mercerism means that they are the other who is not recognised as 'human' and hence whose gaze cannot be returned as fellow subject. Thus, despite its rhetoric about compassion, Mercerism at heart reinstitutes the species boundary, only locating it at the border of organic and inorganic life rather than between the categories of human and animal. Further the novel interrogates the 'reason' of this reification of empathy through Deckard's reflections upon this capacity. He notes that the androids have intelligence but not empathy, suggesting that the latter 'existed only within the human community' (Dick 30) whereas the former existed through 'every phylum and order' (30). He further muses that empathy would in fact be a liability for many animal species as it would make a predator 'conscious of the desire to live on the part of his prey. Hence all predators, even highly developed mammals such as cats, would starve' (31).

Deckard finds comfort in thinking of the androids as predators, thus reassuring himself that 'in retiring – i.e., killing – an andy, he did not violate the rule of life laid down by Mercer. *You shall kill only the killers*' (31); yet he almost immediately realises that since 'it was never clear who or what this evil presence was … a Mercerite was free to locate the nebulous presence of The Killers wherever he saw fit' (32). At first, Deckard responds to this revelation in a manner consistent with Lippit's discussion of the animalisation of outcast others: with disavowal and a re-entrenchment of his identity as a bounty hunter. Yet Deckard himself is troubled by his inability to feel restored by Mercerist fusion, and by the novel's end realises that he needs to reconstitute his subjectivity through a reconfigured relationship to the other in which he no longer demands to recognise himself in order to accept a mutual exchange of gazes, the grounds for empathy and care. Although earlier in the novel he resented his electric sheep, seeing its presence as a sign of his inferiority since he could not afford to care for a real animal, by the novel's end he sees that 'the electric things have their lives, too' (241) and continues to care for his toad, although it too has been revealed to be electric.

Dick's novel also interrogates the relationship to animals that is a consequence of perceiving them as commodities rather than fellow beings.[8] Just as the contemporary sense of the human–animal boundary emerged during the Early Modern period, so, too, did a commodified social relationship with animals. Bruce Boehrer emphasises the tremendous changes wrought by the rise of capitalism and by imperialist expansion, observing that

> more species and breeds of animals became available in Europe during the period from 1400 to 1600 than ever before; they became available in greater numbers, over a wider geographical range, than ever before; and they were put to a broader variety of uses than ever before. As a result, animals in the Renaissance begin to assume the status of mass commodities. (2)

The integration of animals into human social relations of capitalist exchange is one of the chief sites of suffering for animals in contemporary culture. In addition to their commodification as meat and as products such as leather, so-called exotic animals are sold as pets or for sport, and they 'constitute the third largest illegal trade in the world today, after drugs and arms but ahead of women ... the National Network to Fight Traffic in Wild Animals estimates the industry to be worth $15 billion a year' (Braidotti 98). The conditions imposed upon animals reared in factory farms are well known if seldom discussed,[9] and the social relations they imply with another living being whom we consume are disguised by the commodity form as effectively as is the exploitation of labour. In *Making a Killing*, Bob Torres emphasises the extent to which the logic of capital structures such spaces: 'I was taught to view cows as producers ... We learned about how much (or how little) space one could give a dairy cow, and that increasing the number of cows in a space meant increased profit, within certain limits' (18). Such manipulation of animals so as to maximise the extraction of surplus value is a continuation of a process that began in the eighteenth century with the specialised development of breeds in order to increase their mass at slaughter.[10]

In the era of biotechnology, such manipulation occurs on the level of life itself, splicing genes from disparate species in order to create variants that can transcend the limits of nature's productive cycles in order to maximise profit: for example, in the period from 1960 to 1990, broiler chickens were manipulated through changes to their genetics and their environment so that their time from birth to slaughter decreased from twelve weeks to six, their average weight at slaughter increased from 1.4 kg to 1.9 kg, and the ratio between the amount of feed they require and their saleable weight at slaughter decreased; over the same period, they developed increased health problems such as chronic heart failure, ventricular fibrillation, cardiac arrhythmia and the inability to support their own body weight (see Armstrong 'Farming Images' 122). Similar stories can be charted for cattle and pigs.[11] Generally, the commodity form enables us to disavow our knowledge of this exploitation, a process aided by the English language's separation of the animal from its flesh in the distinct and non-overlapping use of words such as 'cattle' versus 'beef'. Yet the cattle industry is also perhaps the most notorious site of the disavowal of the commodity form breaking down, through the spread of 'mad cow disease' or Bovine Spongiform Encephalopathy (BSE) from animals to humans in the form of new variant Creutzfeldt–Jakob disease (nvCJD). The public panic produced by BSE is similar to the Victorian public panic about rabies (see Ritvo 167–202): the disease not only crosses between species, calling into question the human–animal boundary, but it produces in humans 'animal-like' symptoms which further undermine the stability of species difference. The official responses to these problems is massive violence toward the animals involved so as to contain the disease, whether policemen beating dogs to death in the streets of Victorian England or the more recent pyres of burning cattle. But BSE is even more unsettling to the public's imagination because of its association with cannibalism – in the hypothesis that feeding cattle the non-profitable parts of other cattle as filler caused or at least spread the disease – and in the resulting concern that eating beef would thereby similarly infect humans.[12]

The ethics of who eats whom are central to the human–animal boundary and its ideological work. Key to this discourse is not only the understanding that humans can prey on animals but that animals are somehow 'unnatural' if they reverse this relationship. Further, a prohibition against cannibalism is part of the formation of human identity in most cultures.[13] BSE and nvCJD uncomfortably conflate cannibalism with carnivorism; the ease with which the disease-producing prion passes between species reminds us that we share embodiment with the animals we consume. Further, by essentially turning cattle into cannibals, agribusiness has violated the division of herbivores from carnivores, further disrupting a sense of the 'natural' order of the world which clearly places humans at the top of the food chain. In an interview published under the title 'Eating Well', Derrida makes connections between meat-eating and the way in which human subjectivity is constructed via repudiation of the animal. Asked to talk about 'who' comes after the subject in an era in which poststructuralist thought has deconstructed the notion of the stable subject of liberal humanism, Derrida prefers to shift the conversation to the question of what happens to ethics and responsibility once we abandon the conventional metaphysics of subjectivity. Such a focus leads Derrida to 'the essential ontological fragility of the ethical, juridical and political foundations of democracy' ('Eating' 104) based on rights discourse because it always leaves open the possibility of some being wrongfully excluded from the political body and, by definition, excludes all animals.[14] Thus, rather than speculating on who comes after the subject, Derrida focuses on 'analyzing the whole conceptual machinery, and its interestedness, which has allowed us to speak of the "subject" up to now' ('Eating' 109).

This conceptual machinery is similar to what Agamben has called the anthropological machine for producing the human from the animal. The work of deconstruction is thus

> a matter of discerning a place left open, in the very structures of these discourses (which are also 'cultures') for a noncriminal putting to death. Such are the executions of ingestion, incorporation, or introjections of the corpse. An operation as real as it is symbolic when the corpse is 'animal' ... a symbolic operation when the corpse is 'human'. ('Eating' 112)

The homology between symbolic and real ingestions of the other explains why metaphors of consumption are so often used to explain exploitation relationships. As Yi-Fu Tuan points out, we are simultaneously fascinated and repulsed by the intersubjective violence inherent in such exchanges: 'The more civilized we are or think we are, the more uncomfortable we feel toward acts of devouring – especially of flesh – that support our own lives and that, in a more general and larger sense, lie at the foundation of the most refined culture' (80). Our inability to confront this aspect of our existence is what motivates idealised versions of intersubjective relations such as Mercerite empathy which, as Deckard notes, problematically excludes carnivorous animals even though all animals are meant to be embraced within its doctrine. This inability to confront the material foundations of our civilisation and the exploitation upon which is based also enables the continuation of capitalist exploitation of both animals and other humans.

Jonathan Swift's 'A Modest Proposal' (1729) achieves its effects by walking a line that shows how easily the symbolic consumption of other humans drifts into the literal consumption of animals and hence the spectre of cannibalism.[15] Raccoona Sheldon's 'Morality Meat' (1985) uses sf's ability to literalise the metaphorical to similar ends.[16] The story is set in a world facing two crises related to overpopulation: first, a food shortage, especially of meat, since 'the droughts and grain diseases finished off most of the US's meat production' (210); second, overcrowded orphanages, filled with the children of women too young or too poor to raise them, but who could not avoid giving birth due to a moral prohibition against abortion. It is not until the story's disturbing end that we see the connection between these two things. It opens with trucker Hagen delivering a shipment of meat to the Bohemia Club North; his truck skids on the slippery highway, and in the crash he is forced to flee through the broken trailer, where he sees 'a rack of cold slippery things' (211) that 'have little curly ends. Tails – pig-tails. Frozen piglet carcases' (212), he concludes. We then shift to another setting: Maylene, a young African-American woman with 'hollows under her cheek-bones that comes from trying to feed two on wages that barely sustain one' (213), boards a bus with her baby, worried about heading 'into white territory' (213). She gets off at 'RIGHT-TO-LIFE ADOPTION CENTRE NO. 7' (214); when she finally works up the courage to enter, she is told by a nurse who is 'white, like everyone Maylene can see here' (214) that she has come in the wrong door, the one meant for prospective parents rather than birth mothers.

Most of the story focuses on the gap between Maylene's perspective and that of those involved in the adoption institution. Maylene hopes to give her baby a better life and spends the day waiting outside the adoption centre, longing to spot the yellow ribbon she has tied in her daughter's hair and thereby to know who has adopted her. A nurse, meanwhile, is haunted by 'the vision of babies, babies, babies inexorably being born, unrelentingly flooding down … babies at first individual, tragic, then finally only figures' (220), but at the same time has trouble matching a prospective adoptive couple with a child because 'there's such an unthinking demand for blond, blue-eyed babies' (221) and cross-racial adoptions are discouraged in any case. Like 'Sanctuary', this story relies on the shock produced by the realisation that humans are being treated as animals: the end returns us to Hagen, who is approached by two men as he lies injured on the ground beside his overturned truck. When they do not move to help him, he concludes they are hijackers and tries to warn them away from the danger of the burning truck which might explode, crying 'Meat. Only meat. Don't die for meat' (231), an appeal similar to the cry 'it's only an animal' used to exempt violent encounters from the norms of morality. The men murder Hagen, wait for the fire to consume the truck and then carefully check the wreckage for any signs that might link its cargo to the Bohemia Club, in the service of 'ageing oligarchs, who consider it none of the public's business what they choose to do or eat' (232). Among the wreckage they find 'a muddy tag-end of yellow cloth' (233), the ribbon for which Maylene anxiously watches outside the adoption centre.

Like Swift's essay, 'Morality Meat' draws attention to the metaphorical consumption of some classes by others by literalising this relationship. Maylene and those like her are unable to support their children because of a wage structure which prevents them from ever achieving secure employment because 'when you get good and are due for your full salary, they fire you and hire other trainees because it's cheaper and the new girls are almost as good' (228). The story includes two white women who have also given up their babies to the centre, although it makes clear that the combination of racism with the class system in the US means that most of the babies in the centre are non-white, while most of those with means to adopt are white. Yet in addition to its critique of abortion and the hypocrisy of those who insist on the sanctity of human life as a ground for criminalising abortion but yet have no concern for the quality of this life after gestation, the story also draws our attention to the way in which the human–animal boundary is implicated in exploitative hierarchies of class and race. The adoption centre's butchery shop is a materialisation of Agamben's anthropological machine which works to include blond-haired, blue-eyed babies within the category of human and to exclude the excess population of non-white babies for whom there is no place in the economic structure. The meat-packing section of the adoption centre might also remind us of Sinclair Lewis's *The Jungle* (1906) and the parallels it draws between the devalued and dangerous lives of the slaughterhouse immigrant workers and the devalued and sacrificed lives of the slaughtered animals. The story thus functions as an example of the way in which biopower can effectively separate 'the human' from biological life, thereby creating a category of humans whose slaughter is not a crime.

At the end of *Homo Sacer*, Agamben calls for the need to rethink politics such that we can theorise a politics that now includes bare life within sovereign power, a politics of all living things not simply a politics of 'man' as citizen. This does not necessarily mean that we must leap from one extreme of viewing humans and all other living creatures as separated into an absolute and singular binary opposition to the equally extreme conclusion of regarding all living things as precisely equivalent. Instead, as Derrida suggests, we need to rethink the metaphysics of subjectivity and tease out the ways in which binary species division has structured what we have called the subject up until now, a structure of subjectivity that Derrida argues is shaped by *'carno-phallogocentrism'* ('Eating' 113). Derrida's interview is entitled 'Eating Well' because this question of eating – consuming, incorporating, introjecting – the other, symbolically and literally, is at the heart of intersubjectivity and thus of a new politics. Derrida suggests that it is not so simple as embracing vegetarianism, reducing the question to one of whether one should or should not 'eat' the other, nor even to that of what/who one should eat. Rather, because one must eat, the question becomes how does one 'eat well', eating here a metaphor for a way of being in the world, embracing a perspective that is shared. Derrida suggests a starting point is

> respect for the other at the very moment when, in experience (I am
> speaking here of metonymical 'eating' as well as the very concept

> of experience), one must begin to identify with the other, who is to be assimilated, interiorized, understood ideally (something one can never do absolutely without *addressing oneself to the other* and without absolutely limiting understanding itself, the identifying appropriation). (115)

The beginning, then, is perhaps to recognise that consumption is a social relationship and to refuse the disavowal that makes it simply a commodity exchange. Part of this may involve returning to the perspective Berger suggests was lost with modernity, one in which we recognised that animals had a power similar to if not identical to our own, a perspective that has something in common with Native American practices of hunting and consuming animals in ways which acknowledge that this ingestion can have some relationship to understanding, a way of 'addressing oneself to the other' rather than merely appropriating it as object for one's ends.[17] It is part of what Haraway calls confronting 'the multiplicitous necessity and labor of killing' (*When Species Meet* 80) that informs our multispecies communities.

None of this is meant to suggest that another way of thinking about eating well would justify our consumption of the poor classes, those already consumed by starvation and the extraction of surplus value from their labour, as both Swift and Sheldon make clear. Rather, the directive is to begin from the position of respect for the other, but also from a position in which one does not know in advance the answer to the question of what 'eating well' might mean. For Derrida, the question of 'eating well' is one of responsibility and hence of ethics; ethics requires not merely treating everything as resource for one's own needs but instead 'begin[ning] to identify with the other', including those others who may be consumed. Derrida argues that the subject as theorised by Heidegger – that is, subjectivity based on the separation of human being or *Dasein* from all other being – is a subject of rationality and calculation. An ethics that is based on rationality and calculation is an ethics that can know in advance the answer to questions such as whom one can or cannot eat: humans or animals, babies or pork chops, pigs or non-human primates. Such an ethos always defines certain capacities that a subject requires in order to be included within the boundaries of ethical duty, and thus ethical responsibility can be withheld from some living beings. This aporia is what concerns Derrida, both in terms of the structural place it leaves open for excluding some *Homo sapiens* from the moral community, an aporia 'Morality Meat' satirises, and also for the unthinking way in which it lumps all non-human life into a singular category. Taking responsibility seriously, then, requires more than just the unthinking application of the calculation that is the human–animal binary, but at the same time this does not mean that difference collapses into an equally automatic sameness. Instead,

> it is a matter ... of taking that difference into account within the whole differentiated field of experience and of a world of life forms, and of doing that without reducing this differentiated and multiple difference, in a conversely massive and homogenizing manner, to one between the human subject, on the one hand, and the nonsubject that is the animal in general, on the other. (*The Animal* 126).

Paul McAuley's *White Devils* (2004) explores the problematic of this boundary by introducing two species that are meant to represent intermediates between *Homo sapiens* and the rest of the primate species. Set mainly in a fictional African future republic called the Green Congo, the novel also links its interrogation of the human–animal boundary to problematic discourses of colonialism including the spectre of cannibalism and the fear of devolution that has haunted the Western imagination's construction of Africa and Africans since Darwin's day. The white devils of the novel's title are a manufactured version of australopithecines, and they are balanced in the novel by another 'gengineered' hominid, called the Gentle People. Neither created species is precisely a recreation of australopithecines, although approximating their genetic make-up was part of the design. At the same time, however, the novel hypothesises a sort of neural mapping of emotional states called engrams and a technology by which they might be edited (some patterns removed, others reinforced) in order to modify behaviour. The story moves among genetic determinism, the role of engram qualia (a term taken from the philosophy of the mind, where it describes aspects of phenomenological experience) and environment as explanations for human being and the qualities displayed by these created hominids. Although they were to have been made from chimpanzee genetic material, regressed to a point of a common ancestry with austra- lopithecines and then re-evolved forward with additional material to recreate the now-extinct evolutionary path, it is revealed late in the novel that human DNA had to be used because the common ancestor hominid shared with chimpanzees is too far in the past. An engram called cd2, believed to be responsible for violence and xenophobia in primates, is excised from the group called the Gentle People in the belief that this will produce a superior *Homo* species, and reinforced in the white devils, originally, it seems, based on curiosity on the part of their creator, and later exploited as a way to create beings somewhere between bioweapons and super-soldiers.

The novel undermines the human–animal boundary in its emphasis on common ancestors and shared genetic material, and in its embrace of non-*Homo sapiens* as part of the category 'human'; in other ways, however, the novel firmly re-establishes the human–animal boundary, reinforcing choice and self-determination as qualities of the human and suggesting – as does Heidegger's metaphysics of subjectivity – that animals alone remain poor-in-world, trapped by instinctual reaction instead of able to conceive of the world and other beings 'as such'. The creators of both types of hominids think of themselves as fathers to these beings. Matthew Faber, who made the Gentle People, argues that

> the ridiculous absolutist idea that humans are special, that they should be venerated because they possess some kind of precious moral worth that distances them from the rest of the animal kingdom, has been able to flourish only because the intermediates between modern humans and the common ancestor we share with chimpanzees and bonobos are all conveniently dead. (174)

The novel does not give much evidence, however, that his moral vision embraces other species beyond the higher primates, and even then he is more concerned with the recreated hominids than with any other animals. Both he and the Gentle People hunt and consume flesh without moral struggle, for example. Yet the novel betrays links between carnivorous eating habits which entail 'necessary' and perhaps unthoughtful killing of other beings and the origins of violence against others of one's own species. Despite lacking the cd2 engram, as the Gentle People age they begin to display some aggressive behaviour and establish structures of social hierarchy. They begin to make weapons to hunt, but Matthew argues this does not imply cd2 aggression, insisting 'weapon-making isn't in their genes, it's just another example of male appropriation of female kitchen culture' (220). When his daughter, paleoanthropologist Elspeth, later sees a fight between two males, Matthew maintains, 'they get pissed off sometimes, just like us. They'll be squabbling over a tasty bit of crab, they have their kitchen implements in their hands ... It doesn't mean anything' (223, ellipses in original). Yet the implication remains that in learning to hunt and thus kill another being with violence for our own consumption, we also learn the ability to objectify another as an object rather than a fellow subject and thereby enable the violence of warfare and murder.[18]

Elspeth's own research similarly implies a relationship between carnivorous cultures and the capacity for intraspecies violence. She is researching a site in Kenya where three hominid species once shared habitat: *Homo ergaster, Homo habilis* and *Paranthropus boisei*. As the names of these species suggest, the first two are more closely related to man, part of the *Homo* genus, while the last is from a separate genus whose evolution

diverged from that of what became *Homo sapiens*. Elspeth and her team find
evidence of bone damage on the skeletons of each of the *Homo* species that
is consistent with the body having been butchered for food; they conclude
this means that *Homo ergaster*, who inhabited the specific site, preyed upon
other members of its own species as well as upon *Homo habilis* for food, and
that the vegetarian *Paranthropus boisei* were ignored in such exchanges as
they were not in direct competition with the other two hominid species
for resources.[19] The researchers recognise that the evidence of cannibalism
– and hence a lack of respect for the way the human–animal boundary is
meant to exempt humans from the status of food – is the most distressing
aspect of their discovery about these proto-humans. Elspeth cautions
them against presenting an image of early Africans as 'as bone-through-
the-nose, missionary-in-a-pot cannibals' (135), but another of her team
insists 'It's hardly murder. Just one species of hominid killing another for
food' (173).

   This comment returns us to Derrida's interrogation of the metaphysics of
subjectivity in which the human–animal boundary becomes foundational
to the ethical difference between murder and the non-criminal-putting-to-
death of animals. The very term manslaughter, which implies mitigation
of culpability in the killing of another human being, further reinforces
the importance of consumption to interspecies ethics. McAuley's novel
complicates the precision of the boundary by creating a third term, a
species that is not *Homo sapiens* genetically or behaviourally, but yet
which is also not quite an animal. In contrast to the Gentle People, the
white devils are dangerous predators, quick to react with aggression, and
armed with internal modifications that give them a sort of body armour
as well as dangerous claws and teeth. When they encounter humans
they immediately attack them, feeding upon their victims. In short, they
seem an image of pure 'evil'. Yet as soon as it is revealed that they are
derived from human rather than chimpanzee genetic material, some of
the characters in the novel begin to have ethical dilemmas about killing
the white devils. They are no longer simply dangerous animals whose lives
are irrelevant when weighed against the safety of the humans upon whom
they prey; now, they become victims of genetic manipulation they did
not choose, the 'ordinary kids they could have been' (439) uncomfortably
present beneath the external animal appearance.

   Yet, just as *Who Goes There?* struggles to define a firm line between
human and animal, unwittingly revealing that the 'inhuman murderer'
could only ever be a human whose actions put him or her outside the
boundaries of communal moral standards, so too does *White Devils* falter
in its explorations of speciesism and colonialism. The logic Elspeth uses
to argue against killing the white devils is inconsistent: she claims that if

they are 'no more than animals, killing them would be like killing a lion because it's a lion', but when it is pointed out to her that this is precisely how humans treat lions who prey on people – we do not 'try to forgive or redeem' them – she switches to 'people do "bad stuff," too. We're the white devils, the Gentle People' (434). Thus it seems that we cannot condemn violence in the white devils because humans are no better than they and thus to condemn them would entail condemning ourselves. Even the Gentle People begin to display aggressive tendencies, this aspect of primate identity finding a way to express even though the cd2 engram is removed, and more than once the reader is reminded that white devils and the Gentle People are 'two sides of the same coin' (532). Once he learns that the white devils have been made from human genetic material – which quickly becomes conflated in the novel's ethos with *being* human – protagonist Nick finds 'he can't shoot, not in cold blood' (460) a caged white devil; yet later, in the heat of battle, he has no problem shooting soldiers: 'Nick raises the Kalashnikov and drops all four with a single burst. It isn't planned; he simply reacts when they present a clean target' (510).

Rather than the careful rethinking of ethics and responsibility that Derrida calls for, then, which requires taking into account multiplicity and difference, contingency and partial identities, *White Devils* brings the human–animal boundary into question only to all the more firmly endorse it by the novel's end, though not without moments of excess which betray that the world's multiplicity exceeds the categorisations of this moral system. One surviving white devil is brought into bourgeois subjecthood, rescued by survivors Nick and Elspeth, who name him Dogboy and take him to an isolated island where he can live out the rest of his life in peace. The conclusion suggests that Dogboy, despite his unrelenting violence, is no more a monster than the African children (also liberated from the militia encampment) who were subjected to (failed) attempts to engineer them into something approximating the white devils by grafting animal teeth into their mouths and brutalising them so that they become violent, dissociative personalities. More than once the novel compares the white devils (who are physically children although they mature more quickly that *Homo sapiens*) to child soldiers; at first such comparisons are part of a corporate attempt to deny the existence of any gengineeered beings, arguing that witnesses saw merely drug-crazed and brutalised child soldiers. Yet the novel's interrogation of debates about the respective roles of nature and nurture in human violence also suggests connections with the animalised discourse associated with media reports of African children soldiers which began to appear in relation to conflicts in Mozambique in the 1980s, and which have become commonplace in popular culture's representations of African wars since. Like many of these reports, *White Devils* staggers problematically between critiquing the use of speciesist discourse to vilify these children (or the white devils) and pandering to an appetite for horror stories from the 'heart of darkness'.

The novel opens with Nick investigating war crimes, tagging bodies massacred by the Loyalists and reflecting on his inability to

> imagine what it must have been like to hack to death more than forty men, women, and children in one long, hot bloody afternoon. *It was hard work*. The soldiers taking turns, making sure that they were all implicated in the atrocity. Taking no pleasure in the killing, working steadily until it was done. A grim but necessary job. (7)

A witness has earlier told him that the atrocity proceeded 'like they were butchering animals' (4). The unexplored assumption is that there is no moral dilemma in treating the slaughter of animals as work, but something horrifying in the killing of humans approached with a similar refusal to engage ethically, to allow the other to appear as a subject. The novel is careful not to let this be simply a tale of savage Africans capable of such slaughter. Although most of the direct killing is done by other Africans, the wider context makes it clear that it is Western colonialism and neo-imperialism that have so impoverished the continent and left its populations vulnerable to greedy warlords. The continent and its people have already metaphorically been eaten by corporate CEOs who are every bit as bloodthirsty even if they use different tools.

The Green Congo is a country literally owned by a transnational corporation, Obligate, whose name is said to refer to the biological condition of 'being able to exist under only one set of environmental conditions', which the company interprets as symbolising that the human species is 'obligate – absolutely dependent – on the biosphere of good old planet Earth' (271). They thus see themselves as ecological saviours who 'do everything we can to spread the word about the wonderful diversity of our planet, including marketing products derived from plant species unique to threatened ecosystems' (271–272). This transformation of 'good old planet Earth' into commodities betrays the real motivation of such corporations and thus their complicity in the very mechanisms of environ-mental destruction they claim to be subverting, the reduction of nature into standing reserve. This fact is not lost on the African characters within the novel, one of whom explains to Nick:

> Obligate comes to Africa and pretends to want to help us rebuild our lives ... but in fact its people are neo-colonialists. They tell us that they know what is best for our own country. They tell us not to cut down our forests. They tell us not to make plantations of gengineered

trees. They tell us it is bad to use the oil we have under our feet. They tell us not to have too many children. (177)

Later another person suggests that the self-help technology of engrams that is patented by Obligate is merely a way to extract maximum surplus value from the adjusted people in their employ:

> They say they want to help the people, but they break the spirits of men, hypnotize them to make them want to live only in cities, to work in factories for very little money. In the last century, white people came here to steal our diamonds and ivory and rubber; in the century before that they took our young men and women for slaves. Now they want our souls. (234–235)

The literally enslaved zombies produced by alteration of engrams in the militia camp, then, are only the flip side of the coin of corporate labour practices, stripped of their mythology of self-actualisation.

White Devils remains, however, a troubling text. Just as Joseph Conrad located his 'heart of darkness' firmly in the imperial centre of London, but nonetheless required his protagonists to travel to Africa to discover this inner core, so McAuley also at times falls too easily into caricatured representations of African savages. Although the novel stresses that the cannibalistic consumption of some hominids by others is equally evil whether it is done by gun or by patent, and although one of its worst 'human monsters' is a fundamentalist, white Christian from the US who believes it is his god-given mission to destroy all genetically modified beings as an insult to god's creation, nonetheless the dark heart of human violence is still something one finds in Africa. The novel does not see a way out of the anthropological machine that continues to divide the human from the animal, ideological work that, Agamben argues, is always about a division internal to humans. He argues that the urgent political question of our time is not that of human rights, because once we are within a rights discourse we have already ceded a space for the non-human that by definition possesses no rights. Instead, what is required is 'to ask in what way – within man – has man been separated from non-man, and the animal from the human' (*Open* 16). *White Devils* offers no insight into the operation of this ideological division, substituting instead the platitude that moral judgements cannot be black or white, that what makes humans 'so unique' is that we are able to 'extend kinship to the whole wide world' across the species divide, but at the same time are able 'to objectify whole classes of human beings' (386). This is the work of biopolitics, which 'will allow power ... to treat the species, to subdivide the species it controls, into the subspecies known, precisely, as races' (Foucault *Society* 255).

In contrast to this anthropological machine, Donna Haraway and

Rosi Braidotti offer alternative metaphysics of subjectivity that stress becoming over being, that reconfigure the kinship system in ways that no longer require or indeed allow a decision between in-group kin or out-group enemy. Haraway calls this notion 'companion species', a term that is not simply a euphemism for pets, but which implies instead of radical reshaping not only of the human–animal bond but also of our understanding of both the human and the non-human partner in the relationship. For Haraway, 'companion species – coshapings all the way down, in all sorts of temporalities and corporealities' is an 'awkward term for a not-humanism in which species of all sorts are in question' (*When Species Meet* 164). Crucial to her definition of companion species is that both partners in the exchange are companion species, each to the other, rather than the more typical understanding of domesticated animals as species who have become companion to humans. Haraway's emphasis on 'coshapings all the way down' insists that both humans and other animals are changed in this new metaphysics of subjectivity. Similarly, Braidotti argues for a new understanding of 'sustainability' as the basis on which we need to establish new relations among humans and non-humans alike. For her, sustainability

> is a regrounding of the subject in a materially embedded sense of responsibility and ethical accountability for the environments she or he inhabits. What is at stake is the very possibility of the future, of duration or continuity. Becomings are the sustainable shifts or changes undergone by nomadic subjects in their active resistance against being subsumed in the commodification of their own diversity. Becomings are unprogrammed as mutations, disruption, and points of resistance. (137)

The sf texts discussed in this chapter each seem informed by a desire for the possibility of a future that is different from their present, and their interrogation of questions of the human–animal boundary through the ethics of killing and consuming others suggest that they understand a metaphysics of subjectivity based on exclusion of the animal to be part of the problem. They deconstruct to varying degrees the human–animal boundary that Derrida argues is the 'conceptual machinery' ('Eating Well' 109) for the human subject. Yet none move beyond to a posthuman subject of becoming. The emphasis on consumption, both carnivorous culture and the spectre of cannibalism that haunts these texts, suggests that this material basis of our culture is among the most problematic sites that must be addressed in any transformed vision of posthuman companion species.

2. The Mirror Test:
Humans, Animals and Sentience

The mirror test – a classic investigation of consciousness in animal research – has aspects of a typical pulp sf scenario of alien abduction: an animal is rendered unconscious, during which time dye is applied to its face in some way; when it awakes, the animal is given access to a mirror. If the animal then attempts to investigate the mark in some way, such as touching the place or rubbing the marked part of the body on enclosure walls, it is deemed to have passed the mirror test, revealing that it recognises the other in the mirror as self. Coming out of a tradition of ethology rather than philosophy, the mirror test undermines Heidegger's distinction between the *Dasein*, who has the world 'as such', and animals, who are poor-in-world since they respond only to immediate perceptual stimuli. Recognising oneself in the mirror suggests some sort of conception of self in a world of other beings, and thus potentially some capacity for abstract thought. Primates and dolphins have passed the mirror test (Hillix and Rumbaugh 103, 233); many other animals 'fail' this test, either by ignoring the mirror altogether or else by recognising in it another being like oneself but separate from oneself (which can sometimes lead to attempts to attack the other in the mirror).[1] As we have seen in the previous chapter, humans frequently respond to any other as an enemy, which might beg the question of whether or not many would be able to pass such a test did we not live in a social world in which we are regularly accustomed to seeing our own reflections.

This second connotation of mirrors is equally important to thinking about human–animal social relations, especially in the context of a project focused on literary representations of animals. The image of the mirror signifies that we often understand animals as mirrors for ourselves, constructing images of them that glorify some species in whom we see qualities we want to possess (admiring dogs for their 'loyalty'), while simultaneously vilifying others, often by projecting onto them human faults (castigating pigs for their 'gluttony'). Frequently cultural representations of animals, then, will tell us little about the animals themselves and much about the ways animals become caught up in human ideology. At the same time, however, as Haraway cautions, we must not be too quick to dismiss all representations as being entirely disconnected from animal being and human experiences of animals. She insists that 'human beings do, or can, know more than we used to know, and the right to gauge that knowledge is rooted in historical, flawed, generative cross-species practices' (*When Species Meet* 226). She further reminds us that our standards for assessing the sentience of other beings need to take account of changing ideas of human subjectivity: 'we have learned that we are not the "self" or "transparently present to the self" either' (226).

The texts considered in this chapter explore these tensions of the mirror test in various ways, reminding us of the anthropocentrism that has flawed many previous accounts which dismissed animal sentience, and exploring the risks of too quick an identification with animal others that can become an appropriation and thereby erase the specificity of animal being. Like many tests for animal intelligence, the mirror test installs anthropocentrism in advance, presupposing that animals that do not respond as humans might in a similar situation are thereby not thinking beings. We might be reminded here of the example of Clever Hans, a performing horse from the late nineteenth century who demonstrated his ability to do arithmetic by tapping the appropriate count with his foot. His intellect was investigated by a commission set up by the German board of education, which concluded that Hans was not intelligent because he was not performing arithmetic but was instead responding to subtle cues from his owner which informed him when he had reached the appropriate count. From a different point of view, Hans did in fact demonstrate intelligent behaviour as the cues were not something he had been trained to recognise, nor was his trainer cueing him on purpose; instead, Hans demonstrated a sensitivity to social interaction which enabled him to achieve a 'successful' performance, although he made his own sense of what the foot tapping signified. Sf readers, attuned to the difficulties of multispecies communication and the intricacies of polysemic signifi-cation, are well positioned to appreciate this alternative theory of Hans's intelligence. It is also significant that the mirror test for self-awareness measures conscious experience of a particular sort, a way of experiencing the world that allows one to conceptualise self as an entity existing separate from the world (and hence to recognise self in the mirror). As the previous chapter suggests, this metaphysics of subjectivity is brought into question by posthumanist philosophy and HAS.

The mirror test, then, both signifies a measure of self-awareness as indicator of sentience, but also reminds us of the ways in which human representations of animals can be mirrors for our construction of self. Connie Willis's story 'Samaritan' (1985) explores some of the difficulties of this mirroring. In her introduction to the story in the collection *Fire Watch*,

Willis recounts the story of Esau and Jacob from the Old Testament: Jacob, a 'smooth man' cheats his younger brother Esau, who is 'red, all over like an hairy garment' (214), of his rightful inheritance. Willis suggests that Jacob is the ancestor of humanity, and then asks us to consider from whom we have stolen an inheritance, before beginning her story about an orang-utan named Esau and the controversy over his baptism. Esau serves as a handyman at Reverend Hoyt's Ecumenical Church, and new assistant Reverend Natalie Abreu learns American Sign Language (ASL) in order better to communicate with him. Esau belongs to the Cheyenne Mountain Primate Research facility, which breeds orang-utans, a species extinct in the wild, but does not want to incarcerate them as would a zoo. Instead they 'find them useful jobs out in society' (218) where the orang-utans live with their employers. Esau's status is thus ambiguous: in some ways he is recognised as a communicative subject with the same limited range for self-determination as a child might be given, but at the same time he is owned. Natalie announces that Esau has requested baptism following a discussion of confirmation. According to her, Esau said 'I would like very much to be God's beloved child too', but Hoyt finds it 'disconcerting to hear Natalie translate' as he believes she 'changed what was obviously labored and fragmented language into rhapsodies of adjectives, clauses, and modifiers' (216).

The story explores both Natalie's and Hoyt's attitudes toward Esau and this question of baptism with complexity. Although in certain ways Natalie seems the more sympathetic figure as she is willing to include Esau fully within the human community, at the same time the story raises questions about whether her perceptions best serve Esau's interests. For example, she insists that he wear clothing as would a human and that he stand upright, although 'his backbone simply wasn't made for it' (217). Hoyt finds himself unconvinced that Esau truly understands baptism and embraces the sacrament as church doctrine requires, but at the same time realises that any doubts he has about Esau's motivations – 'He's lonely. He needs a strong father figure. He likes the pretty robes and candles. Instinct. Conditioning. Sexual sublimation' (224) – are equally true of many of his human parishioners as well. Before Hoyt comes to any conclusion about proceeding with the baptism, Esau falls from a ladder, which Natalie insisted he use although he could climb to reach high windows of the rectory where he was working. They find him in great pain from injuries too severe for recovery, and Hoyt insists on baptising him before he calls a vet and has Esau euthanised. Natalie is deeply upset by what she sees as the inconsistency in Hoyt's behaviour, insisting 'he *was* a person, you know, not just an animal' (234). Like her insistence that Esau behave in certain ways so that his self-presentation matches what Natalie thinks of as that of a 'person', her defence of Esau in the story's conclusion betrays the anthropocentrism of her vision. She can recognise Esau as a subject only to the degree that he mirrors her own self-image.

Hoyt, in contrast, reflects upon the story of the Good Samaritan, which Natalie taught Esau and to which he referred when questioned about his knowledge of god. The parable is offered in response to the question 'who is my neighbour' asked of Jesus when he is explaining that the path to salvation lies in loving one's neighbour. The bishop who discusses Esau's possible baptism with Hoyt reminds him that in addition to this parable, the Bible contains a reference to another Samaritan, a woman at a well who asks Jesus 'How is it that thou, being a Jew, askest drink of me, which am a woman of Samaria?'(230). Hoyt concludes that Esau does not ask to be baptised based on a failure to recognise that he is not a human,[2] but rather that he is asking for an extension of kinship, of neighbourly love, despite the gap of species difference. Willis's story thus offers a model of interspecies community that does not presuppose anthropocentric standards for achieving personhood and being recognised as sentient. In this way, it reflects work by researchers such as Sue Savage-Rumbaugh, whose work on language in bonobos is conducted in the context of a shared human-bonobo culture rather than on the model of measuring primate ability to demonstrate intelligence within a society organised by human priorities. 'Samaritan' similarly points toward a non-anthro-pocentric vision of community rather than a requirement of sameness in order to recognise sentience, making it an example of the sort of ideal advocated by Derrida and Haraway. The story rejects a binary division between human and animal not in order to collapse into sameness but rather to respect multiple ways of being in the world, multiple modalities of sentience and personhood.

Walter Miller's 'Conditionally Human' (1952) explores this problematic from a more personal and affective point of view, projecting a future in which restricted population regulations mean that many couples wishing to have a child cannot obtain a license to do so. The affective gap in their lives is filled by genetically modified pets, given higher intelligence and the power of speech by the 'evolvotron'. The most elaborate of these beings, neutroids, are altered chimps made to appear as much as possible like human children, the illusion 'broken only by two distinct features: short beaver-like tails decorated with fluffy curls of fur, and an erect thatch of scalp hair that grew up into a bright candle-flame' (21). Neutroids are designed to be sterile and to mature only to a standardised age, no older than equivalent to ten years in a human. The protagonist, Inspector Norris, works for the Bio-Authority and struggles with the emotional and legal ambiguities of these almost-but-not-quite human companions.

He fights with his wife over the euthanisation of unclaimed animals, which she finds immoral but he rationalises as a necessary part of the job, calling himself 'just an up-to-date dogcatcher' (9). The plot is driven by a directive Norris receives to recall certain neutroid serial numbers who have been deemed deviant; regarded as children by their owners, who have 'pseudoparturition parties' (12) to celebrate their arrival,[3] neutroids draw attention to the problematic category of the pet within modern Western societies. They are loved family members, yet they are denied 'hospitalization and expensive treatment' (14) for certain diseases, and might at any time by recalled and destroyed by their manufacturer, as Norris is instructed to do with the deviant neutroids.

Like Deckard in *Do Androids Dream of Electric Sheep?*, Norris gradually finds himself less and less able to adopt the ideology of absolute separation between human and non-human that he requires to do his job. On the one hand, the 'mutants pets fulfilled a basic biological need of Man – of all life, for that matter – the need to have young, or a reasonable facsimile' (36), yet on the other 'neutroids could be bashed with a shovel and buried in the back yard when hard times came' (37). This pathological dualism attempts neatly to sidestep the issue of a culture that refuses inequitable resource distribution and is beset by the consequences of an attitude toward the natural world as commodity for human consumption, but fails to address how to answer human needs for sociality and reproduction through other ways of organising community beyond the bourgeois couple. So long as people's investment in the future remains limited to the future of their own offspring, overpopulation will continue to be a problem because 'when the market became glutted with humans, the merchandise could not be dumped into the sea' (36). Using the category 'animal' for the neutroids and other pets enables the forces of governance to treat them as mere commodities, but Norris's struggles with various owners who do not want to return their 'deviant' family member suggest that affective connections are not so easily rationalised and managed. His culture tries to control this social pathology in part by separating sentience from human-like embodiment. Norris's fight with his wife is focused on killing the neutroids rather than 'the lesser breeds such as Cat-Os, Dog-Fs, dwarf bears, and foot-high lambs that never matured into sheep' (21). Such pets are regarded as 'emotionally safer, than any of the quasi-human models' (11), even though 'the nonhuman pets were brighter than the neutroids' (40).

The story challenges the human–animal boundary with its population of talking dogs and cats, able to express love for their owners, as well as the quasi-human neutroids who occupy a liminal third space between human and animal. The failure of the alibi for violence – 'it's only an animal'

– in relation to them brings into question the deployment of speciesism. Yet 'Conditionally Human', like *White Devils*, in other ways closes down its critique of the human–animal boundary by repositioning its liminal figures firmly on the human side of the binary, thereby limiting critique to questions of who counts as a subject, not the mechanism of human–animal boundary as a way of construing human subjectivity. Norris finally encounters one of the deviant neutroids, named Peony by her family; the deviation, he discovers, is that her age-set and mental capacity have not been limited as required for neutroids. Peony displays advanced language skills, and when told she must leave with Norris she 'began to cry. Standards neutroids never cried, they whimpered and yeeped' (46). The conclusion of the story all the more strongly reinforces the categorical distinction between human and animal. The fights between Norris and his wife intensify, and she insists that he cannot reveal Peony's existence to his superior as that would be 'M, U, R, D, E, R' (48), a characterisation that exceeds her previous objections to killing and which is spelt out so as to spare Peony from realising what they are discussing. Peony's owner/ father, O'Reilly, in despair over her loss, 'take[s] a joint of pipe and a meat cleaver and mass-slaughter[s] about sixty helpless animals' (53) in his pet shop, creatures we had earlier seen talking to him. One dog, who pleads, 'Don' sell me, Dada, don' sell me' (40), is not recognised by O'Reilly as another creature to whom he owes an ethical duty, but the loss of Peony, who is sufficiently human in his eyes, provokes a crisis.

The same is true for Norris. The material example of Peony prevents him from continuing to rationalise his work for the Bio-Authority, and he conspires with his wife to keep Peony and raise her as their child, even murdering his boss to cover up their crime, an incident that (like the killing of soldiers in *White Devils*) indicates problematic aporias in human moral systems where ethics is a matter of rational calculus: 'bad' humans can be killed 'feeling no emotion whatever' (64), as can a 'normal Bermuda K–99' neutroid Norris 'coldly kill[s] … with a wrench' (64) in order to substitute its body for Peony. Norris discovers the deviant neutroids have been deliberately created by a saboteur who both removes the limits set on their intelligence and physical maturation and restores their reproductive capacity. At the story's conclusion, Norris plans to take over the work of sabotage, helping to create new beings who can perhaps 'do better than their makers' (65), a 'new people' who will put 'an end to scheming and pushing and arrogance' and thus create 'a pretty good world then' (66). Miller's story rejects a humanism based on capitalist transformation of the world into raw materials and the expansion of humans to the detriment of all other life on the planet. He believes that Peony is 'rather superior to you and me', as a priest tells him, because she 'hasn't picked an apple yet' (56). Whether or not Peony represents a posthuman subject of becoming – rather than a humanist subject of fixed being, the *Dasein* who must separate itself from all other life – remains to be seen. Reading the story from the perspective of HAS, however, puts a somewhat pessimistic shadow on its conclusion. Peony's own predilections are as yet unknown, but the 'creator' who gives her and her kind a chance, Norris, is working within the same anthropological machine that separates human from animal, simply shifting somewhat the categories of inclusion and exclusion so that Peony and her kind now count as more fully human than do *Homo sapiens*.

The role of pets in modern Western cultures has significant analogies to Miller's future, according to some scholars, who connect pet-keeping cultures to a fragmentation of traditional social bonds caused by capitalist social organisation. Tuan argues that 'humans needed an outlet for their gestures of affection [as] this was becoming more difficult to find in modern society as it began to segment and isolate people into their private spheres' (112). Adrian Franklin sees pets as an antidote for what Zygmunt Bauman has described as the uncertainties of liquid, postmodern society. Arguing that pets provide 'ontological security', Franklin maintains that 'a close relationship with pets is now seen as good for us and perfectly "normal" and acceptable' (85), although he still regards such a relationship as a substitute for more proper bonds with human beings.[4] In contrast, Fudge, drawing on Mary Douglass's work in *Purity and Danger*, argues that 'pets *by their very nature* challenge some of the key boundaries by and in which we live and thus they cannot provide ontological security, but instead undermine it' (*Pets* 19). Pets from this point of view become beings who can potentially challenge our understanding of the human–animal boundary, and perhaps our understanding of what it means to be human. Julie Smith, for example, understands her household as posthuman in her attempts to move beyond the dominance/affection binary that Tuan argues defines the pet relationship. In living with rabbits, Smith has placed some restrictions on the rabbits so that they can live with humans without entirely disrupting the home (such as restricting their access to power cables and bookcases where they might cause damage), but at the same time has also made adjustments to her own way of being in the home so that the rabbits' habits and preferences are also accommodated (such as arranging furniture and other items to suit their liking for clear corridors near walls). This arrangement, she believes, will better facilitate interspecies understanding and communication, transforming her into a posthuman: that is, someone living beyond anthropocentrism and a metaphysics of human subjectivity that emerges from the human–animal distinction.

Pets, like aliens in sf, speak to a longing on the part of the human species to connect with another being we can recognise as a subject, but whose mode of being in the world is nonetheless different from our own. Fudge argues that love for a pet necessarily entails granting that the other is a subject in the world, just as is a human:

> If we cannot access an animal's mind then pet ownership becomes potentially meaningless, for without a mind for us to access (or for us to believe we can access) we cannot really say that a pet loves, as such a claim would be simply anthropomorphic, and we need pets to be able to love if we are to be able to claim that dog love really is a kind of love. (*Pets* 50)

Such approaches to the concept of pet relationships go beyond the binary of human subject and animal non-subject that Derrida argues we must deconstruct in order to move beyond a philosophical tradition that understands the being of animals only as a sort of privation. Based on his absolute separation of human and animal subjectivity, Heidegger suggests that although we may share habitation with pets, we never really live *with* them since they experience a different perceptual and phenomenological world than we do: an animal may sleep in the same bed, walk on the same stair, and eat in the same kitchen as does a human, but the 'being' of the animal's presence in such activities is not that of the human. Rejecting this analysis, Derrida points out 'of course, the animal doesn't eat like us, but neither does any one person eat in the same way ... what I wanted to suggest ... is that these differences are not those between "as such" and "not as such"' (*The Animal* 159).

Deleuze and Guattari's privileging of molecular or fluid modes of becoming over molar or fixed modes of being offers another paradigm through which to think about the differences between humans and animals – and those among humans and among animals – in a way other than privation and not structured around this Heideggerian binary. *A Thousand Plateaus* offers the idea of becoming-animal as a way to challenge the current ideological constructions of society and subjectivity and embrace new identities. Molar identities – fixed in being, able to be grasped as a whole, recognised within the current social formation – differ from molecular identities – always in flux, made up of capacities and tendencies, offering the possibility for transforming identity and society – precisely because they refuse to follow fixed channels. Becoming-animal is one of many examples Deleuze and Guattari use to articulate a transformative politics of subjectivity. Although their arguments are not focused on the subjectivity and welfare of animals per se,[5] as Derrida has argued current conceptions of subjectivity (which produce the molar identities critiqued by Deleuze and Guattari) are predicated upon the exclusion of animal being. Thus a transformative politics of becoming is one model for subjectivity not produced by what Derrida has called 'the whole conceptual machinery, and its interestedness, which has allowed us to speak of the "subject" up to now' ('Eating' 109) or what Agamben calls the 'anthropological machine' (*Open* 29) that attempts to define what is 'proper' to humans. Becoming-animal, then, opens up a space for rethinking politics and ethics in general, which could open up a space for reconceptualising our ethical and social relations with other species.

Becoming-animal is not reducible to simply liking animals or behaving as one thinks an animal might behave. Like Thomas Nagel, Deleuze and Guattari are interested in a deeper transformation: not what it is like to be human and act like a bat, but rather what it is like to *be* a bat. They are careful to point out that becoming is not a relationship, 'but neither is it a resemblance, an imitation, or, at the limit, an identification' (237). Becoming happens on the molecular, not the molar, level, and while 'It is clear that the human being does not "really" become an animal any more than the animal "really" becomes something else', the becoming is nonetheless real. What is real in becoming is a rejection of the false alternative between 'imitate' and 'be' in favour of the reality of the becoming itself, a refusal of 'the supposedly fixed terms through which that which becomes passes' (238). It is important, then, that becoming-animal is not understood as changing from the molar identity of human into the molar identity of a specific animal. Rather, becoming remains on the molecular, fluctuating level, allowing for connections and affinities that reject the distinction between human and animal. Becoming-animal is a cyborg politics in which the ruptured boundary between human and animal signals not the loss of humanity but rather 'disturbingly and pleasurably tight coupling' (Haraway 'Cyborg Manifesto' 152) between human and animal.

The animal is a privileged figure of subjectivity for Deleuze and Guattari because it foregrounds how the subject is always-already multiple. They understand the current 'conceptual machinery' of subjectivity to be a selective narrowing process: the pre-individual is malleable, possessed of potential energy and capable of assuming any number of shapes. Through interactions with the external milieu, certain aspects of this potential energy are reinforced while others are suppressed. Thus, social codes create a stable individual out of the flux of desires, channelling desire into prescribed pathways, a process that is never entirely successful. There are always more potentials than are expressed in a given formation, and both society and the individual are in a constant state of tension between those desires amplified by the social order and those muffled by it. One becomes a stable individual in this order by falling within one of the assigned categories in its grid of value judgements about appropriate and inappropriate desires and connections. Against this, they argue for a continued sense of the subject as multiple and always-in-process, a becoming rather than a being. One way of achieving this state is to embrace a becoming of what one *is not* under this order, and thus becoming-animal represents, as Derrida emphasises, the most foundational challenge possible because it calls into question what is 'proper' to humanity.

As stories such as 'Samaritan' and 'Conditionally Human' suggest, a transformative subjectivity of becoming-animal is both difficult to conceive and threatening to imagine. The stories ask us to stretch our definition of what being a 'person' might mean, but their conclusions strive to restore the human–animal boundary – albeit along slightly different lines of inclusion and exclusion. Although they reconfigure the content of 'the human subject', neither can be read as becoming-animal and thereby challenging the channelling of desire and potentiality into certain culturally sanctioned pathways. Octavia Butler, a writer known for her embrace of alterity and her interest in heterogeneous rather than normative communities, offers a more radical vision in her *Wild Seed* series, particularly in *Clay's Ark* (1984), a novel which asks us to accept the animalised Clayark subjects as people *even though* or perhaps even *because* they refuse to channel their desires closer to what is deemed 'proper' to humans.[6] The Clayarks are infected with a virus that transforms people into beings who desire to eat raw flesh, including human flesh, and who feel compelled to have sex frequently and with multiple partners. The offspring of infected humans are even further animalised, possessing a sphinx-like appearance, eschewing a bipedal gait, and – perhaps most distressingly – not feeling tormented as do the infected humans (who remember their lives before infection) about the ways in which they are different from 'normal' humans. Butler explores the various responses to becoming-animal: many of those infected were outcast from human society and find a new sense of purpose and community in the Clayark family; others cannot face the transformation of what it means to be human and kill themselves or violently attack the new beings.

The novel consistently privileges those able to embrace difference, those willing to work to build heterogeneous, multispecies community. Far from narrating anxieties about degeneration and a loss of humanity as do many narratives of human–animal hybridity – the classic example of which is H.G. Wells's *The Island of Doctor Moreau* (1896) – Butler's text suggests such transformations are the way forward. The animalised characteristics of the Clayarks undo the human–animal boundary as the ground for constructing subjectivity, thereby opening a space for new potential energies, subjects and social formations to emerge. The series is thus an example of 'eating well' in which 'eating' the other is a way of sharing the perspective of the other, of being in the world and relating to others that is respectful instead of destructive of difference. Such a perspective is not a naïve or utopian vision of all subjects being equal or identical, nor of all intersubjective and interspecies relationships being free of conflict. As Derrida points out, one does have to eat. Yet by refusing the human–animal boundary as a site of privileging which subjects are 'to be eaten' and which can only consume, the novel removes a conception of subjectivity that maintains a binary distinction between those included within the ethical community and those excluded from it. Butler's series finds a way outside the anthropological machine. She uses the conceit of becoming-animal to interrogate the ways in which this machine has excluded racial and class others, prohibitions equally as central to her transformative politics as the erasure of the human–animal boundary.

John Crowley similarly uses the idea of hybridity and becoming-animal to critique the exclusions of Western biopolitics in *Beasts* (1976). The novel opens with an epigraph from Act IV of *Timon of Athens*, a play about a generous man who is abandoned by his friends when his money runs out and who comes to curse humanity for its insincere flattery and lack of real community. In a soliloquy earlier in this Act, Timon announces his hatred of mankind and his plan to retreat into the woods

> where he shall find
> The unkindest beast more kinder than mankind. (IV, i, XX)

There he meets another Athenian, Apemantus, and they conclude that had they the power, the best thing to do for the world would be to 'Give it the beasts, to be rid of the men' (IV, iii, XX). When Apemantus indicates his preference for existing as a beast among beasts rather than being set apart as is 'man', Timon responds with a long discussion of the hierarchy among animals, concluding with 'What beast couldst thou be, that were not subject to a beast? and what a beast art thou already, that seest not thy loss in transformation!' (IV, iii, XX). It is this speech which opens the novel, one which is offered by Timon just after he has discovered gold in the woods while digging for food and distributed it to former friends, not out of generosity as was his previous practice, but rather to support their efforts to destroy his former home, Athens. The exchange with Apemantus is typically interpreted as more evidence of the absence of true community in the play because even in their moment of bonding over their shared hatred of humanity, Timon and Apemantus soon fall into an exchange of insults. Even Timon's idealised vision of the animal life is transformed into a more pessimistic vision of the war of all-against-all even among animals.

Crowley shifts the thematic terrain to consider questions of community and friendship not merely among humans but also between humans and other species. This future world includes hybrid beings called leos, a mixture of human and lion DNA produced by the science of 'diagenetics' (9) which originally aimed to increase food production by creating hybrid plants that produce, for example, huge walnuts or 'tough as weeds' (9), high-protein wheat. Written before modern gene-splicing techniques made the chimerical beings with which we are familiar in the twenty-first century, *Beasts'* version of genetic hybridity is different from such real-life examples in one crucial way: rather than positing the insertion of a specific gene from another species so that it can modify what otherwise largely remains a single genetic species – such as a fish gene spliced into tomatoes in order to enable them to better withstand freezing temperatures – Crowley's diagenetics produces fully hybrid beings, each cell possessing equally the genetic qualities of two distinct things. The leos created by this process are not humans with some lion characteristics, nor lions with some human capacities: instead, they are something else entirely, a being that exceeds the categories of the human–animal boundary. They thus offer an example of becoming-animal made literal. The novel focuses on four main characters: Painter, a leo who becomes a political leader for his people as they are increasingly marginalised and criminalised by the mainstream human society; Loren Casaubon, a tutor to the children of the leader of the Union for Social Engineering (USE), who becomes caught up with them in the political battles over the place of engineered beings in society; Reynard, an advisor to the USE's president who later proves to be working for his own agenda and supporting Painter; and Meric, a human activist whose politics become complicated in trying to sort through the difficulties raised by his commitment to animal preserves and their ban on hunting with his sympathy for the leos and education into their desire to adopt a more leonine lifestyle which would include hunting.

The novel foregrounds questions of community and biopolitics in its opening pages. Casaubon reflects upon the new USE ruling that calls for *'quarantine of free-living leos'* (8) and becomes worried about what this increased legislation of life itself might mean for the peregrine falcons he raises. The concern raised about the leos by the human community is the fear that they have exceeded the control of those who made them, able now to reproduce on their own and thus potentially to compete with humans over resources. Their existence also threatens the current social order simply by requiring its reconfiguration. Another character cautions Casaubon that his vision of interspecies relations is outmoded, that

life *is* surprising; *your* era's belief that one sort of life is basically hostile to another has long been disproven, is in fact if you think

about it self-evidently false. We are, each of us living things, nothing
but a consortium of other living things in a kind of continual parliamentary debate, dependent on each other, living on each other, no
matter how ignorant we are of it; penetrating each other's lives. (9)

This vision of the necessary interdependence of all living things can be
read as a politics of becoming, the social body being continually in flux,
a molecular being that is made up of various living beings coupling and
decoupling in diverse interrelations, not requiring the firm divisions of
the human–animal boundary nor biopolitical regulation by the USE.
Casaubon and others who benefit from the current social order resist such
an understanding of life, wanting instead to grasp it in ways analogous
to Linnaeus's cataloguing: a place for every being and each being in its
place. To such people, the leos are threatening not only in their different
embodiment and lifestyle, but also for the challenge they represent to the
taxonomical order and its inevitable privileging of humans (and historically its use to privilege male, white, heterosexual subjects of European
origin). Casaubon is the chief representative of such a view, at least in the
early parts of the novel, and his name is instructive here, reminding us as
it does of George Eliot's Edward Casaubon who is cut off from life, wasting
his days attempting to prove that his Key to All Mythologies can provide
a single explanatory framework that encompasses the whole tradition of
knowledge, what he believes to be fragments of a once pristine ancient
corpus. This privileging of the singular over the multiple is equally an
error in Crowley's work.

   Painter is fleeing to an animal preserve in order to escape confinement
to a lab and thereby his reduction to an object of scientific enquiry. He takes
with him a woman, Caddie, whom he buys as an indentured servant. The
relationship between Caddie and Painter reverses and thereby critiques the
usual relationships between humans and domesticated animals: although
it is only for a period of ten years, Painter nonetheless *owns* Caddie for
the duration of the bond and Caddie resents this relationship. Although
she recognises that her economic choices were indentured servitude or
prostitution, and that she prefers the former, she nonetheless feels 'hatred
that he had with so little thought snatched her from where she had been
– well, comfortable anyway. Hatred of her own powerlessness was what
it was, because he hadn't been cruel. The uses he put her to were what
she was for; it was in the papers; there was no appeal from that and he
made no bones about it' (26). Caddie's anger at her powerlessness and
lack of autonomy reveal to us something of the very inequitable power
relations that exist between humans and animals in most of our social
exchanges with them, even if we are kind and do not mistreat or abuse
them, as Caddie notes. Although she cannot herself clearly articulate her

desires, the novel makes clear that the problem is not Painter but rather the condition of being owned, the reduction of her subjectivity to 'what she was for' as defined by the contract. Later, when Caddie meets someone who tells her that the contract is void because it is illegal for a leo to own a human, regardless of the economic exchange, Caddie has begun to understand something of Painter's own struggle with similar social forces to the ones that oppress her, and she chooses to remain with him although not compelled to do so. In fact, the absence of the inherently exploitative relationship of ownership enables her to embrace life with him – and the other leos they meet on the preserve – in the spirit of a 'consortium of other living things': she is aware that she is not one of them and will never be included in their group on the same terms as a leo, but nonetheless she is included in their group in her own way.

Painter's confrontations with Meric over the leos' activities on the animal preserve suggest a similar privileging of community through multiplicity. Meric lives as part of a religious community isolated from human cities and from other species in caves near the animal preserve. Their founder argued that the best thing humans could do for the Earth is to withdraw from it:

> You have done enough damage to the earth and to yourselves. Your immense, battling ingenuity: turn it inward, make yourselves scarce, you can do that. Leave the earth alone: all its miracles happen when you're not looking. Build a mountain and you can all be troll-kings. The earth will blossom in thanks for it. (68)

Meric and his fellow practitioners are disturbed by the leos' presence because they see them as humans who have invaded a space restricted for animals, and they characterise the leos' hunting of other species as poaching. Meric confronts the community of leos and tries to explain to Painter that this land they occupy belongs to the mountain community; Painter responds in such a way that Meric becomes conscious that he is being forgiven for 'the error of ownership' (85), and he begins to question the ways he has been expressing his commitment to the flourishing of other species. Meric explains to Painter his plan to support the leos by making a documentary that would better enable humans to understand them and thus feel less threatened by them, but quickly realises that 'the creature before him would allow no decisions to be made about him' (85), that is, that a proper community of leos and humans could not emerge from such a context of human control. As he spends more time with the leos, Meric begins to find a way of being in sociality with them that does not presuppose as normal human ways of interrelating, learning that phatic discourse has no meaning for leos, for example, and that his principled rejection of non-vegetarian food offered to him is a rejection of fellowship. Caddie advises, 'Help them when you can, they won't mind. Don't try to understand them' (88), and Meric comes to see that his perception of her as having 'den[ied] so much of her own nature in order to live as they did' is wrong; instead, he realises she 'had only acceded to their presence, lived as nearly as she could at their direction and convenience, like a dog trying to please a beloved, contrary, willful, godlike man, because whatever self-denial that took, whatever inconvenience, there was nothing else worth doing' (89). Meric still perceives the relationship in terms of hierarchy, the preference for the leos over humans a continuation of the ideal of withdrawal valued by his religious community, but he approaches an understanding of multispecies, becoming-animal community in his new ability to perceive that he and Caddie need not mimic the leos in order to live with them as part of the same community.

This isolated community offers a model for a 'continual parliamentary debate' among different beings living with and dependent upon one another, but not necessarily identical to one another. It is disrupted by federal agents who invade the preserve, capturing Painter and killing one of his sons in the attack. Painter is taken back to the city and imprisoned, and here the narrative shifts to the perspective of a dog named Sweet who, like Painter, must survive in the chinks of human-centred civilisation. Sweet thinks of his previous owners as his pack, embracing a model of human–animal domestic relationship that exceeds the exploitation of ownership. It is significant that the novel demonstrates that such a multispecies community is possible not merely between the leos and humans, but also between humans and non-gengineered animals such as Sweet. Separated from his human pack, he must now negotiate a city in which stray dogs are poisoned or else 'routinely shot by the paramilitary gangs, for hygienic reasons it was claimed, but chiefly so the boys could let off steam' (101). Sweet has spent some time as a research animal (the fate Painter fights to avoid), and the experience has led him to conclude that 'It had taken centuries for the bonding of men and dogs to come about, for dogs to come to accept men as of the pack. In the city that bond was being unraveled in a mere decade' (102). Painter and Sweet encounter one another in the city where Painter is similarly on the run after escaping from jail, and the 'lion-man and the once-dog' find themselves able to communicate not through language but through something embodied and affective, a shared sensibility that makes them 'always subtly allied, of one mind. A gift, Painter thought when he later thought about it, of our alteration at men's hands; a gift they had never known about and which, if they could, they would probably try to take back' (111). This bond between

Sweet and Painter suggests that the community ideal toward which the novel gestures includes all living beings if not all in the same way: Sweet who is altered by laboratory experimentation, Painter who is a product of diagenetics, yet also the other dogs in Sweet's pack, and further those humans marginalised by the existing social order. The reason Sweet loses his home and becomes a street dog is that his Chinese owners are moved to a government relocation centre, forced to abandon all their possessions, including Sweet.

The novel's conclusion reveals that Painter has been at the centre of a political struggle orchestrated by Reynard, a character who appears to be human but who is later revealed to be a new strain of diagenetic fox/man hybrid. His name comes from the folklore fox found in popular culture dating from the medieval period. Reynard is a trickster figure, and in the earlier versions of this mythology is typically a folk hero figure that satirises the aristocracy or the clergy. The Reynard character is thus a figure that resonates with transformative becomings, one who resists the sanctioned channels for desire and subjectivity and challenges the hegemonic social order. In *Beasts* Reynard is a Machiavellian figure, hiding his hybridity from humans and thus not subject to the same restrictions as are placed on the leos. He is believed to be an adviser to the president of USE, but he has secretly been working to ensure the president's son, Sten, will grow to have different values than those of his father. Reynard orchestrates a plot to kill the USE president and to ally Sten with the outlaw, Painter, whom he has set up to become a leader of the leos and those humans who unite with them in wanting new social order. Reynard specifically identifies with the trickster figure of mythology in understanding himself and his role in shaping the social world. He feels there is 'no way ... to conceive of himself except as men had conceived of foxes' (50) as he has no history, being the only one of his kind. Yet even here Reynard reconfigures these tales in order to open new potentialities of becoming. He grasps that his identity is not merely a matter of 'how well that character [from medieval legend] fitted his nature', but instead and also the power to 'inven[t] his nature out of those tales' (50). One of these legends concerns the sport of fox hunting and the hunters' construction of this as a mutually enjoyed game of cunning. Fox-hunting folklore insists the fox equally enjoys the chase and 'used not natural terror in its flight but cunning practiced for its own sake' (51).[7] Reynard reverses this self-serving construction of an animal other, suggesting that the humans enjoy the games of political assassination as much as he does.

As the novel makes clear, the real threat the leos represent is not that of different embodiment, but rather that of a different kind of subjectivity and hence a different social order that might emerge from it. USE argues that they must destroy the leos because their sense of community – which is not a liberal, democratic humanist sensibility – inherently constitutes a threat to humanity. Among the leos' sins is that their 'only loyalty was to their pride' rather than to 'the scientific community that had given them birth, and had freed them in order to study them'; their refusal to allow human investigators to treat them as laboratory subjects and thereby to 'verify hypotheses' is equated with a lack of respect for 'human laws' and 'borders' (76). Although official USE discourse suggests that the leos have these flaws as 'the result of an intelligence too low to comprehend human values' (76), one of the humans sympathetic to the leos suggests this is instead 'a heart too great' (76). As is the case with Reynard and his identification with fox-man legends, it is stressed that the leos' different forms of sociality might equally be explained by having 'inherited this trait from their lion ancestors or [having] consciously modeled themselves on lion society' (76). The becoming-animal of the leos, then, and equally of the humans who affiliate themselves with the leo resistance is thus more than an imitation or identification, as Deleuze and Guattari insist. It is not merely the molar being of lions expressed through the hybrid genes, but instead a real becoming. Deleuze and Guattari argue 'the becoming-animal of the human being is real, even if the animal the human being becomes is not; and the becoming-other of the animal is real, even if that something other it becomes is not' (238). The community at the end of *Beasts* – Painter, Caddie, Sten, his sister, Loren, Reynard and even a recently liberated falcon – is a becoming-other of community, what Deleuze and Guattari call filiations of 'alliance' or a relation of 'involution', that is, evolution that is hetero-geneous, 'becoming communicative or contagious' (238). The novel ends at this moment of potentiality, open to a future that is not known and cannot be narrated as it is pure potentiality, not yet channelled into molar subjects and social forms.

The becoming-animal of *Beasts* thus has the energy that Jameson associates with the utopian form and the potentiality brought about by alterity of sf agents. Animals here mark the rupture which opens a space in which the as-yet-unknown might emerge. It is crucial that this space of rupture is a site of both new subjectivity and new community. Part of what Deleuze and Guattari value in becoming-animal is a rejection of a metaphysics of subjectivity premised on individualism, and the recognition that the subject is always-already multiple not only in the sense that it is fragmented, rife with contradiction and ambiguity, determined as much by cultural forces as much as by inner cognitions. Part of the potentiality opened up by a metaphysics of becoming instead of one of being is that we can also understand the subject as always-already multiple in the sense that the subject is a community, in Crowley's terms 'a consortium of other living things'. Jameson argues:

> insofar as our own society has trained us to believe that true disalienation or authenticity only exists in the private or individual realm, it may well be this revelation of collective solidarity which is the freshest one and the most startlingly and overtly Utopian: in Utopia, the ruse of representation whereby the Utopian impulse colonizes purely private fantasy spaces is by definition undone and socialized by their very realization. (230)

Beasts socialises our fantasy of community with other beings, moving it beyond the private spaces of pet-ownership and toward a vision of another sort of community that does not limit subjectivity to those deemed human.

Kirsten Bakis's *Lives of the Monster Dogs* (1997) is similarly interested in the question of intersubjective connection and community. The monster dogs are the outcome of a research project begun in the late nineteenth century by Prussian Augustus Rank under the sponsorship of Wilhelm II. Fearing the loss of control of his project, Rank flees with his research subjects and a group of followers and establishes the town of Rankstadt in an isolated part of Canada; the town and its inhabitants live isolated and unchanged by time, continuing research on the dogs until 1999, when the dogs rebel and kill all the humans. Ten years later the dogs arrive in New York City, where they meet Cleo Pira, a graduate student who becomes their friend and eventually the author of this manuscript, presented as if published in 2017. The monster dogs were meant to be soldiers for an unstoppable Prussian army, 'fierce, numerous, and disposable (for more could always be made), capable of remorseless killing and of loyalty stronger than their instincts for self-preservation' (115). They are bred for greater intelligence, have prosthetic hands in place of their front paws, can speak with the aid of another prosthesis, and have adopted the clothing and habits of the humans of Rankstadt and thus comport themselves like the upper classes of nineteenth-century Prussia. The dogs suffer from what they characterise as a mental illness, and eventually most are killed by a committee appointed to dispatch those who 'want' to die (the gap between the committee's interpretation of these subjects and the subjects' own desires remains ambiguous and shifting). Death is preferable to being

> confined in their laboratories and hospitals, and we will live on there, helpless, alone, humiliated. We may long for death, but they will not allow it. Should we refuse to eat, lose the ability to move, even to breathe, they will attach us to their abominable machines and keep us alive, prisoners. (179)

The dogs fear this fate and seem to prefer death, yet the committee rather than the individual is empowered to ascertain when a limit of madness has been reached.

The novel uses the device of the dogs to explore themes of loneliness and isolation. When they arrive in New York, Cleo is suffering from a broken heart, which she experiences as a literal sense of something in her chest bursting. Part of the manuscript is an excerpt from a history of their creation written by the dog Ludwig, who becomes Cleo's closest friend. He feels isolated from both human and dog communities: the dogs, he says, 'know that they are monsters, but I believe they do not really understand what that means to humans' (7), failing to recognise that 'they will never be seen as anything but caricatures of human beings. There is no place for monsters in this world' (8). Part of Ludwig's history is drawn from journals left by their creator, Augustus Rank, who died in 1916 before seeing the completion of his project. Rank is characterised as a sadist cut off from normal human relations by the death of his mother and a troubled childhood. He discovers connection to others only when he stabs a bird as a child, and this passion for controlling and manipulating life fuels his research on the dogs. He believes that when they are complete he 'won't *need the people anymore. The dogs will be my people, perfect extension of my will'* (4), and Ludwig comments on the irony of this conception of the dogs, one that denies their own subjectivity and thus one that could work only when the dogs 'were no more than an idea in his mind, a desire in his heart. Then we were all together in him and there was no loneliness. There was no difference between master and dog' (30). The material dogs exceed this conception of dog-ness and their eventual rebellion is led by a dog, Mops Hacker, who was meant to be destroyed when a puppy as he was not a good experimental subject, but who is saved and raised by Jebediah Arch, descendent of a North American family who came across the village in its early days and who lived in semi-outcast status on its edges.

The first success in Rankstadt's experiments was a dog named Rupert who spent the beginning of his life as a 'normal' dog before being transformed through surgery. Rupert is later killed by a bear while out hunting with his owner, and mythologies differ between dogs and humans as to whether he was defending his master from the bear or leading the bear to him. Rupert's discontent is linked not only to his suffering as an experimental subject, but also to the incongruity of his position as a monster dog: he is neither human nor fully dog any more, hence the appellation monster, a category of being which, as Elaine Graham notes, violates the taxonomic categories of modernity, polluting its 'ontological hygiene' which separates 'human from non-human, nature from culture, organism from machine' (35). Unlike the hybrid beings in Crowley's *Beasts*, however, the monster dogs are not successful in articulating a new metaphysics of becoming that challenges the molar categories of being sanctioned by the hegemonic culture. Instead, Rupert finds that discovering that he is a dog with his new capacity to understand what being a dog means to human culture was 'like waking up from a pleasant dream to find himself enslaved, as if he had been captured by members of another race while he slept, and taken away to their country' (138). In the novel, therefore, 'dog', functions as a marker of the category of those deemed not fully subjects as much as it represents a category of dog being or animality more generally. Writing of Rupert, Ludwig concludes, 'it is a terrible thing to be a dog and know it' (138). The dogs experience their own being as monstrous because they are so shaped by the molar identities of human and dog that they now relate to their own dog qualities with shame. Their insistence upon adopting human dress and manners even when doing so is uncomfortable is further evidence of how deeply they have been shaped by the human–animal boundary, even though they themselves have no place within this arrangement.

Yet the monster dogs do challenge aspects of the hegemonic anthropocentric order, particularly in relation to the exclusion of animals from those whose putting-to-death is a violation of the ethical order. One of Derrida's objections to the ways animals have been integrated into human systems of knowledge is that producers of such knowledge have never

> taken into account the essential or structural differences among animal species. Not one of them has taken into account, in a serious and determinate manner, the fact that we hunt, kill, exterminate, eat, and sacrifice animals, use them, make them work or submit them to experiments that are forbidden to be carried out on humans. (*The Animal* 89)

Discussing the massacre of the humans at Rankstadt and their discomfort in talking about it with those in New York, one dog tells Cleo

> it's ridiculous that in a place where dogs are killed by the millions for no reason whatsoever and humans are allowed to kill each other *en masse* in wars, though not for perfectly legitimate personal reasons on the street, it's ridiculous that anyone would feel we ought to be brought to justice for settling our own quarrel in Rankstadt, but that's what the worry was. (164)

This dog elaborates that he realises the difficulty is the species boundary: had they been humans killing an oppressive government no one would have cared, but dogs killing humans is another matter, a threat to the metaphysics of subjectivity that produces the human by the exclusion of the animal and thereby a threat to the hegemonic social order based on this conception of the subject.

As the dogs are well aware, the human social order is rife with contradictions and moral aporias, yet such gaps are not perceptible within the logic of species difference. The dogs try to explain to Cleo that

> we feel about fighting and killing that it's a part of life. Sometimes the end of life, to be sure, if you're the one who's killed, but it's all very natural. That's the way we feel, and that's the way we were brought up, too. And we enjoy it. No matter what they have done to our brains we're still dogs. (163)

Yet their embrace of human manners makes it difficult for them to accept the dog aspects of their nature and this is part of what makes them feel isolated and lonely. Despite this defence of open killing as more natural, we never see the dogs engage in any sort of hunting or other aggressive behaviour, except in their battles against one another at the very end of the novel and in the libretto to an opera written about the rebellion. A dog critiques the hypocrisy at the root of human culture's use of killing which exists within a psychic economy of disavowal, arguing that an honest relationship to the reality of killing is 'something I miss in your culture, by the way ... No blood. Everything is so sanitized. There are hardly any butchers' shops. And yet the slaughterhouses that supply your meat, I've seen them on television, they're really appalling, hellish. It's not natural at all' (163). The dogs nonetheless try to adopt the lifestyle of twenty-first century New Yorkers just as they had earlier adopted that of nineteenth-century Prussians, but this only leaves them feeling more monstrous in its inadequacy. Ludwig and Cleo admit to one another that they each try to imagine what it would be like to be the other species, but Ludwig cannot take seriously Cleo's desire, dismissing it as a fantasy projection of human construction of dog existence, not a true understanding of otherness. He argues, 'being a dog is nothing ... Literally. It is nothing but an absence, a negative ... The canine instincts, the soldier instincts, are worse than useless now; they are destructive, ridiculous. But nothing can be done about it' (225).

Lives of the Monster Dogs is thus not a novel of becoming-animal. The dogs do represent a challenge to molar human identity and hence to the existing social order, but this challenge is debilitating rather than energising and an opening up of new potentialities, as in *Clay's Ark* or *Beasts*. At the same time, however, the tragedy of the dogs' lives enables a critique of the species boundary and its metaphysical implications: for subjectivity, for biopolitics and for ethics. At the very end of the novel, Ludwig writes letters to Cleo from his hospital bed (he has been injured in a fall, either an attempted suicide or merely an attempted escape from his apartment where he has been imprisoned to protect him from his own madness). Cleo is also confined in the dogs' castle, Neuhundstein, modelled on the mad Bavarian king's Neuschwanstein,[8] where the dogs have retreated to spend their final days of madness beyond prying human eyes.

Ludwig tells Cleo he has had an epiphany and 'what *I now know could, I believe, save all the dogs if I could explain it to them*' (272): '*hope is motion,*' he tells her, '*curiosity, desire, and hope alone can keep the surface from being drawn back to reveal the terrifying mechanism of the world … In order to live, Cleo, you must feel desire*' (273). These images – hope, desire, curiosity, motion – are modalities of becoming rather than being. They gesture toward molecular identities and social structures, an existence not captured by the molar identities of either dog or human. Ludwig asks Cleo

> *did you ever love me as a living creature? I mean was there anything, ever, about standing next to me that you could not put into words, or keep in your heart? Those are the things that remain unsaid, the little sparks. They cannot exist on their own; they must cling to something else, for they are nothing in themselves; they only make up the spaces in between those things that can be perceived.* (277)

This embodied yet ineffable sense of connection infuses the novel's conclusion. It enables Cleo and Lydia to escape the collapsing castle and to build new lives of community rather than isolation. Cleo is married and has a daughter in 2017, when she writes the preface to the novel, and Lydia lives on a country estate filled with friends. Thus *Lives of the Monsters Dogs*, a tragedy of the failure of becoming for most of its subjects, ends with this gesture of hope which – like all becomings and utopian impulses – remains a spark and a potentiality rather than a fixed and nameable thing.

3. The Animal Responds: Language, Animals and Science Fiction

In Kij Johnson's 'The Evolution of Trickster Stories among the Dogs of North Park after the Change' (2007), dogs suddenly gain the ability to speak. The desire to communicate with another species is a common fantasy in sf, both through the common trope of the alien, as discussed in my introduction, and through the many stories involving modified pets able to communicate with their owners through synthesised speech or telepathy, such as the speaking cat in Suzy McKee Charnas's 'Scorched Supper on New Niger' (1980) or the telepathic dog in Roger Zelazny's *He Who Shapes* (1965). Often such stories are romanticised ideals of perfect union, the pet characters seeing humans the way we would like to be seen, speaking with voices that echo the projections of pet-owners who speak for their animals. Johnson's story is more sceptical that an ideal of interspecies community can be achieved without significant struggle over different ways of being-in-the-world. Her dogs and cats mostly prefer to leave their owners to seek freedom over safety. Cats find humans boring, even the ones who love their owners, and the owners are frightened by the cats' 'pragmatic sociopathy',[1] even the ones who love their pets. The dogs, pack animals, have more difficulty adjusting. Some run away, but many are thrown out by owners made uncomfortable by the new intersubjective dynamic. These dogs, most of whom now live in North Park, will interact with humans but only cautiously, a 'hurt wariness' in their eyes.

The story thus explores the dialectic of dominance and affection that Tuan argues is the essence of the pet dynamic. It gives voice to the animals literally, but also attempts to give them voice by acknowledging that, were the animals to speak, their perspective on the world would be other than our own. It also forcibly confronts us with the fact that our relationship with domesticated animals, however affectionate it might be on the intersubjective level, is also historically a product of humanity's domination of nature and other species. The narrator reminds us

> It's a universal fantasy, isn't it? – that the animals learn to speak, and at last we learn what they're thinking, our cats and dogs and horses: a new era in cross-species understanding. But nothing ever works out quite as we imagine. When the Change happened, it affected all

the mammals we have shaped to meet our own needs. They all could
talk a little, and they all could frame their thoughts well enough to
talk. Cattle, horses, goats, llamas; rats, too. Pigs. Minks. And dogs
and cats. And we found that, really, we prefer our slaves mute.

Johnson thus makes us think not only about the fantasy of communicating with an alien other but also the difficulty of acknowledging that
other as a fellow subject. It is crucial to note that the animals affected by
the Change are those 'we have shaped to meet our own needs'. The dogs in
the park interact with Linna, a young girl who brings them food, and tell
her stories of their own emerging mythology. The stories are always about
'this is the same dog' and they stress the various ways that dogs' worlds
have been limited by their lack of agency: One Dog pulls from a restrictive
collar and is hit by a car in the street; One Dog is hit with a newspaper for
urinating too close to the master; One Dog is shot for mating with a female
whose owner tries to keep her segregated. As the stories evolve, the dogs
begin to integrate into their mythology aspects of human culture they
have learned from their proximity to humans. Their ability to incorporate
aspects of human behaviour into their mythology reminds us that
animals see and have a perspective on us, precisely what Derrida critiques
philosophy for forgetting – or rather, for having to exclude in order for its
metaphysics of subjectivity and ethics to operate. A late story even has
One Dog kill and eat his owner, Hungry Man, because Hungry Man ate all
available food, including the kibble. Like humans, the dogs in the stories
desire connection with the other species, but equally like us they realise
that the two species exist in a dialectic of symbiosis and competition.

One of Wittgenstein's most famous aphorisms regarding language is 'If
a lion could talk, we could not understand him' (qtd in Wolfe *Animal Rites*
44). Johnson's narrator observes that 'perhaps the dogs always told these
stories and we could not understand them' and further 'the cats after the
Change tell stories as well, but no one will ever know what they are'. Thus
Johnson, like Wittgenstein, stresses that it is not that animals cannot or
are not speaking, but rather that they do so in a language that is so alien to
humans that we cannot understand it. This is because language is integrally
tied to a form of life, produced by concrete and embodied experience that
varies among species. Yet this need not be taken only as grounds for despair
and the failure of even the fantasy of communication. As Cary Wolfe
points out, truly communicating with an animal other is about facing a
consciousness that is beyond ours. Wolfe sees promise in Wittgenstein's
account of language because it disrupts 'the ontological difference between
human and animal' which is 'expressed in the philosophical tradition
by the capacity for language' (47). Wolfe finds Wittgenstein's theories of
language productive because in them the question 'what is the difference

between human and animal' is not something that can be solved by a singular answer that can permanently fix a line between two distinct ontological orders; instead, the query is kept 'alive and open by insisting that the differences between participants in specific language games and those "not of their flesh" may be as profound as those usually taken to obtain between the human *as such* and the animal *as such*' (47). Most crucially, from the point of view of sf criticism, Wittgensteinian language games enable us to grasp that the shared dynamics of world and being that emerge through communication are not limited by the human–animal boundary: 'not *the* world but simply *a* world emerges from building a shared form of life through participation in a language game' (47–48).

Yet if humans and animals are to share a language game and build a world which is common to both, we must do so in a way that breaks free of romanticised versions of human–animal relationships under a different regime, as Johnson's story stresses. Perfect knowledge does not immediately and without struggle lead to perfect harmony. After the Change, pets and their owners are more distant: Hope, a dog who mourns the loss of her human family 'compulsively licks her paw as if she were dirty and cannot be cleaned', and 'some dog owners feel a cold place in the pit of their stomachs when they meet their pets' eyes'. Johnson's story challenges us to become posthuman in our interspecies relations, just as Smith has done in her cohabitation with rabbits, shaping her household in ways that accommodate both her and the rabbits' needs. Many of the abandoned dogs in the park long for their owners and want to return: the dogs still love their owners as for them human frailty and limitation is hardly news. The humans, in contrast, all too often prefer 'mute slaves' to engagement with another living being. Only a few 'keep their dogs, even after the Change. Some people have the strength to love, no matter what. But many of us only learn the limits of our love when they have been breached'. The story also reminds us of the long process of forming the human–dog bond through domestication, and of the deeper and older predatory relationship between canines and primates. Hearing the dogs howl one day in the park, Linna is overwhelmed by this embodied memory:

> Adrenaline hits hot as panic. Her heart beats so hard that it feels as though she's torn it. Her monkey-self opens her eyes to watch the dogs through pupils constricted enough to dim the twilight; it clasps her arms tight over her soft belly to protect the intestines and liver that are the first parts eaten; it tucks her head between her shoulders to protect her neck and throat.

She is reminded that the dogs' love of humans is a choice that they have made.

As the story concludes, the dogs and Linna struggle with this complicated history of the dialectic of dominance and affection in human-pet relationships. The dogs conclude that people are both 'nice' and 'not-nice' but seem unable to fathom why. New dogs who arrive at the park begin to see Linna as a representative of the problematic species human rather than as an individual who 'got rid of my collar when it got burrs under it ... took the tick off me ... stroked my head'. As Linna becomes reduced to the sort of discursive category which humans so often use to encompass other beings – Derrida explains 'The animal, what a word! The animal is a word, it is an appellation that men have instituted, a name they have given themselves the right and the authority to give to the living other' (*The Animal* 23) – she feels more and more at risk in the park. Her interactions with the dogs have taken on a quality of abstraction, the sort of reduction of the other to object that has been typical of human social relations with animals. Yet the story offers hope for changing this dialectic. The Change which gave animals language also gave them memory, the narrator tells us, and with memory comes the need for forgiveness. Dogs loved humans before the Change, and could love them after, but humans must become other than humanity as it is currently configured in order for this to be possible:

> Whatever else it is, the Change of the animals – mute to speaking, dumb to dreaming – is a test for us. We pass the test when we accept that their dreams and desires and goals may not be ours. Many people fail this test. But we don't have to, and even failing we can try again. And again. And pass at last.

The dominant humans in the story fail the test. As the dog community in the park grows and the Humane Society shelter is filled to overflowing with abandoned pets, the authorities choose to respond with violence rather than a restructuring of the boundaries of ethics. They poison the dogs in the park and police patrol to shoot any lingering animals whose voice has been reduced to 'the ancient language of pain, wordless yelps and keening'.

But Linna passes the test, adopting a trickster role and pretending to work for animal control so that she might help some of the dogs escape the park. The Change which gives animals speech literally within the story is thus also a metaphorical change in the way that we conceptualise other beings in and through language. The narrator concludes, 'When we first fashioned animals to suit our needs, we treated them as if they were stories and we the authors, and we clung desperately to an imagined copyright that would permit us to change them, sell them, even delete them. But some stories cannot be controlled.' Johnson's story as a whole ends with a final One Dog tale in which One Dog makes the world, a world premised on smell rather than on sight and thus a challenge to anthropo-centric concepts of knowledge and the world itself as constructed through our epistemology.

Language is important in this story and in the intersections of HAS and sf in three ways: first, language is one of the chief capacities which our philosophical tradition has denied animals, and this purported inability to use language has been one of the main rationales deployed to uphold the species boundary; second, as poststructuralist theory has taught us, language has the power to create the perceptual and experiential world in specific ways, structures that are imbued with power relations emerging from the difference between those who have the power to name and those who must speak in another's discourse; finally, language and the recognition of communication in others is one of the key ways that we might begin to rethink and change our relationships with other species and thus produce a more ethical world, an ideal that Johnson's story makes literal in the Change. The desire to communicate with another – and thereby confirm its sentience and prove that humans are not alone in the universe – fuels much of sf, epitomised in such early stories as Stanley Weinbaum's tale of male bonding, 'A Martian Odyssey' (1934), or Murray Leinster's invention of the universal translator made possible through a shared sense of humour (and not incidentally, sexism and xenophobia) in 'First Contact' (1945). Although sf includes stories of communication with another terran species, as I mentioned above, more often than not these narratives concern fictional beings rather than those with whom we already share the planet, perhaps for the reasons Johnson's story suggests: humans have a history of exploiting and marginalising other species and friendship would be difficult to construct out of this history. Yet as Claude Lévi-Strauss laments, 'No situation appears more tragic, more offensive for the heart and the mind ... than that of a humanity that coexists with another species of life on earth which they share in enjoying, but with whom it cannot communicate' (qtd in Lingis 43).

Even without the Change, there is significant evidence that animals can and do communicate with us, from the hybrid dialect of word and gesture we construct with our pets, to experiments which reveal significant language acquisition in other primates and in dolphins.[2] Research on animal cognition and communication confirms Wittgenstein's insight that language is entwined with a form of life. Sf's long history of exploring the intricacies and pitfalls of communicating with another species is instructive here. When aliens meet, they can exchange words and might seem to be sharing a common sense of their meaning, but individual words offered by either species are grounded in concrete and material histories that are not shared.[3] Cross-species communication, in life as in sf, requires our attention to this fact and sensitivity to ways in which different embodiment, different priorities and different ways of perceptually experiencing the world shape language use. Thus all acts of communication among species, even if they speak the same language, are also moments of translation. For example, Terry Carr's 'The Dance of the Changer and the Three' insists that the story of contact between human and Loarra cannot be told 'just as it happened' either in the Loarra's 'shifting wave-dances' (39) or even in human narration. The narrator continually interrupts the story, telling the reader 'I *know* a lot of this doesn't make sense. Maybe that's because I'm trying to tell you about the Loarra in human terms, which is a mistake with creatures as alien as they are' (41). It also reminds us that getting it wrong, failing to retain a sense of the otherness of the non-human, can have tragic consequences. The story of 'The Dance of the Changer and the Three', a legend within Carr's text, is an artwork our human narrator does not understand, whose climax is 'that supremely contradictory moment when the Three destroyed what they had made, when they came away with no more than they had brought with them' (52). The narrator sees the impenetrability of this cultural text as analogous to the Loarra's destruction of the mining operation and forty-two of its human crew, an attack for which their only explanation is 'an answer that doesn't translate. Or if it does, the translation is just "Because"' (53). As in Johnson's story, communication with another entails risk, not merely of misunderstanding but of discovering that one lives in a fundamentally different world, structured by different ideals and imperatives. Yet the fantasy of communicating with our pets is also evident in sf, such as Clifford Simak's 'Desertion' (1944)[4] in which a commander, Fowler, and his dog, Towser, are both transformed into a common sort of embodiment required to live on Jupiter. In this state, they are capable of using their entire brains and thus can communicate. Fowler is amazed to discover that Towser can talk, but Towser tells him 'I always talked to you, but you couldn't hear me' (113); Towser blames himself for this failure of communication, confessing 'I couldn't make the grade', but Fowler's inability to hear another kind of speech is also indicted: 'you knew when I wanted food and when I wanted a drink and when I wanted out, but that's about all you ever managed' (113).

Ursula Le Guin's story 'The Author of the Acacia Seeds' (1974) is a powerful example of the way language creates a world specific to the experience of the language user, and further of how the sf imagination can produce new potentialities for communicating with another species. The story presents itself as a series of excerpts from the *Journal of the Association of Therolinguistics*, a discipline that translates as 'beast linguistics'. The story thus posits as axiomatic that human linguistics is only one semiotic among many, decentring language as one of the warrants of the gap between humans and animals. The first article is a message found in an anthill, 'written in touch-gland exudation on degerminated acacia seeds' (200). The passage is fragmented and thus the journal offers more than one way of interpreting its meaning, the difficulty being that the text uses only the root forms of verbs, and thus might be either an autobiographical statement expressed in the first person, or a manifesto expressed in the imperative. A complex understanding of ant society is conveyed by the reading of the seeds: the journal article observes that this text differs from known dialects of Ant not only in its ambiguous use of person, but further in its unconventional use of certain words, such as a mark usually translated as 'Praise the Queen!' which has been truncated and thus seems to mean only 'Praise!', or the use of a mark that seems to signify 'without ants', which the translators speculate means 'alone' – 'a concept for which no word/mark exists in Ant' (202). The interpretation of Seeds 30–31 requires further contextualisation. They appear to read 'Eat the eggs! Up with the Queen!', but as the journal article points out, this reading may be 'an ethnocentric interpretation of the word "up." To us, "up" is a "good" direction. Not so, or not necessarily so, to an ant' (202). Thus the authors venture, this second seed might be read as expressing the sentiment 'Down with the Queen!' (202). Interpretation of this rebellious sentiment not only gives us a complex understanding of ant semiotics, but also suggests the existence of those who defy the monarchical social order and thus of diversity within ant society.

Le Guin's story uses the extrapolative methods of sf imaginatively to engage with the experience of another terran species rather than inventing – and setting for her characters and readers the puzzle of figuring out – an alien one. The story foregrounds relationships among embodiment, social structure and the emergence of a semiotic system that highlights those things of significance to the particular language user. The next article announces an expedition to observe emperor penguins in order to further develop understanding of the difficult dialects of Penguin. This section of the story emphasises even more strongly than did the first that if we are to communicate with other species, we must expand our definition of what constitutes a language. The Ant language was written in exudation; Penguin is written 'almost entirely in wings, neck, and air' (204). Animal language in the story is also not merely a method of the most pragmatic communication, but instead is also an art form: of the many animal literatures Penguin is 'most elegant and lively', the journal argues, although 'the nuances, and perhaps the essence, must forever elude' (204) non-native speakers. This article gives us some history of the difficult struggle to grasp Penguin, scholars at first being mislead by a similarity to Dolphin 'in *form*' which resulted in the misleading assumption that it would also resemble Dolphin 'in *content*' (204). Similarly, Penguin is a kinetic language of group performance and thus translations can only ever be 'mere notes' that cannot capture 'the all-important *multiplicity* of the original text' (205). Le Guin is able to suggest with admirable economy a rich world of multispecies communication through this brief discussion of Penguin's relation to other languages: like Dolphin, it has 'the same extraordinary wit, the flashes of crazy humor, the inventiveness, and the inimitable grace', which distinguishes it from 'thousands of literatures of the Fish stock' which lack humour, and further from 'the superb gracefulness of Shark or Tarpon [which] is utterly different from the joyous vigor of all Cetacean scripts' (204). Therolinguistics needs to remember the importance of embodiment and social structure, this article's authors conclude, as failing to account fully for these things is what has led them to overestimate the similarities between Penguin and Dolphin: 'The temperature of the blood is a bond. But the construction of the brain, and of the comb, makes a barrier! Dolphins do not lay eggs. A world of difference lies in that simple fact' (204).

'The Author of the Acacia Seeds' thus conveys much more about animal being than merely the premise that animals, too, might have language. The descriptions of the various languages and their specific qualities work against the conflation of all non-human species into the single category 'animal', compelling readers to recall that non-human species are multiple and complex – a fact made evident not merely the differences among the various species from ants through dolphins, but further in the insistence that there is no single Ant or Dolphin language any more than there is a single Human one. Further, the descriptions of the qualities of the literature these various species produce show them to be complex subjects with emotions, a sense of aesthetics and a sense of humour (the quality so crucial to Leinster's characters being able to make contact with an alien species and recognise this other as sentient). In this way, Le Guin's story works against typical representations of animals in human scientific and philosophical history which has reduced them to creatures of instinct alone, imagining their various means of communication (which include but are not limited to vocalisations, as Le Guin insists) to express only the most pragmatic of concerns. Although we can see many similarities between Le Guin's construction of a future in which animal languages are regularly studied by humans and other sf which struggles to find ways to communicate with alien species, there is a crucial difference. While aliens remain creatures of human imagination, speaking to our desire to connect with an other consciousness but unable to create the conditions where that might happen, Le Guin's story posits such exchanges with the sort of beings with whom we already live. The final entry in the journal, an editorial by the president of the Therolinguistics Association, gestures toward this material possibility. The address opens with reflection on the nature of art and language, and cautions against a presumption that misses evidence of communication in other beings because such communication does not resemble human modes.

The reach of Le Guin's story might seem extreme to some readers: for example, the president's message ends envisioning a future in which the entire planet is regarded as communicative, and geolinguists translate the 'delicate, transient lyrics of the lichen' and the 'more passive, wholly atemporal, cold, volcanic poetry of the rocks' (210). Yet readers of both the journal and the story are cautioned not to 'become slaves to our own axioms' (209). Few now doubt that mammals have communicative systems, although the notion that animals might have some aesthetic sensibility is less popularly accepted. Biologist Jakob von Uexküll, who developed the idea of the *Umwelt* to explain each species' perceptually distinct world, argued that even alien animals might be understood by 'scientifically grounded and phenomenologically guided efforts of imagination' (Acampora 'Animal Philosophy' 154). 'The Author of the Acacia Seeds' thus uses a typical trope of sf to encourage its readers to reflect not only on the nature of semiotics, but also on our opportunities – usually missed – to communicate with the other species with whom we share the planet. Yet in striving for such communication, we must not be limited by either our own preformed conclusion that certain species cannot communicate or by forgetting that such communication is never (as in all good sf) transparent or complete.

Paul Ash's 'Big Sword' (1958) starts with the point of view of the alien/animal to explore the difficulty of communicating with an alien being who at first does not appear to be sentient because it does not communicate in the 'normal' way. Our protagonist, Big Sword, is 'a leader from his birth' because 'intelligence was strictly proportional to size' (205) for his species. His People are confronted with an invasion of their forest by Big Folk: they have tried to communicate with these newcomers, but the Big Folk do not speak in 'an ordered succession of symbols' but merely a 'rush of patterns and half-patterns' that are meaningless to the People. Some researchers hypothesise that 'there was some connection between the disappearance of thought and the vibrating wind which the Big Folk would suddenly emit from a split in their heads' (206) but thought and sound waves are so unrelated in the People's experience that little credence is given to this theory. It is only when the point of view shifts to describe the human members of the Second Lambdan Exploratory Party and we see the People from an external perspective that we realise that they are insect-like, resembling some sort of mantis or grasshopper, and the Big Folk are human. Ash's story does much to displace anthropocentric assumptions by beginning with the perspective of the People, thereby enabling readers to see that, from the point of view of a different social and embodied experience, human intelligence and communication are not self-evident. This is similar to Le Guin's stipulation that we consider the existence of such qualities in animals. At the same time, the story is sufficiently immersed in anthropocentric assumptions such that the People never question the conclusion that the Big Folk are sentient beings nor cease in their efforts to communicate with them; the People do, however, begin to speculate that size and intelligence might be inversely related in these new creatures.

Contact is eventually achieved through the mediation of a young boy, Ricky, son of one of the human explorers. The background story of Ricky's troubled relationship with his mother – which is why he is on assignment with his father – and of the trouble Ricky causes among members of the expedition will cue any reader familiar with sf tropes to the fact that Ricky is telepathic. Thus it is no surprise when the People's semiotics of thought turns out to be telepathic communication, and Ricky proves to be the one intermediate who can translate between the two. Less complex than 'The Dance of the Changer and the Three', communication in 'Big Sword' is accomplished fairly smoothly once each species recognises the other as a sentient being (or, more to the point, once the humans begin to see the People as fellow subjects), and this contact averts disaster because Ricky is able to explain to the human party that a tree they planned to destroy forms an integral part of the People's reproductive cycle. In a pattern consistent with early sf lost-race narratives that John Rieder has insightfully diagnosed, the humans come to the rescue of the non-human natives as their biological surveys enable the discovery of a tree that produces the females of the species, from which Big Sword's people have been isolated by terrain changes, and thus humans are able to create a corridor between two sides of a Rift that reconnects the bifurcated species. Discussing Weinbaum's 'A Martian Odyssey', Rieder argues 'one of the marks of colonial-racist ideology on the narrative is the fact that for some unexplained reason Tweel seems to be as much an isolated stranger in this environment as the human narrator does, as if for the good Martian, like the good natives of lost-race fiction, the planet is a wilderness waiting to be humanized' (58). In the context of 'Big Sword' we can see how this ideology, like the colonial and racist discourses from which it emerges, is similarly marked by speciesism.

In the philosophical tradition, speciesism is linked in many ways to language. As I have already discussed, Heidegger's distinction of the

Dasein from animal being is one of the pivotal moments in this intellectual history, and, as Matthew Calarco explains, Heidegger bases this distinction in large part on his assertion that 'animals lack man's specific relation to language ... because they lack "world" ... Plants and animals do not *eksist* outside of themselves in the clearing of Being, but simply *live* within their surrounding environment' (50). Descartes, who before Heidegger was the chief architect of the human–animal boundary, similarly denies to animals a capacity for language – denies in fact a capacity for communicative utterance altogether. In reducing the animal to an automaton, stressing that its communicative behaviours must not be interpreted as meaningful or similar to human communicative behaviours but must instead be dismissed as mere unthinking playing-out of stimuli, Descartes reduces animal communication to 'a language that doesn't respond because it is fixed or stuck in the mechanicity of its programming, and finally lack, defect, deficit, or deprivation' (Derrida *The Animal* 87). Descartes thus establishes the place of animals within the philosophic tradition as one quite similar to that of robots or androids within sf: these beings, despite their apparent similarities to human subjects, are merely executing a programme rather than engaging with the world. At the same time, however, as sf texts from Asimov's robot stories to *Do Androids Dream of Electric Sheep?* continually remind us, the human imagination struggles to accept this boundary between human and machine, finding more promising tales in its breach.

The history of the human–animal boundary is similar, with human self-interest in denying the affinities and thereby justifying our continued exploitation of animals warring with flashes of insight that disarm such rationalisations. Language and the question of what it means to be a being of/in language is critical to this distinction, so much so that Derrida proclaims, 'the said question of the said animal in its entirety comes down to knowing not whether the animal speaks but whether one can know what *respond* means. And how to distinguish a response from a reaction' (*The Animal* 8). The question of language is thus more complex than the presence of a communicative utterance, but instead hinges on this distinction between the (unthinking, instinctual) response and the (sentient, intentional) reaction. How can we decide when what appears to be cognition is merely its simulation, and what might it mean if we were no longer able to draw this boundary with any certainty? The desire to preserve some grounds for human exceptionalism is the unspoken subtext that fuels much of the anxiety circulating around the question of sentience and how we might recognise its presence in a non-human being.

Considering the question from the perspective of research in AI and specifically Rodney Brooks's research on embodied robots, Hayles points out that part of what is potentially distressing about the correspondence between humans and robots is not that they might be able to think as we do, but rather that most of what we do – and think of as defining our humanity – does not require consciousness as the dominant mental activity. In fact, consciousness is 'an emergent property that increases the functionality of the system but is not part of the system's essential architecture' (238), the implication of which is that 'although it thinks it is the main show, [consciousness] is in fact a late-comer, a phenomenon dependent on and arising from deeper and more essential layers of perception and being' (238). Hayles's point is to remind us of the importance of embodiment to the experience of being human and thereby to argue contra theorists such as Hans Moravec who equate human subjectivity with consciousness and suggest that it, like data, might be transferred among media without discernible change (a perspective Hayles regards as a false binary not only as concerns human subjectivity but in relation to data overall).[5] This leads Hayles to a definition of the posthuman which requires us to rethink our conception of human subjectivity and move beyond the mind/body dualism that has been so influential for defining the humanist subject. A further implication of this position not addressed by Brooks or by Hayles is that such a rethinking of the centrality of consciousness to human subjectivity similarly entails a rethinking of the human–animal boundary. This rethinking does not demand a collapse of the human–animal distinction into a singular category of being, but rather implies rejecting the reaction/response division as utterly absolute and determinant of the difference between subject and object status. It involves learning to see that there is more than reaction in animal communication, as well as less than response in much of what humans do.

For Derrida, response and responsibility are linked terms. Because animals lack the 'I think' of the *cogito*, they are presumed also to be deprived of 'understanding and reason, response and responsibility' (*The Animal* 94). Derrida's point is not merely to challenge the presumption that animals lack these capacities and critique an ethics that judges that since an animal is deemed incapable of accepting responsibility there can similarly be no ethical responsibility toward it. Beyond this, Derrida also calls into question the degree to which humans fully possesses the qualities that the philosophical tradition deems 'proper' to humans and absent in animals. Challenging 'the purity, the rigor, and the indivisibility' (*The Animal* 125) of separating reaction from response as concerns humans, Derrida argues, has the consequence of 'casting doubt on all responsibility, all ethics, every decision' when we find that this line cannot hold between 'the human *in general* and the animal *in general*' (*The Animal* 126). The question of language then – specifically the ideal that language is characterised by the response which is wholly different from the reaction – returns us to the ethical function of the human–animal boundary. Discussing Levinas's concept of the ethical appeal of the 'face' of the other and respect for absolute alterity as the grounds for ethical behaviour, Derrida points out a fundamental tension in Levinas's thought because of his refusal to concede that animals fall within the bounds of those to whom we owe an ethical duty. Thus Levinas's ethic 'forbids murder, namely, homicide, but doesn't forbid putting to death in general, no more than it responds to a respect for life, a respect in principle for life in general' (Derrida *The Animal* 110).

In contrast to Heidegger, who posits the special 'being' of the human *Dasein* as that which creates the ethical subject, Levinas posits a break with being that is uniquely human. This break is the recognition of the ethical appeal of the face of the other, a face that says 'I am' and thus confronts the subject which its own, other irreducible being. Humans are uniquely able to see that there is something more important than one's own life – that is, the life of the other, the ethical appeal of the 'I am' which is the face of the other – and hence humans live within a condition of ethics while animals exist merely in a struggle for life outside of ethics. Levinas argues that the animal can never constitute this appeal, that it can call to our sympathy but that its presence never confronts us with the 'I am' of another being to demand of us an ethical response. In his essay 'The Name of a Dog, or Natural Rights' Levinas describes his experience in a slave-labour camp and the prisoners' encounter with a stray dog they name Bobby who greeted them each day as they returned to the camp. Levinas finds incongruous the experience of being categorised as less-than-human by the German guards at the same time that his and the other prisoners' human status is acknowledged by the dog's reaction to them. Far from being comforted by Bobby's reaction, Levinas finds in it instead further evidence for the way Jews were animalised and 'entrapped in their species' (153) by Nazi ideology – part of which, not incidentally, renders them 'beings without language' (153). Bobby's service to the prisoners is to remind them of their humanity and help them break free of the degree to which constant dehumanising treatment was producing a feeling of lost humanity. By responding to the men as men, Bobby reminds them of their humanity.

Yet Levinas insists that Bobby's regard is insufficient because Bobby is 'without the brains needed to universalize maxims and drives' (153) and thus Bobby's response to them as humans is not really a response after all, merely a reaction. The context is significant for understanding why Levinas is anxious not to anthropomorphise Bobby: he fears a homology between humanising animals and animalising humans, and thus recognising Bobby as a fellow being who has a 'face' might seem dangerously close to the logic of Nazi ideology. Yet we need not see the relationship between these two ways of critiquing the human–animal boundary as necessarily leading to the reduction of the human, although certainly historically this has often been the consequence of such moves. Such thinking must move beyond merely shifting where precisely the line between human and animal might be drawn, however, a move which Nazi ideology used to shift Jews and others into the category of those who might be killed without being murdered. As I outlined in the introduction, it is more productive to reconsider the entire logic of the human–animal boundary and the role of this species division in preserving a category of those whose subjectivity might be ignored. Rethinking such a boundary altogether can take us beyond strategies such as 'humanising' and 'anthropomorphising' – and their dark flipside, 'animalising' – and toward the more difficult work of thinking through the ethics of multispecies community, a community in which some will always be killed by others. From a certain point of view, killing is a part of life, a necessary consequence of carnivorous species and perhaps even a necessary aspect of a hierarchical structure in which humans continue to utilise other species for our own ends. The problem is continuing this multispecies community relation within a context where ethics has a limited scope and much killing can be done outside of its bounds. As Haraway succinctly puts it, 'it is not killing that gets us into exterminism, but making beings killable' (*When Species Meet* 80).

Avoiding the category of the 'killable', then, involves acknowledging that animals, too, have a claim on us to acknowledge them as others with a 'face' as much as do human others, even if this claim is not identical. A first step toward achieving this is to return to our conceptions of language and communication, and acknowledge that animals can respond as well as react. One way to do this is to understand language as embodied and material, rather than as a purely abstract semiotic system,[6] and thereby to understand communication as something intercorporeal as much as it is semiotic. Acampora argues that 'by continually immersing ourselves in concrete observation and then connecting our observations to vivid inner images, we enter into a conversation with the animal' (*Corporal Compassion* 36). He sees the similarity of shared embodiment as being equally as important as the imagination in enabling us to grasp something of the animal's point of view. Focusing on shared embodiment provides a better ground for communicating with animals, he suggests, because the materiality of both shared and distinct embodied experiences enables humans to recognise similarities and acknowledge differences, thereby ensuring that while we use our imaginative capacities to connect with animal being, we do not inadvertently erase the specificity of such being in a presumption that animals are identical to humans. Acampora develops the term symphysis (similar embodiment) which he prefers to sympathy (shared feelings) as the foundation for communication. For Acampora, symphysis 'convey[s] the sense of sharing with somebody else a somaesthetic nexus experienced through a direct or systemic (inter)relationship' that is 'mapped onto the medium of flesh', able to 'reflect universal as well as personal experiences – from sexual intimacy as carnal concentricity to panvitalist, quasi-mystical communion with the planet perceived as creaturely "carnosphere"' (76).

Ian Watson's *The Jonah Kit* (1975) explores 'symphysical' communication between humans and whales in its story of an experiment to project human minds onto other brains, including the brain of a sperm whale. The novel's first pages try to convey the sensation of this consciousness that is neither human nor whale, but a combination of the two that both remembers human language but also finds such words inadequate to his current embodied experience. He feels as though 'a "voice" pursued him: arbitrary sounds approaching meaning, like waves on a shoreline, only to fall back in nonsensical jangle – "words" somehow associated with the joyful squirming of his body, with the "smell" of hair flowing under him like weed' (18). This being observes others around him he calls 'ten legs' and 'eight arms', beings we would call giant squid and octopus, but the entity's refusal simply to use the human words calls attention to a characterisation of this new being that recognises that human–whale communication is more complex than merely teaching a whale human language. Whales, like humans, have reasons to distinguish octopi from squid and thus the distinction 'arms' and 'legs' makes sense from the point of view of whale embodiment, and yet the trace of human experience remains in the specific words used. The human consciousness grafted to the whale's brain must negotiate the difficult gaps between his memories of human perceptions and language and his at-times similar but at-times radically distinct physical experiences and perceptions in the whale body. To imprint human consciousness onto the whale's brain is not so simple as 'remove Part A from the whale kit and substitute a corresponding part from your human kit' because 'the whale brain simply isn't built *overall* to process human language' (136). Yet these differences do not entail utter pessimism regarding the possibility of communicating with other species; they merely entail a responsibility to be attentive to differences and what they signify. As one character enthusiastically argues, humans are 'obsessed with objects' but whales are 'interested in flow and vector and relation'; this produces 'a radically different programme from the speech programme built into us humans' but this different programme is nonetheless 'still symbolic thought, articulated in organised sound! There's the point of connexion. We're distant biological cousins, the whale and us' (154).

Another storyline concerns an astronomer, Paul, who continually insists he is interested only in pure mathematics. He dismisses attempts to communicate with alien beings and finds useful the correspondence between radio clicks from the stars and whale song (both of which can be mathematically mapped) only because our failure to communicate with 'own home-grown aliens here on Earth' (35) is used as a rationale to refuse to fund a proposal for a deep space listening project. Paul embodies the stereotype of the scientist abstracted from the living world whose pursuit of knowledge is ultimately destructive of the very thing he sets out to investigate. His attitude is nicely summed up in his invective, 'Personally, I don't give a damn about dolphins. Or nearby stars. Or anything that happened in the past billion years. In my book the only knowledge worth knowing is way out there at the beginning of time' (35). Paul's research leads to the conclusion that what we regard as our material reality is in fact only an illusion, a mathematical echo of the collision of our galaxy with another, real one. He argues, 'A positive, matter universe hatched approximately ten billion years ago, certainly! – and promptly vanished into another mode of being, as soon as it had hatched! Galaxies, stars, ourselves – are only a kind of ghost of it' (69). He believes that his theory proves that god exists (as the original matter that exploded outward to create space had to come from somewhere) but also that god is not interested in our galaxy, which is just an illusion created by the unfolding of equations whose material existence is in this other mode of being. Paul's utter immersion in the world of mathematical abstraction produces a contemptuous attitude toward the physical world of living and suffering beings. He proclaims, 'I'm getting bored with local issues. Moons, planets, milky ways. Astronomy must become the highest form of philosophy – indeed, of religion! It's high time people had their minds torn away from petty squabbles about oil and copper and fish and things' (74).

These two storylines come together over the question of what it would mean for the whale to understand humans. A rival researcher, Richard, finds promise in the idea that the whale sees the world differently than do humans, and argues that in this difference lies an opportunity to transform the world radically. If we believe that reality emerges from the interaction between observer and material particles,[7] then we might understand the entire world as the box in Schrödinger's cat[8] experiment: 'we – the human race, as a consensus of observers – are every moment engaged in choosing the type of universe we inhabit ... At every moment of every day we are collectively free to choose, so it is human *practice* that makes the world what it is' (95). The whales offer an opportunity to shift the consensus of observers and thus to make another sort of world that results from the shared language game, in Wittgenstein's terms, between human and whale. This new hybrid perception will offer 'a fresh view, with fresh observers. Fresh *participants* ... Of *Homo Physeter*, a new mental breed swimming the oceans. Of *Physeter Sapiens* striding out of the sea bringing ocean music to a needy, desiccated land' (184). Richard argues that such a radically other view is possible because of the relationship between language and perception. Discussing a child who is just acquiring language, he uses the metaphor of a house to describe her consciousness. At her early stage of development, she knows the blueprint but cannot yet inhabit the house. Richard wonders 'what other sorts of houses could be built from the same material', and laments that it is the nature of human experience that 'it's only when we've built our house that we can really use it to look out of the windows at the world. And the placement of windows dictates the view'; for him the whales offer the 'possibility of other houses, other views' (40).

The chief difference between the ways in which whales and humans perceive the world is that the whales do not have hands, something that troubles the human/whale entity that becomes Jonah.[9] He has an awareness of having once had hands, but he cannot reconcile this memory with his current perceptual experience:

> But the (hand)-cage is flexible too, caressing hair, the lips, the penis. It even opens up flat and seems not to be a cage at times. Yet it is only the model of a cage, unfolded. Thus it makes fools of us. (But who is *'us'*?) For it seems so open and free, so extensive, always reaching out. We pity those who lack these flat, soft cages. The Cageless Ones, we think of them as. They have no grasp of situations. No grip on the world. (But who is 'WE'!! Who is 'WE'!!) This (hand) has formed the mind, the thoughts, the (words). Minds, thoughts and (words) have all followed the contours of (hand), unwittingly. How could I be aware of this, when awareness is of the same shape as what it should be aware of? One fits the other perfectly, so that one never notices this ... Awareness takes (hand's) fives and tens for numbers. Accepts its grip on things for relations in the world. (Hand) closes round awareness in a cage – and so subtly it is done that cage and awareness appear identical, and call themselves Consciousness ... (143–144, ellipses in original)

Heidegger argues that the distinction between the hand and the paw is one of the markers of the lesser status of animal being.[10] Since the animal is poor-in-world, it is guided only by instinct and its actions have only the goal of continuing the life of the organism. Human action, in contrast, is guided by a mode of being of 'having' the world, a status of being set apart and able to grasp the world through abstraction rather than being immersed in the world. As I outlined in the introduction, a particular relationship to technology that enables humans to perceive nature as an 'unconcealing' and reveal it to be a standing-reserve of possibilities for human action is part of the experience of the *Dasein*. Heidegger's view is precisely the opposite of Acampora's vision of symphysis. For Heidegger, although the hand and the paw may biologically and morphologically appear similar, this does not suggest any homologies between animal being and the *Dasein*. Animal potentialities give rise to paws as a way of interacting with the world which does not have the some potentialities as does the human hand, which emerges only from the being of the *Dasein*.

Watson's novel suggests a similar distinction, or more accurately it acknowledges that different embodiment creates different ways of being in the world, thus the perception of the world as made up of different possibilities for action[11] and a different use of language to describe one's experience of this world. Yet the novel is careful not to privilege the human perspective, here not the contrast between hand and paw but the more radical one of the having or not of a appendage that grasps. Jonah notes that the '(hand)' – a word whose referent no longer makes full sense to him, hence the word appears as set apart in his narration – constrains as much as it enables. It might be used to caress but it is equally a cage. The hand reaches out and could signify a relation to the world that is 'so open and free, so extensive', but it equally and invisibly 'closes round awareness' like a cage, conflating awareness and its limitation into what gets called 'Consciousness', a consciousness that is never aware of its own limitations. Thus, human consciousness 'accepts its grip on things for relations in the world' and never recognises the error of reducing the multiplicity of the world to its own singular way of experiencing this materiality. Instead, like Heidegger, human consciousness tends to construe as inferior those who do not share human ways of perceiving and human priorities in communication, seeing these 'Cageless Ones' as inferior, as having 'no grasp of situations'.

For Heidegger, the *Dasein*'s 'having' of the world by being apart from it was a sign of superiority, but in *The Jonah Kit* the implications of this human way of being are more dire, summed up by Paul's dismissive attitude to anything that does not serve his interest in abstract astrophysics. Paul becomes the epitome of a peculiarly human way of seeing the world which is also expressed in our language. For humans, 'apprehension is *prehension*: the hand reaching out to grasp' and thus 'the human sentence *manipulates* objects and events' (180). Whales, in contrast, have no need for 'reaching out and grasping' (180) to construe a relation to world, as they have no hands. The more significant implication is that a whale consequently does not experience 'the distancing of his mind from the world' (180).

This means that whales do not have technology or a scientific episte-mology as do humans, but similarly whales do not exploit and destroy the environment in which they live because they do not conceive of it as a standing-reserve, separate from themselves. Richard hypothesises that 'there may be no "things" as such for [the whale], but only "states of being"' (180). He hopes this insight into how the whale's brain processes language and construes reality will enable better communication between whales and humans, and sees in Jonah an ideal of a consciousness that can more fully perceive the world than can either humans or whales because his experience is 'apprehension, *plus* prehension: a new skyscraper with firm new windows on reality – along with the old human ones – a four-dimensional building, almost' (184).

Yet just as this experiment better enables humans to understand whales, it also seems to better enable whales to understand humans. Jonah becomes part of a star formation among whales, which the humans hypothesise is a sort of biological analogue of a computer, a union which enables them to process data collectively in a far more advanced way than could any one alone. Following Jonah's participation in the star formation, a trans-species alarm is sent out along cetacean communication channels, and these species collectively begin beaching themselves. The novel ends with the humans puzzling over what this action might signify. Some see it as a reaction to the presence of human consciousness within their cultural community, an 'invasion of alien beings into the whales' souls', moreover beings 'who were poisoning [their] world' (206). Earlier in the novel, some characters visit a dolphin exhibit at a zoo which is described as a 'great dismal hall' and a 'tomblike place' (52), an experience of animal being among humans which gives some credence to this proposition. A reporter who had asked Paul to consider that the entire universe was a version of Schrödinger's paradox – a view Paul rejected as he believes biological entities and their observations have nothing to do with the pure, mathematical structure of reality – hopes that the whales have collectively chosen a different reality, collapsing the wave to observe a world different than the one made by human practice, escaping to 'a different way. To a positive world' (209). A priest who refuses to accept Paul's conclusion that this reality is not god's universe sees in the animals' death a Christ-like sacrifice, their lives offered to restore 'Faith in reality! They have sacrificed their reality, so that we can believe in this world once more, and care about her. Our world' (213).

The novel offers us no way to select among these theories; it is interesting to note, however, that what they all have in common is a reduction of the whales and their lives to the level of symbol, their actions having meaning to confirm or deny a particular way for humans to experience the world.

Such characters are unable to imagine not only that the world might be organised otherwise from the cetaceans' point of view, but further that there might be some way of grasping what these creatures have done other than through analogy to one's own experience. One of the final hypotheses offered is a grim one as relates to the ideal of interspecies communication: that 'it was simply their first true knowledge of *us* – of this race they share the planet with: Humanity, no less. Suppose that you were a Jew trapped in Nazi Germany –' (218). *The Jonah Kit*, like 'The Evolution of Trickster Stories among the Dogs of North Park after the Change', reminds us that just as we see animals and fantasise about communicating with them, animals also see us and evaluate our actions toward them. A future of human–animal dialogue will require humans to accept their responsibility for acts of exploitation and abuse. Watson's novel ends on a somewhat pessimistic note. One character asks why after centuries of human slaughter of whales and dolphins they suddenly decided to remove themselves from the planet, and is told 'maybe they didn't interpret our actions the way we would? Maybe they thought we'd grow out of it? I don't know. But what we finally did do, through our Jonah, is found a way of showing the exact nature of our minds to them ... The result –' (219).

The critique of the anthropocentric and grasping perspective of those with hands, however, suggests that merely retreating from an attempt to communicate with the other is not an adequate response. If we are to learn to see animals as others who can make ethical appeals upon us, and if we want to enact the fantasy of communicating with an alien being by striving to communicate with some of those with whom we share the planet, humans have to accept that much of what animals may want to communicate to humanity is not what we might like to hear. To refuse this communication, however, puts humans at the level of reacting rather than responding, according to Haraway, and thus reduces human subjectivity to the level of an unthinking application of a calculation, where Descartes relegated animals:

> To claim not to be able to communicate with and to know each other and other critters, however imperfectly, is a denial of mortal entanglements for which we are responsible and in which we respond ... Response is getting it that subject-making connection is real. Response is face to face in the contact zone of an entangled relationship. (*When Species Meet* 227)

Entangled relationships are never innocent or easy, as Haraway argues and the texts discussed in this chapter make clear. They involve facing difficult truths of exploitation and projection, owning histories of misunderstanding and conflict. And yet if the distinction between reaction and response is to have any meaning and if we are to embrace an identity as ethical beings capable of response, we must not allow the automatic division of the human–animal boundary to guide our communication with other beings. Derrida is adamant that ethics is possible only when we risk ourselves in the uncertainty of not knowing in advance how to respond to the other: 'the unrescindable essence of ethics, decisions, and responsibility. All firm knowledge, certainty, and assurance on this subject [which emerges from a fixed human–animal boundary] would suffice, precisely, to confirm the very thing one wishes to disavow, namely, the reactionality in the response' (*The Animal* 126).

Roger Zelazny's ''Kjwalll'kje'k'koothaïlll'kje'k' (1973) is a story of negotiating this ethical difficulty, exemplifying a way of thinking about animals and language which Derrida has argued is not a question of giving speech back to animals but 'of acceding to a thinking, however fabulous and chimerical in might be, that thinks the absence of the name and of the word otherwise and as something other than a privation' (48). The novella opens with a mystery: two humans appear to have been killed by dolphins; yet all human knowledge about dolphin behaviour suggests this is impossible. Humans do not understand what they mean to dolphins, but observe that 'we seem to be quite important to them, so important that I even believe one of them might rather die himself than see one of us killed' (95). An investigator, Madison, sent to resolve the case learns more about dolphin nature as he probes the circumstances of the men's deaths. He is informed that dolphins are characterised by *ludus*, a sort of serious attitude toward recreation and play that 'might conduce to virtue by making the body fit, promoting a certain ethos, and enabling us to enjoy things in the proper way', ideals Aristotle associated with music, as the text notes, and which perhaps might even 'promote a certain ethos and foster a particular way of enjoying things' (100). The mystery plot is resolved as such things typically are, uncovering a plot to smuggle diamonds which has led to a falling out among thieves, with an attempted cover-up of the resultant murders by faking dolphin bites and attempting to blame nearby dolphin pods. But in the interstices of this thriller plot, Madison discovers something more interesting than these human machinations through befriending an artist, Martha Millay, who lives and works near the dolphins. Millay is physically disabled, a legacy of the atomic bomb dropped on Hiroshima. She lives isolated from most humans and is telepathic.

Millay's telepathy enables her to experience dolphin art, something that no other human can perceive. The novella's title comes from the name of the greatest of their creators, a being who is 'prophet, seer, philosopher, musician – there is no man-made word' (135) that can effectively capture his role. The dolphin's ludic sensibility makes Millay feel accepted, finding their embrace of her 'uncluttered with the pity that demeans' (135) that she experiences with fellow humans. Millay's telepathy enables her to share in the perceptions of other humans as well, and it was through the thieves that she was first led to the place where 'Kjwalll'kje'k'koothaïlll 'kje'k's works are heard. The dolphin's relationship to place is such that his art would not be the same were he to be removed from this location, and since it coincides with the location of the diamonds, the thieves were attempting to drive the dolphins away, willing to use violence if necessary. Millay has used her telepathic ability to help Madison solve the crime in order to protect the dolphins, but she later attacks him when he seems to be getting too close to a truth she wants to protect; yet this further resolution of the mystery is not the novella's point either. The climax comes not when Millay finally reveals the 'truth', but rather when she and Madison decide upon a truce which emerges once she is able to show him what she is 'seeking to preserve, to defend' (139). Madison feels 'delight in this dance of thought, rational though not logical' (139); immersed in the art, he forgets his isolated human existence and swims 'in a sea that was neither dark nor light, formed nor formless, yet knowing [his] way, subsumed, as it were, within a perceptual act of that thing we had decided to call *ludus*' (140).

The experience of dolphin art leaves Madison feeling 'the infinite potentialities that fill the moment, surrounding and infusing the tiny stream of existence, and joyous, joyous, joyous ...' (140, ellipses in original). Here, communication with animals enables a becoming-animal, an existence open to other potential models of subjectivity, other ways of constructing the world through language, other affective ways of enjoying the world and other beings in it. Despite the difficulties and risks, then, of speaking to the animal other, there is also hope for another future, a world less damaged than the one produced by the heritage of the human–animal boundary. Yet these potentialities can be achieved only if we insist on the responsibility of response, of allowing ourselves to become entangled in the contact zone of interspecies communication. Animal trainer Vicki Hearne contends that communication can only emerge from a relationship in which both partners are open to the subjectivity of the other. If we continue to conceptualise and interact with animals as if they did not have language or thought because it is not identical to our own, we will never be able to perceive the world through what Zelazny calls *ludus* or Watson calls 'a four-dimensional building, almost'. Hearne argues

> to the extent that the behaviorist manages to deny any belief in a
> dog's potential for believing, intending or meaning, there will be no
> flow of intention, meaning, believing, hoping going on. The dog may

THE ANIMAL RESPONDS 89

try to respond to the behaviorist but the behaviorist will not respond
to the dog's response ... The behaviorist's dog will not only seem
stupid. She will be stupid. (58)

Refusing the reactionality in our response to animals, and allowing
for their responses to be more than reactions, enables another sort of
exchange. Sf's ability literally to enable animals to respond helps us to
reach for this complex, non-innocent, and enabling fantasy, and HAS
helps us to see that we might achieve this dream of speaking to an alien
right here on Earth.

4. 'The Female Is Somewhat Duller': Gender and Animals[1]

The relationship between animals and human categories of gender has a long and complicated history in Western culture. The binary male–female is as central to our intellectual and cultural history as is that of human–animal, and the parallels which link human more closely with male and female more closely with animal are part of this complex affiliation.[2] Women have often been at the forefront of animal welfare activism, particularly in the anti-vivisectionist movement of the Victorian era. Yet at the same time, the discourse of feminism has had a fraught relationship with the category 'animal' – if not with actual, material animals – because the term, along with others such as 'body' and 'nature', has been used to denigrate women and deny them full status as political citizens. Animals become part of human discourses of gender through language in the prevalent use of animal names as sexual appellations for women (fox, chick, bird) and also in the way domesticated animals are often differentiated by specific terms for the male versus the female of the species (bull/cow, dog/bitch, stallion/mare). We control animals' sexuality through specific breeding programmes and the use of castration to render more docile many domesticated animals (often with specific words for such altered animals, such as gelding or steer); domestic pets are spayed or neutered, to control overpopulation of dependent animals, but also to render them more convenient housemates for humans. At the same time, we project fantasies of sexual prowess onto certain animals, often with the consequence that they might be farmed or hunted for some small portion of their anatomy believed to convey such power to a consuming human, as happens with bear and tigers.

The intersections between discourses of gender and the human–animal boundary are multiple and contradictory. One of the most important points of intersection is the overlap between patriarchal discourses of masculine power and superiority and species discourses of human exceptionalism. Derrida's deconstructive analysis has followed a trajectory, as he notes in the concluding section of *The Animal that Therefore I Am*, from considering logocentrism, to phallologocentrism, and finally to carnophallogo-centrism; yet he insists that although his work has historically traced this progression, nonetheless it was 'destined in advance, and quite deliberately, to cross the frontiers of anthropocentrism' (104). In the interview 'Eating Well', Derrida develops at more length his conception of the relationships among language, masculine identity and the human–animal boundary, explaining that philosophical history 'install[s] the virile figure at the determinative centre of the subject' (280) and abjects all those (such as women and homosexuals) who do not have the same 'appetites' as these 'men' (281) – that is, those who are not fully human because they have not sufficiently distanced themselves from animal, embodied being. This same logic enables the sacrifice of animals in such a way that their putting-to-death is not considered killing (283). Thus, Derrida makes clear, 'Power over the animal is the essence of the "I" or the "person," the essence of the human' (93). Women can only ever tenuously occupy this carnophallogo-centric 'I' position.

One of the discourses Derrida evokes as constituting 'man'[3] in this way and 'marking his authority over living creatures' (93) is Genesis, where man is given the power to name the animals. The role of language is crucial here for two reasons: first because, as Derrida consistently stresses, the human–animal boundary is made through discourse, the linguistic and institutional history by which humans have given themselves one name and animals another and insisted that the difference in terminology stood in for a wide number of other qualities; second because, as Derrida equally insists, language is something that exceeds, precedes and subjugates individual humans just as Adam subjugates animals. Thus the Genesis story of naming and having dominion over the animals is one of the ways in which humans try to produce the species boundary, and thereby man is able to give himself 'the infinitely elevated power of presenting himself as an "I," of presenting himself and just that, or presenting himself to himself, by means of a form of presence to himself that accompanies every presentation and representation' (*The Animal* 93). Part of Derrida's point here is that this power over animals which creates the 'I' is a way for the human subject to try to fix its identity as stable and present, to escape the traces of language which fragment and undo this conception of self.

Ursula Le Guin's story 'She Unnames Them' (1985), the final story in her *Buffalo Gals* collection, similarly explores how patriarchal power, language and power over animals are linked. In the introduction to this collection, Le Guin observes that 'in literature as in "real life," women, children, and animals are the obscure matter upon which Civilization erects itself, phallologically. That they are Other is (*vide* Lacan *et al.*) the foundation of language' (9). She positions her stories as part of an effort to give voice to these excluded others, to find another way to speak a language that is not premised on their othering, a concept that has some affinity with Deleuze and Guattari's notion of becoming-animal as a way to construe subjectivity outside and beyond the normative cultural channelling of desire, a normativity that is '(*vide* Lacan *et al.*)' the Law of the Father. In the introduction to 'She Unnames Them', Le Guin notes that she had to put this story last in the book because '*it states (equivocally, of course) whose side (so long as sides must be taken) I am on and what the consequences (maybe) are*' (229). Her hesitations and qualifications speak volumes to the difficulty of negotiating these discourses. The story begins with the animals' reaction to the ritual of unnaming, recounting 'most of them accepted namelessness with the perfect indifference with which they had so long accepted and ignored their names' (233). The world in which the story is set presumes both animal consciousness and linguistic capability. Although most animals feel no connection to names, the yaks feel their name 'sounded right' and thus they 'discussed the matter all summer' (233) before concluding that the name was really for the sake of others and 'so redundant from the yak point of view that they never spoke it themselves, and hence might as well dispense with it' (233). Most of the other animals agree enthusiastically to give back their names to 'the people to whom – as they put it – they belonged' (234).

As Marian Scholtmeijer has argued, the story emphasises the specificity of animal identity by evoking behavioural traits, habitats or physical features in its descriptions of how the animals give up their names (235). Kasi Jackson insightfully argues that this fact is part of an overall pattern in Le Guin's animal stories that 'grounds her fiction in an attempt to inhabit the worldview of the animal that is informed by science, and yet critiques the "habitual ways" that scientific accounts sometimes deny animal subjectivity and agency' (208). Yet there is also an issue of specific resistance to the power of language as well, one of whose consequences concerning animals is to erase individuality, conflating all members of a species to the generic species name, or in fact at times conflating all living beings into a singular non-human category, one of Derrida's critiques of the word 'animal'. He describes it as 'an appellation that men have instituted, a name they have given themselves the right and the authority to give to the living other' (*The Animal* 23), and substitutes in his own discourse the word *animot* which he argues incorporates three important corrections: it implies a plurality of other beings as compared to the singularity of 'the animal'; it reminds us of the role of language in constituting the other through its use of the French *mot*; and it enables us to think of the absence of names (given by humans) and speech (as understood by humans) in animal being 'as something other than a privation' (48). *Animot* – which includes humans

– is 'neither a species nor a gender nor an individual, it is an irreducible living multiplicity of mortals' (*The Animal* 41). It is thus something like the openness of becoming-animal.

Pet animals pose a particular problem in the world of Le Guin's story as they are named in human discourse in two ways, a generic name invoking their species and an individual name invoking their place in social relations with humans: although, of course, the notoriously independent cats, like those in Johnson's story discussed in the last chapter, 'den[y] ever having had any name other than those self-given' (234). The hesitation felt by some pets draws our attention again to the inadequacies of the word 'animal' and its inability to designate the wide varieties of social relations we have with other beings, which range from interacting with them as everything from food sources to family members. Yet even dogs are happy to escape from a discourse of naming once 'they understood that the issue was precisely one of individual choice, and that anybody who wanted to be called Rover, or Froufrou, or Polly, or even Birdie in the personal sense, was perfectly free to do so' (234). A human point of view enters this story only near the end, when a first-person narrative voice remarks 'how close I felt to them' (235) as she (one presumes from the title) truly observes the animals rather than perceives them through the shorthand of language which names them and thus forestalls any further exchange: 'they seemed far closer than when their names had stood between myself and them like a clear barrier' (235). This new closeness enables fear and attraction to mingle equally and creates a new interspecies dynamic where 'the hunter could not be told from the hunted, nor the eater from the food' (235), precisely the sort of becoming-animal or becoming-other subjectivity that I discussed in the previous chapter, an encounter among entities in which ethics has not already been decided in advance.

The connection between this transformative subjectivity and gender becomes apparent in the story's final paragraphs. The narrator tells us that she could not 'in all conscience, make an exception for myself' (235), and she goes to Adam and returns – refuses – the name he and '[his] father' had given her: it is 'useful, but it doesn't exactly seem to fit very well lately' (236), she tells them. Like the animals, women have been named in patriarchal discourse, given identities and roles that capture perhaps only a part or perhaps none of their being. Just as a new relationship between She (no longer Eve) and the animals is enabled by the refusal of this discursive history of naming and the identities and social relations it gives in advance, so too might a new structure of gender identity and social relations emerge from this change. Yet it takes both human and animal awareness and openness to create interspecies communication, and it will take Adam's acknowledgement that his name does not suit She for a transformative subjectivity to emerge, something he seems disinclined to give in the story. Scholtmeijer argues that 'animal indifference to language shows a woman the way out of the stories culture tells about women and animals' (255), stressing the emancipatory aspect of women's identification with animals. The story ends with She struggling to embrace how radical the refusal of names and the discourses of gender and species they carry will be, realising 'I could not chatter away as I used to do, taking it all for granted. My words now must be slow, as new, as single, as tentative as the steps I took going down the path away from the house' (236). Both She and the animals must learn to speak this new language that is not founded on their otherness, a language that compels engagement with the world, slow and singular, and thereby avoids the violence of preformed linguistic categories that impose their logic on the multiplicity of the world. Derrida argues that 'what forbids words, is not a muteness and the experience of a powerlessness, an inability ever to name; it is, in the first place, the fact of *receiving one's name*' (*The Animal* 19–20). Without a name, women and animals might speak their own experience.

One of the chief discourses in which both women and animals have been named and constrained by Western patriarchal culture is that of sociobiology. Barbara Herrnstein Smith notes that one of the paradoxes regarding how human culture understands its kinship to animals is the degree to which we at times resist acknowledging continuity between ourselves and other species, while at others – such as the popular embrace of sociobiology – we capitulate to the inevitability of our 'genetic' or 'animal' nature and posit as unchangeable certain behaviours, such as the idea that males need to maximise their reproductive potential by maximising their number of sexual partners. She calls this incongruity a 'settlement of the question of our kinship with other animals (and a characterisation of humanity – that is, like beasts in our social and sexual behaviour and like computers in how we think) that currently appeals to a great many people' (163). Such a settlement, she argues, gives us an inadequate concept of both human and animal, reducing the complexities of gender politics and social justice to issues of biological determination, and creating a view of 'the human mind as a computational mechanism designed to solve environmentally posed problems *and* ... [a view] of art, philosophy and other cultural activities as, at best, secondary and superficial elements of the conduct and conditions of human life' (162). Sociobiology sees all behaviour as explicable in evolutionary terms, and thus looks for the evolutionary advantage that will unlock the key to all culture. Given its focus on the survival of the species – in its most extreme version, the survival of individual genes – sociobiology tends to focus on behaviours that are also the ground of biopolitics: reproduction and warfare, techniques regarding the power to 'make live or let die', in Foucault's phrasing.

Sociobiology's use of animal models is intriguing and problematic for a number of reasons. First, as arguments made earlier in this book explain, such a limited and deterministic vision of motivation and social relations is insufficient not only as an account of human subjectivity, but as one of animal subjects as well. Second, the reduction of human behaviour to something exactly identical to animal behaviour and thus understood solely through genes is as partial and illusory an understanding of human–animal kinship as is the philosophical axiom that humans and animals belong to entirely separate modes of being. Finally, sociobiology is often inconsistent in its use of animal models, deciding in advance, it seems, which animals are permissible models for explaining human society and which are not. Thus, primates such as chimpanzees who organise around a patriarchal leader are seen as 'pure' models of natural behaviour, while those such as bonobos whose social organisation includes stronger roles for women and a preference for sexuality rather than violence to resolve conflict are viewed as aberrations. Sociobiology is far too limited in the explanations it is willing to consider and far too quick to reduce complexity to single causes.[4] Among the problems are a tendency to separate the organism from its environment as if the organism confronted an autonomous environment rather than was something shaped by and shaping its environment; a sense that genes are all-powerful codes that determine the sum of human behaviour instead of one in a set of explanatory elements; a refusal to acknowledge that genes themselves are complexly influenced by environment, interpreting instructions in more than one way according to criteria not well understood; a tendency to separate out various possible 'causes' for things and manipulate them independently so that their interaction is never sufficiently a focus of research; explanations by animal analogy which lose sight of the fact that they *are* analogies, contingent acts of interpretation; and an epistemological separation of nature from culture which produces impoverished notions of both and creates 'a politics in which most political activity justifies itself by referring to nature' (Latour *Pandora's Hope* 258).

One of the principal popularisers and defenders of sociobiology is Edward O. Wilson, whose works such as *Sociobiology* (1975) and *On Human Nature* (1979) founded the new discipline and paved the way for understanding human society and behaviour through evolution in this field and the related one of evolutionary psychology. Wilson's work is controversial for a number of reasons, among them his insistence that nature is the final determinant of all behaviour, including human behaviour, thereby discounting any role for nurture or the cultural environment in producing subjectivity. This view has the consequence of both conceptualising the social order as something ahistorical, necessary and inevitable (because it is the expression of overwhelming biological imperatives), and further of severing any critique of social relationships from the possibility of transformative action (since the given order must be 'right' since it is 'natural' and thus unchangeable). Wilson thus situates social behaviour as beyond good and evil, not in the Nietzschean sense of moving past conventional and unthinking morality, but in the sense of putting humans so firmly within a deterministic account of nature that concepts of 'right', 'wrong' or 'justice' are not relevant measures: human behaviour simply is what it must be, from the point of view of sociobiology. Sociobiology tends not to reflect on its tendency to endorse the status quo of patriarchy, a social arrangement that it portrays as reached not by a historical power struggle and the exclusion of animals and women as Le Guin's story highlights, but rather by the playing out of the unavoidable expression of human's primate identity. The discipline's interest in biological reproduction as the ultimate goal of any living organism's behaviour justifies its interest in arrangements of sexuality and gender, and thus gendered power relations are a particular blindspot of this explanation of human behaviour.

Professionally, Wilson is a myrmecologist, someone who studies ants.[5] His work in this field, and in sociobiology more widely, emerges from his belief that 'ants can be studied for the meaning of their social interaction, whereas the most impressively trained chimp is only performing individual tricks, devoid of any social or ecological import' (Sleigh *Ant* 8–9). Gender is a prominent theme in Bob Olsen's 'Peril among the Drivers' (1934), one of several ant-focused pieces that Olsen published in *Amazing Stories* in the early pulp period. This earlier text's interest in both conservative gender social relations and a detailed account of ant social organisation puts sociobiology's interest in explaining especially human sexual behaviour through biological determinism in a new light. The focus of Wilson's own research on ant societies is perhaps more foundational to the discipline than has been previously acknowledged.

Olsen, as well, was quite knowledgeable about ant behaviour and many of the minutiae of ant ecology are lovingly detailed in his stories, including the use of extensive footnotes to ensure that readers fully appreciate the sheer wonder of these creatures. Yet at the same time, the themes of 'Peril among the Drivers' have little to do with ants or solid scientific knowledge of their behaviour: instead, the scientific detail forms the background to an adventure story whose main theme is appropriate and differentiated gender roles. In drawing attention to this story in the context of the feminist critique of sociobiology, part of my purpose is to suggest that a similar logic operates in the 'stories'[6] that sociobiologists tell about animal and human behaviour. Like Olsen, they do understand and accurately describe the 'facts' of animal (in this case, ant) behaviour, but like Olsen they also do so from a position deeply informed by the cultural assumptions, preferences and prejudices of their particular historical moment and their specific subject position. Thus, this sf tale about ants (and humans) can tell us something not only about the problematic gender roles in much pulp sf, but also about the problematic gender ideology of sociobiology and something about how ants became caught up in these discursive moves.

The story is a simple enough adventure tale: Diana, 'a projectile of pink and gold' (38) has been raised by her entomologist father to a life of adventure and thus has not settled down as should a proper middle-class woman, even though she is in love with and engaged to Gordon Cabot – who rescued her from the downed seaplane crash in which her father died. A 'transmitigating machine' that can 'jar lose the soul, spirit, ego, or whatever you wish to call the consciousness of an animal, and ... separate this spirit from the physical body' (44) enables Diana to fulfil her dream of truly understanding ant society by becoming one of them. Diana insists upon being a driver ant as they live the 'most adventurous lives' and further that she should be a 'princess ant' (that is, a queen-in-waiting) as 'they don't have to work and they don't have to fight' (49). Despite claiming that Diana wishes to follow her father's work, the story thus characterises her as spoiled and frivolous, unable to comprehend ant society in a complex way and motivated instead of her own romanticism and impulsiveness. Gordon also transmitigates into an ant so that he can protect Diana on her adventures. The bulk of the story concerns the various perils they face in the ant colony, incidents which serve the dual purpose of conveying information about ant social organisation and simultaneously representing Diana's foolishness and helplessness: time and again she takes unnecessary risks, fails to perceive danger or otherwise gets into trouble, only to be rescued by Gordon at great physical risk (and at times injury) to himself, none of which she perceives or appreciates. Chaos clearly attends a lack of patriarchal order, and Diana is lost without a strong paternal figure in unambiguous authority over her.

Most of the difficulties are caused by Diana's biological susceptibility to regressing to animal behaviour. Gordon has no difficulty maintaining an awareness of his human identity and priorities when embodied as an ant, but as soon as Diana enters her 'princess ant' body, she becomes jealous of the queen and bent on fulfilling a biological imperative to become fecund: 'the cumulative instincts of ages were concentrated in Diana's ant body, developed with such power that they overwhelmed her human will, which strong as it was, became feeble in comparison' (55). The more time Diana spends in the ant body, the more she becomes reduced to her biological being until a climatic fight with Gordon in which she petulantly rejects his attempts to protect her, announcing, 'I don't want to be rescued … I want to remain as I am – a queen ant destined to become the mother of a great nation!' (77). Gordon, fortunately, knows that he understands Diana's needs better than she and refuses to let this rejection daunt him. When Diana is menaced by an ant lion, he is able to protect her and kill the ant lion – what should be an impossible feat for the type of ant he is – and then, despite his injury and fatigue, fly both himself and Diana to safety and the site where they return to human status. When she awakes in her human body, Diana begins 'to weep hysterically' (81), apologises and tells him 'how noble – how patient – how wonderful you were to get me through it all' (82–83).

The story ends somewhat ambivalently: Diana says she now wants to get married, which seems to affirm Gordon's role as paternal figure, his authority soon to be formalised. At the same time, however, she announces that she wants to do something exciting before she settles down as a sedate wife, which can be read merely as a further characterisation of her immaturity (she has learned nothing from her near-death) but might also suggest that she does recognise that life as a proper middle-class wife is as limiting as the role of ant queen: perhaps symbolically valorised but lacking in any real power or agency. At the time this story was published, the social organisation of ant reproduction was understood as a sign of appropriate gender behaviour, the ritual of the 'princess ant' shedding her wings to become a reproductive queen established as 'a metaphor for a woman's transition into the serious business of motherhood and the abandonment of flirtation' (Sleigh *Ant* 80). This sense of gendered destiny fits well with Wilson's construct of ant society overall as being organised efficiently based on fixed and unchanging roles for each type of ant worker, something also evident in Olsen's story in the various encounters Diana and Gordon have with other ants[7]: for a woman, this fixed role is motherhood. On its surface, the story seems to reinforce the dominant sociobiological narrative which rationalises a gendered division of labour and women's culturally inferior status. It also seems to reinforce the construction of women's subjectivity as closer to the body, nature and animals (given Diana's greater susceptibility to ant being), and thus further to support an ideology which posits women as inferior to men, just as body, nature and animal are inferior to mind, culture and human. Yet the story itself exceeds these ideologies in Diana's continued refusal to capitulate to the gendered order of the human realm upon its conclusion.

Alice Sheldon is the sf writer most associated with challenging gender roles and the gendered assumptions that have shaped which subjects have and have not, historically, been able to achieve full humanity.

'The Screwfly Solution' (1977), published under her Raccoona Sheldon pseudonym, nicely captures the way models of science drawn from our manipulation of animals and their reproduction can be turned back upon humans. The story opens with Alan reading a letter from his wife, Anne: he is off on a 'biological pest control' (435) research project and she is at home taking care of domestic duties (as well as her own research, although it is rarely mentioned in the letters that she too is a scientist). Part of Anne's letter contains news of the Sons of Adam cult whose violence against women has advanced, as one newspaper account quips, from 'murder' to 'a life-style' (437). As Anne continues to update Alan on the declining situation, Alan looks for *'the vulnerable link in the behavioural chain'* (436) in his research trying to destroy disease-spreading caneflies. The Sons of Adam characterise the women they attack as 'crypto' females and believe they are doing god's work in 'purif[ying] the situation': men without women will form a more perfect society, one that need not be concerned with trifling biological matters such as male dependence upon women for reproduction, because 'as long as man depends on the old filthy animal way God won't help him. When man gets rid of his animal part which is woman, this is the signal God is awaiting. Then God will reveal the new true clean way' (440). In addition to drawing attention to the links between misogyny and speciesism in this discursive construction of the masculinised human subject, Sheldon's story calls attention to the fact that Western science (privileged over its binary other, irrationalism) is similarly a product of this logic of misogyny in the parallels she constructs between Anne's and Alan's narratives.

Linda Birke argues that critiquing the way animals are used – materially and metaphorically – within science practice is an important priority for feminism's goal of challenging systems of domination and injustice. She and other feminist critics of science have traced how the development of Western science and technology has gone hand in hand with the domination and expropriation of nature, which includes the domination of non-human animals. Such systems of domination 'remain intertwined so to understand human oppressions more fully requires us to consider also how those oppressions are related to nature's domination' (134), and thereby to see human cruelty to and control over animals not as individual incidents of depravity or isolated examples justified by the species in question, but rather as the product of 'the location of science in the world of late twentieth century industrialized capitalism' (134– 135). Donna Haraway provocatively suggests that an awareness of these parallels through first-hand experience might have been part of what informed Sheldon's work. She points out that Alice Sheldon was a student at Rutgers' Poultry Science Department in the late 1940s and ran a small chicken farm in New Jersey from 1946–1952 with her husband, as well as writing 'science fiction that toyed mercilessly with species, alternation of generations, reproduction, infection, gender, genre, and many kinds of genocide'; is it possible, Haraway wonders, that 'those chickens inspire[d] some of her quirky sf imagination and unsettling feminist thought experiments?' (*When Species Meet* 272).

'The Screwfly Solution' does convey some sense of what it may be like to be a chicken, or a canefly or any number of species under a regime of the binary division between humans and other animals. Anne begins to refer to women as 'an endangered species' (441), trying to joke in her letters but nonetheless revealing her fear. In addition to Anne's letters, Alan catches glimpses of a world increasingly polarised by gender division through other media: a funeral home's refusal to accept 'female cadavers' (444), the terminology itself indicating the bolstering of an ideology that moves beyond a construction of women as slightly less securely occupying the category of 'human' than do men toward severing them completely from the category; the Catholic church's position that women are not defined as human but merely as 'a temporary companion and instrument of Man' (445); an analysis of geographical distribution of cases of 'femicide' which suggest 'a physical cause' (446) although none has yet been found. As Alan travels home and imagines his reunion with his wife, he is shocked to discover his sexual fantasies taking a violent turn, the collapse of sexual lust into bloodlust. In a conclusion that turns sociobiological capitulations to the supposed inevitability of certain behaviours neatly on their head, the story reveals that a vulnerable link in the human behavioural chain has been exploited by an alien species who wish to rid the planet of the human pest, namely 'the close linkage between the behavioral expression of aggression/predation and sexual reproduction in the male' (448). The story ends with Anne having fled civilisation, 'eating perch raw so nobody will see [her] smoke' (452), realising that for her 'we' used to mean her nuclear family, but now means 'women' because 'being killed selectively encourages group identification' (451).

The story's feminist themes are quite evident, but my purpose here is to draw attention to the ways in which the human–animal boundary is also central to the story's meanings in complex and sometimes contradictory ways. Many aspects of the story challenge the human–animal boundary, centrally the demonstration of what it is like to be a species eradicated via manipulation of one's reproduction by putting humans in this position of the manipulated animal. Further, the rhetoric of the Sons of Adam shows how the discourse of animality has been used against women and thus the story serves to remind us why this boundary is of ethical significance, even if one is not concerned about the welfare of actual animals, that is, of non-*Homo sapiens*. Finally, by showing a sort of race suicide to be the consequence of the conflation of male aggression and sexuality, the story undermines the ways in which sociobiological discourses have been used as alibis for male violence, including sexual violence such as rape. When Alan discovers his own bloodlust, he chooses not to return to his family but instead calls Anne and explains his conclusions to her, advising that she will have to treat him 'like a fucking wild animal' (448) instead of a loved companion from this point on (their daughter, Amy, unable to rationally understand this change, is later killed by him when she goes to his lab). This description of Alan might be taken to reinforce the human–animal boundary. Another way of reading this comment, however, is that it simply acknowledges the reality of that boundary as a part of the world in which they live (Alan had been working on wiping out the canefly, for example), and expresses an aspect of the horror and disorientation they feel when that 'natural' boundary is undermined and humans begin to express the behaviour we normally project onto other species in our construction of ourselves. Rosi Braidotti argues that the common structural position shared by women and animals as the excluded of patriarchal power provides grounds for common causes in the struggle for social justice, and also compels us 'to think from within the awareness that the market price of exotic birds and quasi extinct animals are comparable, often to the advantage of the plumed species, to that of the disposable bodies of women, children and others in the global sex trade and industry' (100).

It is also significant that it is human gendered behaviour that appears monstrous in this story – the sort of behaviour we often label with adjectives such as 'inhuman' or 'animal' but which is, paradoxically, abhorrent behaviour of which only humans are capable ('inhuman', for example, is never applied to acts by animals as there is no presumption that they would behave according to human moral codes). The category 'human' is constructed from exclusions and projections, an effort of purification that offers a more flattering portrait of the range of 'natural' human behaviours than those to which our history testifies. John Kessel's story 'Animals' (1997), from a collection suitably titled *The Pure Product*, also takes the troubled relationship between the genders as its topic. The story is told from the point of view of a human pet, Matthew, who refers to his owner as the Tall One. It opens with his encounter with a non-owned human, Philip, one of many who forage on the edges of a world dominated by the Owners. The narrator is the Tall One's philosopher, his job to study the works of human philosophers and offer commentary when asked by the Tall One. He is unaware of the more immediate historical past and has no clear account of the arrival of the Owners; all he knows is that 'the lives of my philosophical predecessors, and the aggressive and complex world they lived in, were swept away – not without violent resistance' (161). Philip is defiant about his identity as a free human, yet accepts food and shelter from Matthew's owner when he is spotted in the house. Philip comes and goes as he pleases, while Matthew works to serve his Owner by explicating the philosophical texts he is given.

The Owners can shift their form, and often 'will take on the appearance of beasts' (163). Matthew exchanges ideas about the proposition 'existence precedes essence' with his Owner while the Tall One is in the form of a silver cat. Matthew parrots the typical axiom of the human–animal boundary that he has learned from his philosophical education: that 'our existence as human – as beings – comes before all other statements of what we are here for or what we may become. Our only definition lies in this fact of existence' (164). Matthew's belief in this human existence and its uniqueness, rather like Heidegger's statements about the *Dasein*, leads him to struggle with how to reconcile his conviction that man (his term for human) is both 'fundamentally free in an absurd universe' and yet 'in practice … cannot deny the influence of external … ah … influences' (164, ellipses in original). Dismayed by his collapse into tautology, Matthew tries to redeem himself by falling back on another truism gleaned from his education – 'man is alone' (164) – which his Owner interrogates, reminding Matthew that he is not alone since Philip moved into the home. Matthew attempts to manipulate this exchange into the acquisition of Madeline, a woman with whom he has developed an infatuation, as a companion, which leads the Owner to propose a meeting between Philip and Madeline, an idea Matthew adamantly resists.

As the remainder of the story unfolds, we hear of Matthew's growing disgust for living with Philip whom he characterises as animal-like, distinguished by 'the sour stink of his sweat' and his 'coarse black hair', in contrast to Matthew's growing obsession with Madeline who is 'beautiful … slender, with full hips, thick brown hair, an easy grace' (165). When Matthew works out that the Owner means for Phillip and Madeline to breed, his 'distaste climbed to the edge of hatred' (165), a hatred that expresses itself in violent dreams when he returns one day to observe Philip and Madeline 'rutting away on the floor, sweating, fumbling, grunting' (167). In the dream, the slight and academic Matthew is able to crush the skull of his male opponent, but when he later, in waking life, shouts at Philip for touching his books, Philip is able easily to overpower Mathew and taunt, 'I'll read anything I please. I'll *screw* anything I please' (167). The next day, Matthew follows when Philip goes to visit Madeline, and confronts her as soon as Philip leaves. He now finds her 'disheveled' and believes 'she had become coarse herself' through her contact with

Philip; eschewing a verbal argument about Philip, Matthew instead attacks Madeline and attempts to strangle her: finding he is not strong enough to accomplish it, he tells us, 'I shoved my fist into her mouth, ground the thumb of my other hand into her throat, lifted, and slammed her down again, throwing the whole force of my weight behind it. There was an awful dull splitting, and she lay still' (169).

Matthew escapes punishment for this crime, the blame for which 'naturally fell to Philip' whose 'violence had been evident even in his lovemaking' (170). Yet the very end of the story casts Matthew's sense of having got away with something into question, when the Owner comes to talk to him in the form of a human and asks why Philip killed Madeline. Matthew suddenly has 'the wild fear that the Tall One had arranged everything, from the beginning – that this had all been a little game to him' (171). The discourse of species figures in this story in a number of ways. First, the story destabilises and draws attention to the construction of the human through projection of certain traits onto the excluded animal, in this case making it all the more clear that such a metaphysics of subjectivity is a product of our philosophical history. Second, the conclusion, like that of Sheldon's story, disturbs anthropocentrism by suggesting that humans might be the objects of the scientific and investigatory gaze of non-human others. It is striking that the first form adopted by the Owner is that of a cat, a creature often seen to challenge human authority due to its independent nature and thus one often vilified as cold and calculating, perhaps like a research scientist manipulating living beings. In addition to the physical suffering experienced by animals in laboratory conditions, there have also been numerous investigations of the psychological consequences of various mistreatments and social stresses, most famously Harry Harlow's experiments on mother–infant bonding using rhesus monkeys.[8] Perhaps most pertinent for the topic of this chapter, the story draws attention to the parallels between this kind of philosophical subject whose identity is construed on the 'tragedy' of man's isolated status as sole sentient being in a world of dumb objects and a tendency to destroy violently those same dumb objects – including animalised women – when their expression of their own agency disrupts this fantasy of man as the measure of all things.

Carol Adams argues in *The Sexual Politics of Meat* (1990) that there is a structural homology between the slaughter of animals and violence toward women, seeing both as products of a logic of patriarchal cultures and the human–animal boundary as the foundation for human subjectivity. She sees women and animals as both absent referents in the popular cultural imagination, both reduced to and metonymically substituted by fragmented body parts in pornography and food advertising. This link, she contends, explains the animalising of women in much contemporary culture and the sexualising of animals used for food. Her work counters the reduction of both women and animals – albeit in slightly different ways – to 'meat' in the vernacular of these discourses. A similar link between the exploitation of animals and the exploitation of women is suggested by Cordwainer Smith's 'Think Blue, Count Two'. Smith is better known for his underpeople stories about a race of people derived from animal stock who form a devalued underclass in a society dominated by humans. These tales, as I will discuss in more detail in the next chapter, repeatedly foreground the exploitative nature of the human/underpeople relationship and critique the ideology of speciesism that justifies and perpetuates this exploitation as a version of class difference. But gender is also relevant to the world of Smith's stories and his characterisation of the relations between underpeople and humans.

'Think Blue, Count Two' is about a number of humans in deep space transit; most are being shipped for the improbable reason that a distant colony's human stock is 'running dreadfully ugly' and thus they are being sent 'better-looking people' (131) to repair their gene pool. A few individuals are taken out of stasis, serving as monitors to run the ship's systems in shifts. One of the awakened, Talatashar, has had his looks spoiled by the cold sleep process, apparently a common risk, while another is a girl who has 'no skill in herself, no learning, no trained capacities' but is considered valuable because her appeal is such that she can 'remotivate almost anyone older than herself' (131) and thereby inspire them to heroic efforts for her sake. Rather than having specific skills in an emergency, she is a sort of desire catalyst. Talatashar proves to be among the tiny percentage of the population who can resist her appeal because he is psychotic and can recognise others only as objects, not fellow subjects. He begins to torture the girl, and his rationale is much like that of those who discount the subjectivity of animals, suggesting a link between this story's portrait of a psychotic and misogynistic personality and the pathological way in which humanity treats animal others, with which Smith is more broadly concerned:

> You're not a person. Girls aren't people. They are soft and pretty and cute and cuddly and warm, but they have no feelings. I was handsome before my face spoiled, but that didn't matter. I always knew that girls weren't people. They're something like robots. They have all the power in the world and none of the worry. Men have to obey, men have to beg, men have to suffer, because they are built to suffer and to be sorry and to obey. All a girl has to do is to smile her pretty smile or to cross her pretty legs, and the man gives up everything he has ever wanted and fought for, just to be her slave. (145)

Like the human subject's denial of animal agency and suffering, Talatashar cannot recognise woman as humans because they are neither identical to him nor absolutely passive in the face of his controlling will. It is his own desire that he attempts to subdue in her, his resentment of her power to make men 'suffer' or 'beg', just as Matthew murdered Madeline because he could neither prevent his desire for her nor compel her to reciprocate.

Yet the propensity toward violence in masculine identity is not always critiqued: it can also be glamorised and serve as a positive point of identification with animals. In *Elizabeth Costello*, Coetzee has his fictional professor discuss this tendency, associating it with writers, such as D.H. Lawrence, who 'celebrate the primitive and repudiate the Western bias toward abstract thought' via an attentiveness to animal others that 'our faraway ancestors possessed and we have lost' (149). Costello is critical of this attitude, however, suggesting that 'despite the vividness and earthiness' of its texts, there 'remains something Platonic about it' (149), a distance from the material reality of other beings as fellow subjects: animals are still the absent referent in this discourse, replaced not by their own consumable bodies but rather by the abstract notion of something that might be labelled masculine virility. Philip Armstrong calls this a redemptive ideal of therio-primitivism, and associates its most simplistic version with the work of Ernest Hemingway, in which particular modes of repeated animal killing 'are conceived as re-enactments of primal rituals, regenerative links to the anthropological and ontological foundations of human being' (150). Such modes of animal identification reinforce rather than revise both the existing social relationship that humans have with animal others (the killing in Hemingway's rituals, for example, is all but exclusively done by humans in bullfighting rings, deep-sea fishing or on safari) as well as the construction of the human subject based on what Derrida has labelled carnophallogocentric logic.

Harlan Ellison's 'A Boy and His Dog' exemplifies these therio-primitivist tendencies. In a future polarised between the feminised, effete world of the downunders and the masculine, brutal world above, a boy struggles to survive with the aid of his faithful dog, Blood. Blood is a man's dog, self-reliant and pugnacious, dining on rather than sharing species with a 'manicured poodle, lost off a leash' (905). He is the dominant one in the relationship, more intelligent and street savvy than the boy, the result of a Third World War bioweapons research programme that created telepathic dogs 'able to track gasoline or troops or poison gas or radiation', the twenty-first century's 'shock commandos of a new kind of war' (910). They meet Quilla June when she emerges from downunder, seemingly a helpless girl whose adventurous nature has led her to forsake the safety of the family-values-inspired enclave. After a series of adventures with other male predators in which the boy demonstrates his fighting prowess and ability to dominate Quilla June physically and sexually, boy and dog are separated when he follows Quilla June to her downunder home, bent upon revenge for her attack upon and escape from him. Predictably, life in downunder does not suit the boy: he discovers that Quilla June was part of a complicated scheme to lure 'certain special kind of men' (930) into the community to rejuvenate the gene pool, and he is bored not only by the quotidian middle-class banality of downunder life, but further by the rapidity with which his presence is accepted within the community. He and Quilla June, declaring their love for one another, escape and return to the surface, where he promptly feeds Quilla June to Blood, who is weak from starvation and injury, but who is nonetheless waiting for his boy.

The story's final line is his answer to Quilla June's question *do you know what love is?*': he replies, 'a boy loves his dog' (938). Here, the animalisation of women to which Adams points joins with a humanisation of animal pets as the boy, faced with a choice between his girl and his dog, chooses that loyal companion, man's best friend. Yet what does it mean for the boy to have chosen Blood? We might see this as a refusal of the species boundary which would automatically privilege Quilla June as the human subject, as an embrace instead of Blood's arguments to the boy before the descent into the downunder which called upon the boy to recognise and respect their long friendship and co-operative relationship. At the same time, however, the boy's descriptions of his casual violence toward Quilla June and what he believes to be his rape of her (the status of the act is complicated by the later revelation of Quilla June's complicity in the entire capture/escape/tracking scenario) suggest misogyny is also a huge part of the boy's worldview. Further, Quilla June is characterised as manipulative in her attempt to ensnare the boy in downunder life, and cloying and childish later when they jointly leave the downunder. Blood, in contrast, is characterised as a steadfast, loyal and tough companion who can hold his own in a fight and stoically endure the pain of injuries. Thus the preference for Blood over Quilla June is as much about choosing a masculine companion as it is about choosing a canine one, if not more so. Finally, there is a degree of selfishness in the boy's love for Blood based on their mutual struggle for survival. As he laconically explains, in some ways he had no choice because 'we couldn't go back, and with Blood in that condition we couldn't go forward. And I knew, good as I was solo, I couldn't make it without him' (937). Blood's survival means his own survival, and in this calculation Quilla June must become meat because Blood 'had to have food at once' (937) to survive.

This story's embrace of the animal other, then, challenges to a degree the human–animal binary, but leaves firmly in place the male/female one. Given the correspondences between them, we might want to question the degree to which such a tale really deconstructs the species division, or the degree to which it, like Hemingway's therio-primitivism, merely reconfigures the boundary in ways that romanticise certain aspects of animality and masculinity. Like the human–animal boundary itself, the binary choice between these two reading is insufficient. Instead of a single line between progressive and reactionary readings, we need to acknowledge the dialectic between them. Herrnstein Smith reminds us that mythic constructions such as the 'ontological thrill' of the hunt, in which the hunted animal is posited as a worthy adversary for the equally feral hunter, are not so easily purified from 'the impulses that constitute our most intellectually subtle and ethically potent institutions of animals or, thereby, our most reflective and respectful relations with them' (157). As the texts discussed in this chapter make clear, human culture is replete with 'fantasies of coupling with, being or becoming' animals, desires that re-imagine our social relations with other species in ways enabling and constraining, productive and reductive, transformative and stagnating.

Leigh Kennedy's fascinating 'Her Furry Face' (1983) teases out some of the complex entwining of desire, identification, exploitation, projection and even love that inform our social relations with animal others. The story centres on Douglas, a researcher who works with primates. He is particularly attached to his orang-utan prodigy, Annie, who has had a story accepted for publication and who becomes something of a celebrity; Annie's achievement is taken by Douglas as evidence of continuity between humans and other primates. The media treats Annie's accomplishment more as a sort of novelty: her text is marketed as a children's story (and Douglas's infantilisation of Annie is significant here) and most of the attention focuses on the fact that the editor did not realise the story was written by an orang-utan when she selected it. Douglas's girlfriend, Therese, lacks interest in the orang-utans and – at least in Douglas's view – feels resentful that any accomplishment by one of them is treated as more significant than things accomplished by her deaf students. Douglas and Therese have a strained relationship which at first seems to be in part because she has no understanding of his work or sympathy with his defence of orang-utan intelligence; yet as the story develops, we are given reasons to doubt Douglas's perceptions more than Therese's: he attributes deeper meaning to many of Annie's statements than she seems to intend and ignores her lapses into 'animal' behaviour, such as violently destroying a toy and running up a tree when she is upset.

By degrees, the story conveys the impression that Douglas is not necessarily responding to Annie's subjectivity or serving her best interests in his insistence on her capacities: she reacts violently when a newspaper article refers to her as an animal, sitting by herself and signing 'not animal' repeatedly; he is disappointed that her report on Lawrence's *Sons and Lovers* can grasp the novel only on the level of plot and Annie feels rejected as she notes his response. As well, Douglas admires Annie far in excess of what he sees in any other orang-utan and his feelings for her are increasingly expressed in sexual terms, noting her 'glossy and coppery' (6) fur and 'expressive and intelligent' (6) eyes. His feelings for Annie grow as those for Therese decrease, and it is clear that Annie's attempts to please him in her training sessions are part of what fuels his sexual desire, while Therese's refusal simply to capitulate to his interpretation of all events makes him withdraw from what he characterises as her constant criticism. Douglas begins to construct Therese as an excessively fragile person, rationalising that his inability to connect with her is a consequence of her not being 'as tough as Annie' (11). He feels that this vulnerable quality in Therese is something 'he'd never seen ... until it was too late' and 'their lives were too tangled up to keep clear of it' (11). He believes that he feels for her what 'anyone would call "love"' but that he is also 'helplessly angry with her most of the time' (15). He finds her needs and feelings something beyond his understanding and her misunderstanding of his good intentions toward her something 'beyond his repair' (15).

With Annie, in contrast, Douglas feels a closer and closer connection, a perfect symmetry of his desires and hers, and particularly appreciates 'the unconditional joy in her face when she saw him' (15). The more he thinks of Annie in these terms, the more Douglas withdraws from Therese. He believes Annie 'was bright and warm and unafraid. She didn't read things into what he said, but listened and talked with him. They were so natural together' (15); yet when he decides to act upon his love for Annie in a physical way, believing 'she understood what he wanted, that her breath on his neck was anticipation' (17), Douglas is confronted with the fact that he understands Annie no more than he understood Therese. Douglas turns their hug into a sexual encounter, but 'Annie went rigid when he entered her' and then pulls away, telling him 'no' and 'not you' (17). The next day, he tries to talk to Annie and explain but finds communication 'wasn't any easier than it had been to talk to Oona, or Wendy, or Shelley, or Therese', that 'he didn't understand her any more than he'd understood them' (19). He grasps neither why she rejected him nor what she is thinking. Instead of finding Annie 'filled with vitality' (15) as he had before, Douglas now feels exhausted by 'all the effort he would have to make to repair their relationship' (19). Annie's response to the rape is to retreat from the behaviour that had pleased Douglas – behaviour we might interpret as imitating humans: she says she has no more interest in reading books or writing stories, but just wants to 'Sit tree. Eat bananas, chocolate. Drink brandy' (19). She also aggressively refuses any physical contact between them, although previously their relationship was characterised by frequent non-sexual contact. While the reader is given considerable insight into these parallels, Douglas remains blind to his own projections and constructions. Just as he sees Therese's needs and subjectivity only in terms of the demands they make on him, he similarly has no understanding that Annie has a perspective on the situation different from his own. He fantasies about a romance with Annie that would have been 'them against the world, a new kind of relationship. The first intelligent interspecial love affair ...' (21, ellipses in original) and regrets that it is not possible because 'Annie didn't seem any different than Therese, after all' (21). Douglas's rationalisations move quickly from self-pity regarding his rejection to blaming Annie for seducing him: 'Annie was no child. She'd given him all those signals, flirting, then not carrying through. Acting like he'd raped her or something' (21).

Douglas's character reveals a number of interesting things about the relationship between the human–animal boundary and the Western cultural construction of women as closer to the being of animals. As Adams suggests, both are deeply implicated in a patriarchal desire for dominance over another. Douglas's mode of relating to women shares much with the dialectic of dominance and affection that Tuan argues characterises the pet relationship. Douglas sees women as there to serve his needs – to understand him, talk to him and give him affection – which is often how we perceive the role of domestic pets. Although Douglas likes to see himself as adventurously embarking upon an interspecies love affair, his desire for Annie has everything to do with his perception of her unconditional love for him. Dogs are often praised for their slavish devotion to their masters and the absence of such evidence of subser-vience to human desires explains the corresponding lack of reverence for (and often prejudice against) cats. Ritvo argues that Victorian society's high regard for dogs was linked to a sense that the species 'understood and accepted its position so thoroughly that it did not resist punishment if it failed in its duty' (21), going so far as to regard the malleable body of the dog (which could be bred to many sizes and uses) as a symbol of its desire to please; hunting cats, in comparison, who 'did not seem disposed to acknowledge human dominion' (22), were regarded as poachers. It is instructive that Douglas sees his relationship with Annie within the same framework as he sees his relationship to Therese: like the Victorian differentiation between dogs and cats, one is (at least initially) a good pet who wants to please her master, while the other is frustratingly insistent upon pursuing her own life and priorities, even if she is choosing and trying to share this life with him. 'Her Furry Face' thus reveals that the animalising of women in much philosophical and popular discourse is not merely about their political disenfranchisement or buttressing the privileges of patriarchal domination, although it is of course about these things: equally, however, it is about producing a certain self conception of man that enables him to feel complete because loved and understood by a non-critical other.

Kennedy's story brings together in the figure of Annie the way that Western man, as well as Western civilisation, produces itself out of the 'obscure matter', in Le Guin's phrase, of 'women, children and animals'. Given that Douglas's vision proves so self-serving and unreliable, it might be easy to conclude that the story speaks only to his attitudes toward women and not to issues of animal sentience and agency. Certainly one of its main themes is the revelation of the degree to which Douglas is incapable of love for either human or animal other, and the way that his initial preference for Annie suggests a patriarchal imaginary that prefers women to be subservient and dependent, needing to please their male 'masters' and willing to see men through the filter of unconditional love that we project onto our understanding of pets' view of humans. Yet at the same time, the story's critique of Douglas's projections onto both Annie and Therese also comments on the limited way that he views the orang-utans, never seeing Annie as a subject any more than a vivisectionist sees his specimen as one. Although Douglas's narrative differs from that of others who discount animal subjectivity, ultimately he no more sees her as a separate being possessed of agency than do those who regard animals as merely part of the raw materials put on Earth for man's use, however he pleases. Even though Douglas asserts the value of orang-utan sentience – and the story does give us concrete reasons for believing in a version of this outside of his projections – his view is ultimately as biased as that of those who refuse to recognise any possibility of sentience in animal others. He is incapable of seeing Annie because he can see only what he requires her to be in order to support his construction of self. What makes Kennedy's portrayal of this vision all the more insightful and disturbing is her exposure of the degree to which patriachally identified men see women in precisely the same ways. Annie does show agency in the story and thus its portrayal of her capacities exceeds Douglas's perceptions: she not only refuses his sexual overture but also retreats from trying to mould herself into an imitation-human for him. The story's conclusion thereby comments on the way we interact with other species and on our need to accept them as fellow subjects *even if* they do not express their subjectivity precisely as we do ours.

As all of the texts discussed in this chapter reveal, there are many parallels between the ways in which women have been constructed, controlled, spoken for and objectified by patriarchal culture, and similar constraints placed on animals by Western culture more generally. Achieving better insights into this overlapping and intersecting oppression is valuable for both feminism and those interested in animal welfare. Rather than fearing a further animalisation of women by making common cause with those interested in animal welfare, then, feminists might gain new tools for resisting gender discrimination by interrogating the logic of carnophallogocentrism evident in both the human–animal boundary and discrimination against women.[9] Rosi Braidotti maintains that contesting the existing definition of the human, including its exclusion of animals, is a core feminist priority 'given that this concept of "the human" was colonized by phallogocentrism, [and] it has come to be identified with male, white, heterosexual, Christian, property-owning, standard-language-speaking citizens'; she argues that transformative potential lies in the embrace of all living being, life as *zoe*, which 'marks the outside of this vision of the subject, in spite of the efforts of evolutionary theory to strike a new relationship to the non-human' (37). There is more to both women's and animals' being than is accounted for in man's philosophical and scientific discourses, as the tests discussed in this chapter make clear.

5. Sapien Orientalism:
Animals, Colonialism, Science Fiction

Building on Edward Said's observation that the orient in the Western imagination is not an entity with specific properties but rather is that which remains after the occident has produced itself through contrast, Donna Haraway argues that 'western primatology is simian orientalism' (*Primate* 10). That that is to say, 'knowledge' of the orient has to do with how the occidental imagination has chosen to construct itself as the opposite, and little to do with the actual existence of those called oriental. As outlined earlier in this book, Derrida similarly argues that philosophy bases its concept of what it calls 'animal' on little to no contact with other species and thus the meaning of the term 'animal' itself is a kind of orientalism, labelling the raw material out of which the human is produced. Nowhere is this logic more evident than in the intersections of the human–animal boundary and the discourse of colonialism. John Rieder argues that the logic of colonialism is central to the emergence of sf as a recognisable genre – apparent in the tales of conquest and exploration that fuel early sf, as well as in 'the relevance of colonialism and imperialism to the science in science fiction' (54). The centrality of animals to these historical and intellectual developments is similarly crucial to note. For Victorian British citizens 'the connection between triumphing over a dangerous animal and subduing unwilling natives was direct and obvious, and the association of the big game hunter with the march of empire was literal as well as metonymic' (Ritvo 254). Animals were among the main resources taken from the colonies during the period of imperial conquest, and encounters with both strange new animals and strangely different humans were crucial in the development of the social relations that emerged under colonialism.

Rieder links the emergence of sf to 'the disturbance of ethnocentrism' (2) that resulted from such encounters, in which Europeans were confronted with the realisation that their culture is only one of a number of possible cultures. The human–animal boundary was similarly destabilised by contact with other constructions of interspecies relations, and many of the cultural shifts that accompanied the imperial expansion had significant consequences for the construction of the category animal in the Western imagination. The Victorian display of the power of empire was jointly aimed at domination of the land itself and of the subject people: animals occupied an ambiguous and fluctuating third space in this system, at times being reduced to part of 'nature' or the land, and at other times serving as metonyms for subjugated natives in displays of imperial power at zoos and menageries – some of which included both exotic animals and their exotic keepers. The developing bourgeois culture of animal welfare looked to the protection of many species (although ignoring some and simply removing the suffering of others from public view, such as in the relocation of slaughtering to city margins). Yet at the same time the newly discovered sentiment for animals was often secondary to the motive of policing the 'pleasures' and habits of the working class (Lansbury 23), one of the reasons why practices such as bear-baiting were targeted while fox-hunting has survived into the twenty-first century as a leisure activity. Such class politics played out over the status of animals were also informed by anxieties about the potentially degenerative consequences of too much time spent among the 'savages' and about the role of immigrants in shifting the home country's culture. Ritvo notes that by the 1830s 'the English humane movement had begun to claim kindness to animals as a native trait and to associate cruelty to animals with foreigners' (127).

The rhetorical division of animals into domestic and wild species – categories that do have some material validity given the behaviour and genetic changes induced in some species through their long cohabitation with humans – maps easily onto colonial discourse to a division between civilised and savage societies. Animals were inevitably caught up in such struggles, the supposed savagery of creatures such as the tiger, for example, serving to symbolise the supposed savagery of their homelands. The historical domestication of animals also played a significant role in shaping human cultures and producing the context for imperialist expansion. Jim Mason notes that the very emergence of a herding culture through the domestication of animals in antiquity can be linked to greater aggression between groups of humans: herd animals provided both economic advantages and a more secure source of food, but also the concept of property that transformed parts of the natural word into owned things, and further greater militarism to defend territory needed by grazing animals – and often to expand it (Mason 35). Animal domestication also changed both the daily structures of human life – providing a prompt to the invention of other technologies such as the horseshoe or the stirrup, which changed the ways animals were integrated into human society and warfare – and also shifted the human–animal relation away from more totemic ways of seeing animals as having their own cultures alongside human ones. Such attitudes toward other beings as appropriable

resource, as well as the social relations attendant upon a new human way
of living separate from other species, both created the conditions for a class
system of labour and informed colonial encounters. It is not inconceivable
to trace the emergence of modernity to the domestication of animals
which

> allowed for not only development of early city-states with their
> complex division of labor and high degrees of inequality (thanks
> to the large numbers of people who could be fed with domesticated
> plants and animals), but eventually the political and economic
> dominance of a handful of European and Asian societies over much
> of the rest of the world (thanks to their unique geography and the
> animals and plants available to them, not to mention the epidemic
> diseases carried by domestic animals that helped to wipe out much of
> Native America). (DeMello 68)

Animals are vital to this material history and its imaginative discourse.
H.G. Wells's early critique of colonialism in *War of the Worlds* involved a
reversal not only in the sense that England was the invaded instead of
colonising nation, but further in suggesting that the Martians did not
recognise the native British as human/sentient subjects, treating them
as we treat animals 'not just in the many analogical comparisons of the
Martian invasion to humans' unthinking destruction of animal lives and
habitats, but literally, in their role as livestock feeding the Martians' thirst
for blood, and as domestic pets for the triumphant conquerors' (Rieder
111). The Martians' conquest points to the central role of the category of
property in shaping colonial encounters and human–animal relations.
Gary Francione argues that it is the status of animals as property that lies
at the root of their exclusion from many legal protections,[1] and conflicts
over human 'ownership' of the land and its resources inform many human
campaigns against 'pest' species. This is similar to the conflicts between
colonisers and natives in which native occupation of a territory or use
of a resource is not deemed to constitute a property relationship and
Europeans can thereby construct themselves from having a right to own
the resource exclusively based on their 'proper' use of it. Animal lives
continue to be bound up with such discursive struggles and even when
colonial agencies operate in a benevolent way toward them, property lies
at the root of the relationship. Ritvo argues that the end of the Victorian
period saw a decrease in safari hunting, for example, as the status of
colonial techniques changed because 'the need to conquer through force
had almost disappeared, leaving an urgent new need to husband and
manage, to protect and exploit' (288).

Slavery is one of the most problematic meeting points of these discursive formations, with the animalised Africans being treated as a resource whose labour might be as justly appropriated from the colony as any other resource. The model for American slavery is linked to the techniques gained from the experience of domesticating animals, and comparisons between it and the exploitation of animals remain a fertile and controversial site of enquiry.[2] Clare Winger Harris's 'The Ape Cycle' (1930) raises the question of whether or not enslaving animals for their labour is any more just than was enslaving humans. The story opens with a father and son fresh from an expedition in Africa deciding to devote their resources to the problem of domesticating the ape through selective breeding among a number of species they have brought back with them. The father reasons 'the horse, the ox, the camel, the elephant, the dog, and other animals less intelligent have all contributed towards man's emancipation from the external problem of working for his subsistence' (390) and so it is only sensible that the ape should do so as well. He specifically posits the need for ape labour as a consequence of the loss of slave labour to prime the economic system, a solution that had been 'quite satisfactory until man became awakened to the moral wrong' (390). With apes, he opines, no such difficulties exist; yet the rest of the story casts doubt upon this certainty. Quickly skipping ahead three generations to 2216, we find that primate labour is normalised and grandson Wilhoit has found a way to increase ape intelligence and to breed specific lines of 'gardeners, domestic servants, chauffeurs, mechanics' (395). The increased intelligence, though, brings as many challenges as benefits, and Wilhoit fears a disruption of the social order based on the reduction of the primates to labour power alone, essentially to the status of slaves.

Wilhoit's fears have foundation. The apes have been given a ruined area of Death Valley and they create an independent primate society they call Reclamation City. Here they begin to develop their own interpretation of the proper relation between ape and man and organise a revolution. Human leaders trace the root of this unrest to 'Man's first vital mistake, after the initial error of educating monkey at all', namely training 'certain apes for the sole purpose of controlling and superintending others of inferior intellect' (397). Such apes become leaders of a successful revolution, overthrowing and killing their human oppressors and – since most humans are elsewhere, their presence long unnecessary at a site of labour – occupying most of the country's industry. The story does have a happy ending for humans: Wilhoit and his girlfriend, who have the most knowledge about the apes because Wilhoit's family has created them, manage to infiltrate the ape governing structure, set up a meeting between themselves and the ape president by impersonating a key resistance leader and then destroy the entire ape leadership with explosives. Without the elite leaders, the apes quickly collapse back into disorder; they are contained, the labour hierarchy is reinstated, but with much less responsibility for ape labourers and a return of human management, and Wilhoit is made president by a grateful America.

Yet despite this facile restoration of order in its conclusion, the story has raised uncomfortable questions about the social relations between a dominant class and an exploited labouring class. The apes are liminal figures, somewhat like slaves, somewhat like the colonial subject trained into playing a role in British and other imperial civic structures, and yet at the same time they are wholly owned entities that have been bred and patented by Wilhoit's family. One way of reading the story is as a cautionary tale that insists that what is 'proper' to the human/elite – such as decision-making, managerial roles – should remain with the human/ elite, a retrenchment of hierarchy both in terms of the division of labour and the human–animal boundary. At the same time, however, the story might also be read as a critique, not of these divisions but rather through the revelation that such roles must be jealously guarded for the human/ elite, that the subordinated other is just as capable. Before the defeat of the ape revolution, one news reporter wonders if it is not indeed the appropriate moment for an 'Ape Cycle': humans have had our time and while this shift looks like the death of civilisation from the human point of view, ascendance of abjected others might be inevitable and evidence of progress, both from their point of view but also perhaps overall if evolution as viewed as teleology. The reporter concludes that it would be 'good for our race that we usher it in gracefully' (401). Thus 'Ape Cycle' might be read as a critique of the unnaturalness of colonial and anthropocentric social orders and a warning about the costs of policing them.

Colonialism commodified not only the bodies of animals and natives, but also their knowledge, discounting native ownership of techniques as much as of the land itself. This is a problem that continues under the neo-colonialist regimes of biopolitics where the genetic properties of plants and animals are patented by pharmaceutical or agribusiness corporations, ignoring any native claim to having bred a specific strain of plant or animal, an information age continuation of colonial resource transfer.[3] David H. Keller's 'The Steam Shovel' (1931) exemplifies these conflicts over property in its tale of commodified knowledge, colonialist racism and the status of animals in human cultures. It begins as 'the great Oriental surgeon' (510) Wing Loo visits his engineering friend Francis Smith at a project site in India. Wing Loo has been educated in Britain and thus he occupies an ambiguous position in the colonial class system: he is a professional and is able to converse with British subjects on their own terms, yet his exotic background also gives him insight into the 'irrationalities' of the native mind. His appearance also marks him as not quite a proper British subject: he wears 'jewelry that would serve to ransom a king' including 'rings his ancestors had worn for more than two thousand years' (510). Smith is frustrated by the lack of progress on the project, feeling 'it was one thing to build a railroad in a temperate climate with white labor, and decidedly another to build even a short road in Burma' (510). He blames the Indian labourers for their superstitious refusal to work when they perceive bad omens from the gods and argues that 'the job would be finished by now if they were white men' (51). These opening descriptions establish the colonial hierarchies and convey a casual racism the reader is presumed to share.

The narrative focuses on an elephant named Mabut Rae who is part of the work crew. Over 100 years old, Mabut operates the site's steam shovel and is constructed by Smith as a more reliable worker than the humans. Unfortunately, the incompetent Rajah – another superstitious and irrational native – visits the work site and sees Mabut, remembering him as the elephant that had humiliated him on a hunt many years ago, and thus orders Mabut killed. Smith is in despair at this loss of his most efficient worker, but Dr Loo is able to save his old friend by performing surgery to transplant the elephant's brain (and hence its knowledge of the steam shovel operation) into the mechanism itself. They then kill the elephant to fulfil the Rajah's orders, although not before getting Mabut high on opium so as to minimise his suffering. The story's denouement has the Rajah visit the completed road: as he is mistreating his horse, blaming it for his own error in judgement, the steam shovel mysteriously 'malfunctions' and kills him. Clearly meant as a humorous tale of revenge, the story nonetheless betrays a more complex set of conflicting attitudes toward animals and colonial others. Smith is kind to Mabut in a way he is not toward his human labourers, an attitude that attempts to convey sympathy for animals as a trait of civilised cultures (and hence the contrast with the Rajah's brutality); yet at the same time, Mabut is preferred because his agency is more easily discounted than is that of the human workers[4]: he does not disrupt the work schedule based on his 'superstitious' practices, and he can be killed for the sake of convenience without moral qualm.

Mabut becomes the perfect labourer whose knowledge can be commodified and embedded in the machine itself, thus aligning him with more recent innovations in laboratory animals such as knock-out gene mice, animal bodies that are created by human technoscience (such as Dr Loo's surgery on Mabut). For such creatures, their status as living beings is overwritten by their status as created laboratory tools. The colonial imagination has more difficulty reducing the native to the status of passive resource available for appropriation, hence the preference for animal labour. Walter Kateley's 'Remote Control' (1930) exemplifies this fantasy all the more clearly. It creates a future in which the line between animals and machines has collapsed because humans have learned 'the great secrets of Nature' (24) and thus are able to compel all living beings to form a vast network of labour awaiting human instruction: whales and sharks pull cargo, primates and elephants unload barges, squirrels operate 'typing and computating machines' (27). The financial benefits extend beyond merely free labour but include also the absence of a depreciating machinic infrastructure. This utopia is a product of genius amateur scientist Kingston, who has 'a deeper insight into the physical properties of all matter than any other man' (28) despite his lack of formal scientific training, assisted by his friend and our narrator, who not incidentally works for the patent office. As well as being a fantasy of the perfect domination of animal life to human ends, then, 'Remote Control' is also an exemplar of the sort of sf promoted by Gernsback which celebrates the power of the amateur tinkerer to participate equally with professionals in creating the technology that will bring a better human future.

The narrator tells the story of the discovery/invention of this technology that has radically transformed labour and human–animal relations. Kingston and his friend were observing ants and marvelling at their industrious achievements, all of which seem to be accomplished 'by instinct alone', their behaviour 'controlled by something more deeply seated than intelligence' (30). Among the ants all is 'orderly and efficient' despite the fact that 'in all the public works, in all the engineering projects carried on, no one has ever been able to discover anything remotely resembling supervision' (31). Unlike humans, ants appear to need no master builder to conceive of and develop a plan; each ant seems to do her[5] own thing and yet the finished project coheres, leading Kingston to conclude 'a single ant is not an entire individual ... these units that we see are not the entire entity, but only parts of a larger animal, other parts of which escape our notice' (33). These amateur experimenters are able serendipitously to discover thin threads of 'silvery, shimmering blue' (36), usually not perceptible to human senses, which connect all the ants they observe, and trace these threads back to 'an imperfectly formed brain' (38) that controls the entire colony. They investigate and quickly patent this 'nerve energy' and develop a technology to 'apply the force to all animals' and thereby 'revolutionize all industry!' (39). Their success produces the utopian world of infinitely exploitable animal labour upon which the story opens, a world in which animal agency is entirely overwritten by human control of the force that 'actuates the nervous system of all animals', enabling them to 'convey messages to the nerve centers and ganglia of an animal in such a way that they will come in stronger than those from the animal's own brain' (40).

The ants have thus provided a model of the perfect exploitation of labour, where the existence of all living creatures is reduced to that of labour power alone, the imperatives of the industrial control mechanism able to overwrite their volition at the level of ganglia. This fantasy of infinitely exploitable animal labour is like the mechanised social relations produced under capital, where humans are alienated from the products of their own labour, their own bodies and their fellow creatures. Capital's exploitation of surplus value separates humans from their creative agency, just as the ants are presumed to have no control or agency in their engineering products, the result belonging to the centralised control mechanism and not to the individual labourers. Thus the ants' productivity, like that of all animals in this story's world and that of workers under capitalism, is alienated from them and assumes a separate, autonomous existence. As Marx argues, under this system an uncanny exchange takes place in which the workers (human only, in Marx's view) lose their animate qualities as full beings, while the commodities they produce take on seemingly magical qualities of liveliness, via what Marx terms the commodity fetish.[6] This logic of maximising one's appropriation of labour power from other living beings parallels the logic of colonialist appropriation of resources, including labour power and both human and animal bodies. Paul Burkett argues:

> capital's damaging effects on labor power and nature result from its tendency to take advantage of this elasticity [of limits to exploitation due to limitations of the body, the speed of work, the amount of resources] as the pressure of competitive monetary accumulation stretch human and extra-human forces to the breaking point. (133–134)

Looking to twenty-first-century technoscience, Melinda Cooper sees a similar manipulation of life itself at the level of biopolitics in order to enable living bodies to transcend their limits and thereby prevent those limits from becoming an obstacle to capital's continued expansion. Cooper points to 'a whole series of legislative and regulatory measures designed to relocate economic production at the genetic, microbial, and cellular level, so that life becomes, literally, annexed within capitalist processes of accumulation' (19), including interventions 'in line with the standard rules of assembly line production, [whereby] animal reproductive science seeks to eliminate unproductive (or rather *unreproductive*) time, by extending the fertility of animals' (132–133), a logic she also sees extended to humans through biomedical interventions.

The politics of colonialism are thus deeply entwined with the politics of labour exploitation. Ants have been a favoured cultural symbol for interrogating the related logics of imperialism and capitalism. E.O. Wilson, more famous for his sociobiological pronouncements than his myrmecology, has argued that 'the competitive edge that led to the rise of the ants as a world-dominant group is their highly developed, self-sacrificial colonial existence', provocatively suggesting 'it would appear that socialism really works under some circumstances. Karl Marx just had the wrong species' (9).[7] Leaving to one side Wilson's egregious but common misreading of the nature of work as understood by Marxism, it says much about human cultural priorities that the ant has so frequently been a figure of imaginative identification and admiration, in sf and elsewhere. H.G. Wells's 'The Empire of the Ants' (1905) is the exemplar text of this tendency within the genre. Creole Captain Gerilleau initially suspects mockery when he is ordered to take his gunboat into the South American interior and help the natives defend against 'a plague of ants' (47). Yet as he and his multi-ethnic crew move up the river, they encounter a world that increasingly seems distant from the orderly world of the imperial centre, one in which the dilapidated remnants of colonial incursions seem 'a little thing lost in this wilderness of Nature' (49), especially to British engineer Holroyd who becomes the captain's confidante. Holroyd finds his first view of the tropics disturbing, too unlike 'England, where Nature is hedged, ditched, and drained into the perfection of submission' (49). Land in the colonies is thus a wilderness, not a landscape, evidence of the uncivilised location.

The very notion of landscape, as Raymond Williams has argued, implies a particular sort of relationship to place based on 'separation and observation' (120), a relation that Williams links to class divisions but which is equally applicable to differences between colonial spaces and those of the imperial centre. Williams emphasises the imposition of order that is part of the production of the landscape, the division of space into the 'mathematical grids of the enclosure awards, with their straight hedges and straight roads' and into 'the natural curves and scatterings of park scenery' (124). This order is as much social and economic as physical: the beauty of park landscape is 'organised for consumption' (124) as much as the agricultural land is organised for production, and the people within the landscape are similarly sorted and categorised, with workers being removed from the park prospect. Similarly, the colonies are organised as something akin to a park for imperial subjects. Their wildness is carefully contrasted to the ordered grids of the urban imperial centre and their fauna, including humans, are meant to serve as backdrop for adventures but not to exercise agency in ways that threaten European possession of the landscape. Rieder emphasises the importance of looking to the ideology of imperialism, which 'distributes knowledge and power to the subject who looks, while denying or minimizing access to power for its object, the one looked at' (7). Yet the land in Wells's story resists this imposition of order and its reassuring vision of a conquered nature, instead making Holroyd feel 'that man is indeed a rare animal, having but a precarious hold upon this land' (49).

The ants both challenge the imperialists' hegemony and serve as an emblem for their techniques. In her reading of the story, Charlotte Sleigh notes that contemporary travel literature presents 'ants in far-flung places as familiar and domestic; they were reassuringly English compared to the lazy and incompetent natives' ('Empire' 33). Yet at the same time, the ants represent a threat to empire in their formation of their own colonies and their insistence upon occupying the territory Europeans have deeded to themselves. Sleigh notes that ants were a significant obstacle to European colonisation of Africa, both destroying settlers' crops and serving as vectors to spread disease among native labourers and white settlers alike ('Empire' 37). This unpredictability of the ants is apparent in Wells's story. Some 'plagues of ants' prove helpful: 'ant armies come into your houses ... you go and dey clean the house. Den you come back again; – the house is clean, like new! No cockroaches, no fleas, no jiggers in the floor' (48); at the same time, these new ants that Gerilleau is sent to investigate present a threat as they 'don't go' (52) and thus violate a presumed 'natural' hierarchy in which humans are meant to have dominion over all animals, extended in the Victorian period into a logic by which European humans also had dominion over animalised natives. The ants and the land as a whole disturb Holroyd by their indifference to his goals, an 'inhuman immensity' that confronts him with the fact that the land is not owned by the imperial centre, even though 'in an atlas, too, the land is man's and all colored to show his claim to it – in vivid contrast to the universal independent blueness of the sea' (53). The ants are thus in part aligned with the natives,[8] inhabitants of the land whose claim trumps that of the colonisers, drawing into question the entire imperial project by which 'everywhere about the earth, plough and culture, light tramways and good roads, an ordered security, would prevail' (53). Yet the ants are simultaneously an image of the colonisers in their relentless drive to occupy all territory and displace the previous inhabitants, their methods 'oddly suggestive of the rushes of modern infantry advancing under fire' (59). The ants thus doubly call the imperial project into question by offering an uncanny, dark image of the other side of such 'progress', similar to the image of the Martians in *The War of the Worlds*.

Just as the ants challenge the hierarchical logic of colonialism, they challenge the human–animal boundary by their displays of intelligence, a quality which, in the form of reason, Europeans are meant to possess over savages as well as animals, as Sleigh also notes. The ants are not simply unthinking, instinctual hordes that overrun the rational order established by the colonial power, but more disturbingly are an enemy that displays a capacity to plan equal to the Europeans' own. They move with 'a steady deliberation very different from the mechanical fussiness of the common ant' (57) and appear to have tools and clothes, two of the chief signifiers of civilised status. When Holroyd confronts a group of them over the body of a fallen man, they look at him 'as a rallying crowd of men might look at some gigantic monster that had dispersed it' (58). The ants thus destabilise the human–animal boundary that grounds Western subjectivity, just as the tropical landscape destabilised a sense of imperial order and ownership. The overlapping logics of colonial ideology and the human–animal boundary are signalled when Holroyd thinks of the boat's crew as an 'unappetizing mixture of races' (62). Distressingly, the ants seem indifferent to the weapons technology that has ensured European dominance over colonised natives, failing to react at all when the captain fires 'de big gun ... with great sternness and ceremony' (63). Yet what is most disturbing about the ants' intelligence is that they use it to enact precisely the same sort of expansionist aggression that characterises colonial nations, the link between the ability 'to store knowledge' and to 'use weapons, form great empires, sustain a planned and organized war' (54) seeming inevitable.

The story ends with the Europeans fleeing the area, abandoning it to the ants who have 'driven men out completely, occupied plantations and settlements, and boarded and captured at least one ship' (64). The story's final line ominously projects that the ants will not stop their conquest in South America, but by '1950 or 1960 at the latest' will discover Europe, a potential conquest ironically made possible by the transportation networks of the 'European capitalist' (65). It is their very ability to imitate the aggressive and expansionist aspects of Western society that predict the ants' domination, and thus Wells uses the horror evoked by them to underscore the horror of colonialist and capitalist expansion. Many other pulp stories similarly feature the fantasy of ants attempting conquest of the Earth or the related one of ants as future rulers of the Earth, but frequently such stories lack Wells's implicit critique. In them, fear of ant dominion is frequently mixed with almost equal measure of admiration for the order and discipline of ant society, such as in Louise Rice and Tonjoroff-Roberts's 'The Astounding Enemy' (1930), which similarly conflates insect infestation with the petulance of natives and the 'pestiferous Labour Unions' (78) as common barriers to the orderly progress of civilisation. Modernism itself seems to be under threat from this 'astonishing enemy' which attacks all metal and thus threatens transportation and other infrastructure, as well as machinery-dependent agricultural production. Although native sabotage is at first suspected as the culprit, it is revealed that 'an heir' to human's dominion is behind the problems: 'the creative urge has not been idle since man emerged from the animal world, its master and rival. Following the production of his master, nature has continued her work. The accident of humanity may repeat itself tomorrow' (81).

At first this story seems to reject the human–animal boundary and even take some delight in the wondrous power of invention that has enabled the ants to achieve such organised sabotage of human enterprise. Like Wells's ants, these are frightening because they have produced a metal-eating acid not through chance or random selection but via the scientific method. When one military advisor expresses shock that ants understand chemistry, he is told 'they have always understood it ... it is ourselves who have not understood them' (82). Humanity's entire sense of self, based on the protection of those things deemed 'proper' to humans, is disrupted by these ants who have the power of 'invading man's realm, and understanding that realm as well' (83). Yet no sooner is this potential erasure of the human–animal boundary put forward than the story immediately turns to an adventure narrative about finding a way for humanity to 'win the world all over again', not this time through 'millions of slow and stupid years' of evolution but instead immediately through the superior power of technology, the force by which humans are set apart from the world rather than subject to its vicissitudes. Unless modernity can be salvaged, 'man will be so crippled that his world will all but be lost to him and again he will be at the mercy of the animals, which he once put under his heel' (83). The similarities between ant and human social organisation thus make the struggle one with a worthy opponent in this story, not a disruption of the hierarchical logic of colonialist expansion as in 'Empire of the Ants'. Our hero, Colonel Fortescue, insists that human civilisation has reached a stage where 'we know that the scientist, in all branches of human needs, is the true educator and teacher' (90), and he specifically celebrates this power of the scientist to save humanity as compared to the lesser power of those whose status comes with wealth. The story's conclusion drifts away from issues of scientific conquest and ant social order, depicting instead a multispecies insect society and the heroic rescue of a white woman from rape by a giant ant bent on conquest through miscegenation, betraying even more of such tales' tendency to conflate anxiety about non-white hordes with images of teeming insects.

The ant menace is safely contained in 'The Astounding Enemy', reasserting the very hierarchies that are drawn into question by 'Empire of the Ants'. Yet although such hierarchies include privileging humans over animals, just as they privilege the colonisers over natives, there nonetheless remains a sense of admiration for the industry of the ants who proved a more formidable enemy than the 'oriental' menace originally presumed to be behind the sabotage. This admiration for ant society suggests something about the value placed on the division of labour and its attendant class systems. Admiration for ants focuses on two things: their ability to accomplish feats of conquest and engineering that seem superhuman when measured against what proportionately sized humans might achieve, and their rigid (and therefore presumed ideal and efficient) social organisation. Although Wilson characterises ants' co-operative organisation of labour as Marxist, his conception of the rigidity of their class system in which an individual ant is defined entirely by its labour role is in fact precisely the opposite of Marx's ideal of a classless society. Instead, ants typify the status of alienated labour under conditions of capitalist production, except they seem magically to remove the deleterious effects of alienation by virtue of their 'essence' being truly that of their labour role, rather than this reduction to labour power alone being a stunted and stultifying existence, as it is for humans subjugated by the class system. What is constructed as admiration for ant society, then, is more often than not endorsement of expansionism both colonialist and capitalist. Bob Olsen's 'The Ant with a Human Soul' (1932) exemplifies these tendencies.

Narrator Kenneth Williams attempts to commit suicide because he has lost his faith in god by going to university and finding education and faith incompatible, thereby leaving him 'at the mercy of every passing gale of opinion' (235), trapped in a meaningless existence. He is rescued by a scientist who plans to use him as an experimental subject for a memory transference procedure that will enable Williams to inhabit the body of an ant and thereby better study the species, which the scientist contends are 'from the standpoint of behavior – of social activities, mental development, constructive intelligence and similar "human" traits ... far ahead of the ape in development' (237). Most of the story is an exposition of ant behaviour, which continually emphasises their industry and superiority: driver ants are praised as housecleaners as in Wells's story, but here the relationship with human occupants of the house is entirely co-operative; the ant is celebrated as 'the most charitable of creatures' (245) for what Sleigh calls its 'social stomach' (77), that is, the use of the bodies of some ants to store food that is shared with the entire colony; the interloping 'Hobo Bugs' (246) that are parasites on the colony are disparaged for their failure to contribute to industrious production; and the diligence of enterprising 'farmer ants', who plant crops, 'cowboy ants', who tend and milk aphids, and 'slaver ants', who compel those captured from other colonies to do their work, are admired. Like human society, it seems, ant types are organised in a hierarchy in which the 'most primitive races' are hunters, 'represented today by the African savages (for the men) and by Driver Ants (for the insects)'; these are followed by 'semi-savage tribes of men who live principally on fruit, nuts and other vegetable foods that grow wild', paralleled by gatherer ants; next follow tribal warrior races; then 'semi-civilised' pastoral ants and people; and finally the development of agriculture that allows for the emergence of true civilisation. The ants who plant and tend their crops 'have reached a very high stage of development – much higher than any animal, except man, has ever attained', but humans have a higher stage yet, not thus far achieved by ants, which is 'the industrial and cultural age, which is characterized by the use of machinery and by the acquisition and recording of knowledge' (256).

As with the other ant stories, Olsen's neatly encapsulates imperialist ideology and manages to combine admiration for the ants with a celebration of the superiority of tool-use and the domination of nature that otherwise buttresses the human–animal boundary. Williams enjoys his many adventures throughout the ant world and finds he is always physically and mentally stimulated by the various roles he occupies, failing to note that the ant social order he venerates is presumed not to offer such chances for social mobility. The implicit privileging of both his human sensibilities and the colonial racism that underpins the representations of the ants is revealed in the one risky encounter he faces as a 'honey pot' ant used to store the colony's food. He finds this experience so intoxicating that he becomes 'like a white man who, attracted by the care-free life of a South Sea Islander, tasted the lotus of forgetfulness and "went native"', and thus he 'almost lost white man's heritage' (262). Fortunately his superior intellect is able to recall him to a life beyond his immediate absorption in the 'honey pot' role – and we might recall here that in the Olsen story discussed in the previous chapter, the female, Diana, living in an ant's body, was not able to overcome this domination by instinct – and return to his human embodiment where he discovers a newfound passion for life as a consequence of his experiences among the ants. His loss of Christian faith is replaced by 'Myrmacism' which he defines as 'a norm for guiding the conduct of any person under any circumstances ... Do whatsoever will bring the greatest amount of happiness to the largest number of people' (279). Throughout the tale Williams emphasises the fulfilment found in whatever labour role defined his current ant existence. The story thus functions as a sort of alibi for capitalist social relations, suggesting the problem lies not in reducing humans to labour power alone but in construing human existence in such a way that this role as labourer is unfulfilling; for ants, the greatest happiness is brought to the greatest number by subordinating oneself entirely to one's productive role, and the only villains are those labelled hobos who use the resources of the colony without contributing to their production.

The connections between colonial exploitation and the more general exploitation of wage labour is also the topic of Karel Čapek's animal allegory *War with the Newts* (1936). Like the ant stories, the novel has a colonial backdrop, opening with Captain von Toch lamenting that the Cuban/ Portuguese agent is the only white man among 'lousy Bataks' he must deal with on this voyage, and further lamenting the influence of the 'damned Jews' (9) who control money back home, as he is busy 'loading some of the blessings of the island (copra, pepper, camphor, gutta-percha, palm oil, tobacco and labour)' (18–19). Labour is just one commodity among many being extracted from the colonies, and its embodiment in living beings registers on von Toch only insofar as he is inconvenienced. The newts, called tapas by the Batak, enter the story when von Toch observes them watching the natives open oyster shells; later they approach him on the beach and seem to ask him to use his knife to help them do likewise. In a familiar conflation of the racial ideology of colonialism with the human–animal boundary, von Toch expresses a preference for the newts, who seem dependent and know their place in the 'natural' hierarchy, over the unreliable labour of natives. Von Toch insists 'those lizards have more brains than a Singhalese or a Batak because they tried to learn something. Whereas a Batak will never learn anything except by crookery' (35), and explains 'I made something ... something like a contract with those tapa-boys. That's to say I gave them my word that if they would bring me those pearl-oysters I would give them those harpoons and knives to defend themselves with. See? An honest deal, sir' (41, ellipses in original).

Yet von Toch's version of 'an honest deal' involves dealing with a labourer who – like Olsen's ideal ant – is presumed fulfilled entirely by the act of service to the human master through labour. His contract with the newts soon involves removing them from their homes to labour elsewhere, and although he insists that the crews of the transport ships do not mistreat them, the newts at the same time have no autonomy: unlike native labour, the newts' lack of human status is presumed to exempt their employers from the moral quandaries of reducing an other to labour power alone. Yet the dream of free labour continually runs up against the material constraints caused by the fact that the newts are living beings and not simply the embodiment of labour power: once they can defend themselves against sharks with the knives supplied through their 'deal' with von Toch, their numbers grow and they demand the right to immigrate. The struggle to determine on which side of the human–animal boundary the newts belong is central to these issues of labour. If the newts are animals, they cannot be exploited and thus any degree of mistreatment is justified, but if they demonstrate qualities deemed 'human' then other considerations become pertinent. One newt kept at a zoo develops the ability to speak and takes the name Andrew Scheuchzer, a Christianised version of the species name *Andrias scheuchzeri*, named for the similarity between their skeletons and one discovered by a Dr Scheuchzer, which he 'regarded ... as the remains of *antediluvian man*' (75). Andrew is able to converse with those who visit his cage at the zoo and he regularly assists the friendly janitor with the performance of his duties, yet scientists insist this 'so-called animal intelligence' is the product of 'how popular belief overrated the intellectual activity of animals' (81).

Andrew dies from being fed chocolate by a zoo visitor, an echo of the fate of many zoo animals who have been fed unhealthy substances either maliciously or ignorantly by zoo visitors.[9] Other newts kept as novelties, pets and circus attractions similarly suffer at the hands of ignorant or indifferent owners who continually ignore signs of these creatures' intelligence even while profiting from them. Scientists experiment on newts in ways that tend to destroy rather than test for intelligence, such as experiments in which 'some sensory canal in Andrias's brain is severed' or a test to see 'how Andrias would behave if the mechanism corresponding to the labyrinth of the inner ear were crushed' (136), leading our narrator to retort, 'just then a thought flashed through my mind: what kind of disturbances would appear in Professor Devrient if I removed his right frontal lobe?' (136–137). He continues,

> I was tormented by doubt on whether we were entitled (in the strict scientific sense) to speak about our (I mean: human) mental life unless we first removed each other's cerebral lobes and cut each other's sensory canals. Strictly speaking, we should pounce on each other, scalpel in hand, to study each other and our own mentality. (137)

Although this commentary is offered with the bitterest of sarcasm, it might also be read more seriously in light of Derrida's deconstruction of the human–animal boundary in philosophy, particularly his questioning of the right by which humans attribute to themselves that which they deny 'the animal'. Derrida argues 'the gaze called "animal" offers to my sight the abyssal limit of the human: the inhuman or the ahuman, the ends of man, that is to say, the bordercrossing from which vantage man dares to announce himself to himself, thereby calling himself by the name that he believes he gives himself' (*The Animal* 12). The experiments performed on the newts despite their evident 'humanity' are made all the more disturbing if we consider that this novel is published almost contemporaneously with similar Nazi experimentation on Jews, experiments that are justified by this logic of the human–animal boundary and the positing of Jews on the inhuman or ahuman side of such a line.

Despite these ways in which the newts suffer similar to how animals suffer within human cultures, the novel nonetheless does not precisely challenge the human–animal boundary but rather challenges specific applications of this boundary which have excluded human-like subjects from the human category. The newts are culturally positioned as if they are animals, or at least nearer animal than human, yet the novel continually points out that this is a category error. Like colonised subjects, the newts are trained into Western cultural norms but reminded 'we were not the same as humans' (143) by sexual and other taboos. Newt flesh is not suitable for human consumption unless it is treated via an elaborate process of soaking and boiling to make it palatable, and then only as a cheap source of protein for the working classes or armed forces. A newt laboratory subject, Hans, is described as 'an educated and clever animal with a special talent for scientific work'; Hans works as a laboratory assistant and can 'be trusted with the most exacting chemical analyses' and participate in discussions with the human researchers in which they are 'amused by the insatiable thirst for knowledge' (140) he displays. Yet despite all this evident of 'human' behaviour, Hans remains categorised as an animal and is sacrificed – in scientific idiom – once he loses his eyesight in an experiment and thus can no longer serve the scientists' ends. All observation confirms that the newt 'in purely biological terms ... [is] just as decadent an animal as man, and like him it tried to overcompensate its biological inferiority by what was called the intellect' (136). Other incidents in the novel confirm that the newts are used to challenge how the human–animal boundary is drawn rather than the existence of such a line between 'proper' subjects and exploitable objects: like colonised subjects the newts are kidnapped from their homes and enslaved; like the working classes, they are subjected to harsh working conditions that destroy their bodies and health; like enslaved Africans, they are transported in overcrowded ship holds and many die in transit.

Analogous to the robots in Čapek's R.U.R., the marginalised other for whom the newts most evidently stand in for is the working class. A significant shift occurs in the novel when von Toch dies and with him a paternalistic attitude toward the exploited newts. This shift coincides with concern about the falling price of pearls due to overproduction using newt labour and anxiety about maintaining the company's profitability within changed market conditions. The newts are now declared wholly owned by the company rather than under contract and no longer restricted to harvesting pearls; instead the newts will 'be sold as labour to whoever planned to conduct any operation in or under water' (102), a move that ensures the company retains a marketable product. The company is unable to patent the newts – who unfortunately can reproduce themselves – but it does have the foresight to set up a vertical trust, The Salamander Syndicate, which ensures it controls contracts for the special, patented instruments the Newts use as well as for their food and transportation, all of which involve technologies that can be patented. The company sees its responsibility lying not with the newts who no longer have a contract but in fulfilling a 'promise that a dividend of at least 10 per cent would be paid out that year on the shares of the Pacific Export Company' (106). Increased attention is paid to the newts' reproductive physiology in order to ensure labour supply meets demand, an aspect of the biopolitics of governance. Foucault argues that biopolitics is focused on 'the population as political problem' (*Society* 245) and that it uses racism to allow 'power to treat that population as a mixture of races ... to subdivide the species it controls, into the subspecies known, precisely, as races' (*Society* 255). The management of populations requires that power operate in terms of security rather than sovereignty, and crucially this style of governance addresses not 'a collection of juridical subjects in an individual or collective relationship with a sovereign will' but rather 'a set of elements in which we can note constants and regularities even in accidents, in which we can identify the universal of desire regularly producing the benefit of all, and with regard to which we can identify a number of modifiable variables on which it depends' (*Security* 74).

Governance of populations rather than people takes as its object 'to improve the condition of the population, to increase its wealth, its longevity, and its health' (*Security* 105) and with it is born political economy, an ideology that presumes what is best for humanity conceived as 'population' (an aggregate mass, not as a collection of individuals whose subjectivity exceeds their economic role) is what is best for the smooth functioning of the economy. Management at the level of population requires mechanisms such as scarcity (and its attendant suffering) but intervening in such matters is not the role of governance under this model. The economic system takes priority over the governed subjects and 'the idea is not, given the state of things, how can we find the economic system that will be able to take account of the basic facts'; instead the question becomes 'given the economic-political regulation can only take place through the market, how can we modify these material, cultural, technical, and legal bases ... how can we modify these facts, this framework so that the market economy can come into play?' (141). It is unsurprising that Čapek uses an animal other to stand in for workers in such conditions as animals are frequently managed in terms of populations, the focus on statistical averages rather than on the individual happiness of each being. The vocabulary of newt markets emphasises this point: only *leading* newts trained for specialised labour are sold one at a time; others are all sold in aggregate units – *heavy*, athletic newts in groups of six; *team* standard newts in lots of twenty; and *trash*, defective ones, are sold 'collectively by weight' (126). As the narrator tells us, 'the moment the Newts had become a mass-scale and commonplace phenomenon the whole question of the Newts, if we may so call it, underwent a change' (141). Newt labour and their management as a workforce population for a time maintain the company's profitability even in the face of a depressed pearl market.

Newt labour physically transforms the world through their dredging of canals or construction of more land mass in oceans and rivers, thereby allowing human settlement to exceed the limits otherwise placed upon it. Like the logic of biopolitics, this is nature made over into a capitalist model of productivity. As one character puts it, 'nature is not, and never has been, as enterprising and purposeful as human production and commerce' (123). Yet as the title of the novel suggests, this management of newts as labour power alone ultimately fails and humans find themselves at war with the newts. Human labour, rather than seeing common cause with the newts, see them as unfair competition and seek to ban or limit their use, thereby allowing capitalism to profit from a speciesism that fragments the working classes, as racism historically functioned in American labour politics.[10] The newts also come to symbolise the destruction of human life as all is subordinated to an expanding capitalism, one in which previously uncommodified areas of social life increasingly fall under its logic. The so-called

> Newt Age ... will be concerned solely with numbers and mass production. The world's entire future lies in a continually increased consumption and production – so we need even more Newts to produce even more and consume even more. The Newts are quite simply Quantity: their epoch-making achievement lies in their huge numbers. (166)

Newts begin to fight back against human aggression, attacking those who attempt to kidnap them into slavery and demanding the right to dismantle continents in order to make more shoreline for newt habitation, reversing their previous work creating land masses for human occupation. They start to use the munitions they have been given for construction projects as weapons against humans, all the while insisting that they are not aggressive or expansionist, merely exerting their right to live.

An excerpt from a philosophical work on the decline of mankind suggests that the newts will be victorious because they are a united people, not divided by class and national differences: 'biological necessity as well as historical logic demand that the Newts, being subjugated, will have to liberate themselves; that being homogeneous, they will have to unite; and that, thereby becoming the greatest power the world has ever seen, they will *have to* take dominion over it' (200). The newts in this final section of the novel seem fully severed from animal origins and thus from questions related to the species boundary. The very last chapter, entitled 'The Author Talks to Himself', is an exchange between two voices: one wants to retreat from such a dire vision of humankind subjugated by its former slaves and proposes that the newts might die out as the consequence of some virus; the other rejects this *The War of the Worlds*-style solution as 'too facile', asking 'why should Nature put right what man has messed up?' (237). The problem is that the real enemy is not the newts, but the desire for profit which pits 'people against people – that's something you cannot stop' (237). Even though humans are aware that many of their social practices and the products of modernity are diminishing human happiness, nonetheless 'Every factory in the world. Every bank. Every country' (237) will continue so long as they feel they might profit. The newts are destroyed in the end not by a virus but by their own similarity to human culture: they too begin to form nations, to fragment as a species and thereby destroy themselves.

Although Čapek's newts seem clearly intended to draw attention to the exploitation of marginalised human subjects such as the colonised and the working classes, the metaphor of animal other used to accomplish this critique is instructive. Animals too have been exploited as labour power by capital, and the social relations possible between humans and other species have been deformed by this exploitative exchange. The exploitation of animals as labour and the exploitation of animalised working classes are highlighted by Berger in his discussion of factory farms. He notes 'This reduction of the animal, which has a theoretical as well as economic history, is part of the same process as that by which men have been reduced to isolated productive and consuming units ... The mechanical view of the animal's work capacity was later applied to that of workers' (11). Cordwainer Smith's *Instrumentality of Mankind* stories also raise issues of labour and the exploitation of a working class that emerges from animal being, but Smith retains a dual focus on the animals themselves as historically exploited by human culture, as well as on their exploitation as workers in this future.[11] Smith's interconnected series of stories tell of a future human society that has overcome poverty and suffering for humans, but which has also created a permanent underclass of workers, the underpeople, 'animals in the shape of human beings, who did the heavy and the weary work which remained as the *caput mortuum* of a really perfected economy' ('Dead Lady' 224).

Smith thus combines the permanently impoverished and uncertainly employed class required by capitalist production methods with the bias expressed in the human–animal boundary. Because the underpeople are derived from animal stock, one does not need to be concerned for their welfare or consider them as fellow beings with whom one engages in social relations. Instead

> Human beings and hominids had lived so long in an affluent society that they did not know what it meant to be poor. But the Lords of the Instrumentality had decreed that underpeople – derived from animal stock – should live under the economics of the Ancient World; they had to have their own kind of money to pay for their rooms, their food, their possessions, and the education of their children. If they became bankrupt, they went to the Poorhouse, where they were killed painlessly by means of gas. ('Ballad' 403)[12]

The underpeople are thus a perfect, expendable working class; it is illegal to treat them in hospitals because 'It was easier to breed new underpeople for the jobs than it was to repair sick ones' ('Dead Lady' 224), a situation which is identical to the lives of animals in agribusiness who are killed as soon as they stop producing eggs or milk, often ground up for fertiliser or otherwise subjected to the extraction of the last possible bit of profit from the sale of their corpses. Health crises such as BSE (mad cow disease), as discussed in Chapter 1, are a direct consequence of such capitalist practices, developing because the ground-up bodies of dead cattle were fed to living stock.[13]

Although Smith makes explicit the connections between the underpeople and the permanent underclass of humans required by capitalist production methods, he is also insistent that the underpeople equally represent animals who are regularly exploited by human culture. In *Norstrilia*, the rebelling underpeople construct their revolution in terms of resisting the long history of human–animal social relations that have been disavowed by human culture:

> How many cats have served and loved men, and for how long? How many cattle have worked for men, been eaten by men, been milked by men across the ages, and have still followed where men went, even to the stars? And dogs. I do not have to tell you about the love of dogs for men. We call ourselves the Holy Insurgency because we are rebels. We are a government. (248–249)

The revolution begins in a period long before that in which most of the stories are set, and when it is recounted in 'The Dead Lady of Clown Town' (1964) we are continually reminded that this is a story of ancient history and that 'we must remember that centuries passed before mankind finally came to grips with the problem of the underpeople and decided what "life" was within the limits of the human community' (276). The revolution itself is rather anticlimactic; it 'lasted six minutes and covered one hundred and twelve meters' (168) and ended with the slaughter of most of those involved on the spot and later the burning of the leader, D'joan, a dog-girl. Yet Smith suggests that the revolution cannot be measured in minutes and metres, but instead needs to be assessed with reference to the long, slow transformation of consciousness that it sparked. The revolutionaries in *Norstrilia* believe they are finally seeing the end of this transformation of social relations and conditions of production, and argue that their achievement is 'not ending time ... We are just altering the material conditions of Man's situation for the present historical period' (249). Smith further emphasises that this transformation of social relations is not possible without collective struggle, that 'mankind would [not] ever get around to correcting ancient wrongs unless the underpeople had some of the tools of power – weapons, conspiracy, wealth, and (above all) organization with which to challenge man' ('Ballad' 403–404).

The seed of social change that D'joan plants during her short-lived revolution is an idea of a transformed and non-alienated relationship between humans and other life on the planet (or, in this future, planets). D'joan's message is about resisting a relationship with all other life that sees value only in the accumulation of capital:

> I bring you life-with. It's more than love. Love's a hard, sad, dirty word, a cold word, an old word. It says too much and it promises too little. I bring you something much bigger than love. If you're alive, you're alive. If you're alive-with, then you know the other life is there too – both of you, any of you, all of you. Don't do anything, Don't grab, don't clench, don't possess. Just be. That's the weapon. ('Dead Lady' 256–257)

Smith's revolutionary underpeople recognise that the way to a better and non-alienated life is the acknowledgement of the other as a subject not merely an object, what Donna Haraway has called letting 'the question of how animals engage *one another's gaze responsively* tak[e] center stage' (*When Species Meet* 22). Being alive-with lets humans return to nature, not as conquerors and not merely to 'grab ... clench ... possess' but instead to 'just be' as part of a larger social collective, as part of an existence that does not put capitalist accumulation at its centre. The state of alive-with allows all species to flourish, humans and animals. This logic equally critiques what Rieder calls the 'series of acquisitions – of wisdom, wealth, and power' (36) that inform the fiction of empire. Smith's work is unlike many of the examples discussed in this chapter, which either endorse an ideology that rationalises the unequal distribution of power and resources or else merely wring their hands at the prospect that humans might someday find themselves on the marginalised side of the binary. Instead it exemplifies what Rosi Braidotti calls 'bio-centred egalitarianism', a philosophy whose core value is 'the principle of *non-profit*, which means a stand against individualism and exploitation, in favour of self-expression and communally held property rights over both biological and cultural artefacts' (110). The colonial and labour conflicts dramatised through animal others in the stories discussed in this chapter have at their root a common engine of capitalist production and its role in producing social relations which alienate us from animals because they have the status of commodities. Smith's revolutionary tale proposes a link between dismantling the deleterious effects of the human–animal boundary and rejecting the social order of capitalism.

6. Existing for Their Own Reasons: Animal Aliens

Alice Walker's pronouncement that 'The animals of the world exist for their own reasons. They were not made for humans any more than black people were made for whites or women for men', is a dictum frequently repeated among animal welfare activists.[1] Most of the history of human–animal relations, however, proceeds from the opposite logic. Walker's linking of the human–animal boundary with similar historical exclusions that have presumed non-whites and women had lesser existences than full subjects – heterosexual, property-owning, white men – reminds us that just as these once-axiomatic hierarchies have been dismantled by cultural change, so too might the sense that animals exist only for human use. The twenty-first century is a particularly fruitful time in which to explore such questions. On the one hand, we are living through a current mass-extinction event[2] caused by human action, including habitat destruction, overconsumption of animals and human overpopulation; at the same time, factory farms subject more animals to worse conditions than ever before in the history of human agriculture,[3] and laboratory use of animals has gone beyond utilisation of those found in nature for human ends into the realm of modifying or manufacturing animals so that they are more useful laboratory tools.[4] On the other hand, animal welfare and environmental activisms have grown steadily since the institution of Earth Day in 1970, and pet ownership and the standard of care lavished on pets has exponentially increased.

The disparity between these two poles of our current social relations with animals hardly needs emphasis. Yet despite wide differences on the axes of comfort and affect for animals' experiences of human–animal interrelations in the twenty-first century, both treating animals as part of a human family and treating them as mere commodities might be thought of as examples of animals existing for human reasons, not their own. Even conservation efforts such as zoos or wildlife preserves often cite an educational rationale as part of their mandate, just as Kant once asserted that we should be kind to animals not for their own sake but so that human capacity for compassion is not damaged by the exercise of cruelty.[5] Current research on violence, especially domestic violence toward women and children, confirms a link between abuse of animals and a propensity to act violently toward humans;[6] at times, animal welfare legislation justifies its provisions based on such a link, further pointing to the complex nexus of animal and human concerns that shape our cultural moment. The tremendous conflicts over land use as animals are increasingly squeezed into smaller and smaller areas of the globe can at times make it appear as if human needs and animal needs are inevitably locked into a zero-sum game.

Representations of aliens in sf are one of the places where these tensions and contradictions are worked through culturally. As I suggested in my introduction, the very concept of the alien is one that expresses a human interest in – and struggle with – the reality of living with a different being. Yet as well as this broad homology between animals and aliens, some sf also specifically figures its aliens as animal-like and thus invites more direct comparison with how human society relates to its animal others. This trope of animal aliens and that of reversing the hierarchy between humans and animals (which will be discussed in the next chapter) are the most evident ways that animals enter sf. Many of the stories already discussed in this book fall under this rubric and thus it should already be apparent that animal aliens represent both humanity's desire for connection to another being and its fear that all others represent a threat to self and hence must be destroyed. With regard to animal aliens in particular, the various prejudices and preferences that have emerged from our long co-evolution with other species enter and shape the characterisation of animal aliens, a very obvious example being the prevalence of stories in which dogs figure as steadfast companions – such as Simak's 'Desertion' (1944) – as compared to the number of malevolent aliens who have cat-like characteristics – such as the antagonists of *Man-Kzin Wars* series (1966–2006), by Larry Niven and others; the Victorian preference for malleable dogs over sovereign cats shapes such choices. The complex history of human–animal relations thus informs the animal aliens who appear in sf, drawing on 'the multiplicity and variability of the repertoires of responses we build up with respect to the relevant categories (animal, human, mammal, primate, beast, brute, living being and so forth)' and the ways in which such categories challenge or reinforce 'our ideas of propriety, naturalness, fitness and justice' or those of 'absurdity, cruelty, inhumanity or injustice' (Herrnstein Smith 156).

Mack Reynolds's 'The Discord Makers' (1950) plays with such correspondences. Ross Wooley reports to his boss, Director of the Department of Security, that he has 'reasons to suspect there might be aliens in the United States': those 'from space, some other planet' (134), he clarifies, not the expected illegal immigrants. Wooley is not believed by his superiors and his evidence is scant: 'an article here, a news item there, some quotations from obscure scientists' (135). He finds an ally in professor André Dumar who has been studying what he terms 'unnatural life forms on Earth' that 'revolt other animals, including Man' (137), thus betraying their foreign nature. Dumar identifies as part of the invasion force those species commonly detested in human discourse: the spider, the snake, the rat, the cockroach. When contemplating such beings, he explains, 'there's an instinctive loathing that nine out of ten persons feel … because we know they don't *belong*' (138), that they are alien to Earth. Dumar offers a number of theories to explain how such seemingly unaccomplished beings might have developed the technology to travel to Earth from another planet, his favourite being that they are 'guinea pigs', a term whose generic equation of a certain species of rodent with the concept of expendable test subject speaks volumes about a certain way of conceiving interspecies relations. Thus, the animal beings in the story remain conceived of as animals, now 'inferior life forms from their planet' (139), sent here by that planet's sentient beings to test the prospect of colonising Earth. Wooley next visits a 'nationally known lecturer and commentator' (139), Morton Harrison, who contends that humanity's progress is being sabotaged by alien forces that encourage us to ridicule and dismiss those whose ideas would lead to 'fighting for such things as the end of war, a better social system, for an end to intolerance and racial discrimination' (141).

Finally, Wooley finds further support for his theories with Dr Kenneth Keith, President of the Western Rocket Society, who believes the aliens have come as conquerors, poised to assert their dominance now that humans have developed 'along the lines they thought best'; these aliens have produced a territory worth conquering with a population 'you can exploit' (143). Keith's litany of things humans might fear from the aliens is similar to the way animals (and animalised humans) have been exploited by the hegemonic class, including being bred 'for soldiers to be used in their interplanetary or interstellar wars' (143) or as slaves. His theory that the aliens have already infiltrated 'positions of power in our governments, our communication centers, our education systems' (143) proves sound when Wooley makes his report to his boss who reveals himself to be an alien from Aldebaran, promptly executes Wooley and sends out teams to dispose of Dumar and Keith. Animals disappear quite quickly from this story which ultimately focuses on the conflict between humans and Aldebarans, conveniently offering an alibi for human aggression in its construction of an alien influence as that which keeps humanity focused on war and thus failing to develop a culture of social justice. Yet the presence of reviled species such as spiders and cockroaches in the theory of alien occupation is revealing nonetheless. The oppressive Aldebaran invaders demonstrate an attitude toward other beings that is comparable to the human attitude toward animals: these 'inferior life forms' were sacrificed by Aldebaran colonial efforts just as human culture has sacrificed many animal lives in its pursuit of progress, whether this be those used in laboratory experiments (including space-flight research) or the insects who challenge the colonial nations' ability to possess the land, as discussed in the previous chapter.

Although 'The Discord Makers' seems intended to villainise the Aldebarans, it also inadvertently reveals that its model for sentient species presumes an antagonistic relationship to other species. The Aldebarans, one presumes, will justify their oppression of *Homo sapiens* just as humanity has justified its oppression of animal others, and as hegemonic humans have justified oppression of those presumed less advanced. Animals remain animals in this story and those who have demonstrated their sentience are considered analogous to humans, including in unflattering ways that perhaps exceed the story's intent. Other stories, however, retain animal features in their alien others which can either force us to reconsider the ways in which we dismiss the possibility of animal sentience (if we are willing to acknowledge this sentience in the animal aliens), or reinforce a sense of antagonism between humans and the animal world by projecting this conflict on to one with animal aliens. Howard Fast's 'The Large Ant' (1960) uses the first mode effectively to unsettle human certainty and expose human prejudice. Like Reynolds's story, Fast's is concerned with interrogating what seems to be humanity's self-destructive tendency. The narrator, Morgan, speculates in the story's first pages about 'how it would end', conveying a sense of hopelessness in the recognition that 'we were what we were', that although we might solve the immediate problems of food scarcity and nuclear annihilation, 'we have never been any good at changing ourselves or the way we behave' (124). He goes on to emphasise his own typical qualities as a human being: he is not 'a bad man or a cruel man' and loves his family; he is like most men and does 'the things they would do and just as thoughtlessly' (124). This autonomic aspect of human behaviour is emphasised in the story's introduction before Morgan proceeds to tell us his tale.

The first incident is an encounter with a large ant, 'fourteen, fifteen inches long' (128), whom Morgan finds on the foot of his bed one evening. He immediately grabs his nearby golf club and strikes 'a savage and accurate blow, and kill[s] it'; he tells us, 'what I referred to before: Whatever kind of a man I am, I react as a man does. I think that any man, black, white or yellow, in China, Africa or Russia, would have done the same thing' (125). This violence makes Morgan feel nauseous, something he has not experienced since travelling to Europe 'on the tub of a Liberty Ship' (124) in 1943, suggesting that this autonomic violence response is connected to warfare. Disturbed by the experience, he takes the ant specimen to Bertram Lieberman, a curator of insects at the museum, a meeting also attended by a government agent and a US senator. They query him about his response to the ant, enquiring if it seemed 'about to attack' or made 'any sudden motion' (129) toward him. Morgan is at first confused by this line of questioning, responding, 'No. It was just there' (129). Lieberman concludes 'the answer is very simple ... You killed it because you are a human being' (129), turning to a specimen cupboard with eight similar ants, all violently killed. He informs Morgan that these are not merely a new species of ant but instead intelligent beings from elsewhere. Each ant wears an appendage that contains 'little tools or instruments or weapons' that are 'beautiful the way any object of functional purpose and loving creation is beautiful – the way the creature itself would have been beautiful, had it not been an insect and myself a man' (130). The creature's brain matter further suggests intelligence and, combined with the creature's presumed collective social organisation, is 'something beyond our wildest dreams. To us – well, what we are to an ordinary ant' (130–131).

In this moment of confrontation with the other, Morgan realises 'you can't look at anything through a screen of hatred' (130) and that he had not looked carefully at the ant in his bedroom because he allowed his automatic judgement of repugnance to dominate. The group conclude that the ant beings are superior to humans because the humans cannot understand the ant instruments they have discovered and have 'no idea of what they can or should do' (131). Morgan protests that were the creature intelligent it should have used a weapon to defend itself from his attack, but Lieberman counters that the inability to 'conceive of a mentality that does not include weapons as a prime necessity' (131) is a human limitation. The story ends with the group contemplating 'the problem of murder and what to do with it' (132) as they presume that many of these creatures have been killed by humans across the globe and thus their whole society might be on trial as a culture of inherent murderers. The story closes with Morgan trying to picture his encounter with the ant in order to determine 'whether behind that chitinous face and the two gently waving antennae there was any evidence of fear and anger' (133), recalling only 'dignity and repose' and concluding that 'like a criminal who can no longer live with himself, [he] is content to be judged' (133).

Like many contemporary stories, 'The Large Ant' is concerned with the threat of nuclear war which is the focus of the group's discussion at the end. The characterisation of the alien being as an ant ties into the ways that ants have been admired as perfectly social beings, as discussed in the last chapter, although it overlooks the degree to which ants are also martial. Like 'The Discord Makers', this story uses an animal other to foreground the problems of human aggression, a technique suggestive of a repressed connection between the qualities that produced the culture of the Cold War and other examples of human aggression, and the longer history of human aggression toward animals. The story implies that such characteristics are inevitable expressions of human nature, but they are better understood as an expression of the culturally specific construction of human subjectivity that has been critiqued throughout this book. The threat of nuclear annihilation is linked to a metaphysics of subjectivity that relies on the logic of sacrifice, as Derrida has argued. This version of the human is structured around a necessary 'outside' of those who might be put to death without ethical import. Similarly, the human as conceived of via this metaphysics is one for whom the rest of the world exists as appropriable resource. 'The Large Ant' critiques more than our treatment of ants and other creatures at whom we do not truly look: it extends its critique to the very logic of human subjectivity as produced by the human–animal boundary.

Examples of animal aliens in sf are not necessarily critical of such metaphysics, however. Just as representations of colonial others in H. Rider Haggard's work and similar stories work to buttress an exploitative ideology, examples of animal aliens in sf can similarly be used to reinforce the human–animal boundary. Such work uses animals for our own rather than their own reasons, often creating animal aliens without paying attention to the specific attributes of the animal itself. Larry Niven and Jerry Pournelle's *Footfall* (1985) is an obvious example of such fiction and it is particularly instructive that the work of writers who pride themselves on being hard sf writers – that is, writers who understand science and extrapolate from it rationally – would create animal aliens without conducting sufficient research into the nature of the animal. *Footfall*, a tale of alien invasion and heroic human resistance against the odds, takes great care to explain its physics, but does not give comparable notice to ethology, thereby revealing its priority is not animal being nor human–animal relations, but rather what Tom Godwin has called 'The Cold Equations' of the universe. Like Godwin's story,[7] Niven and Pournelle's novel tries to excise contingent human social arrangements from its scope and focus instead on more manageable engineering problems. The novel is about an alien species called the fithp, who resemble small elephants but have branching trunks thus giving them the digits presumed necessary for tool development. They come to Earth intending to conquer it.[8] The aliens are a herd species and at times their characterisation factors in the difference such an origin would create: for example, individual fithp go mad or 'rogue' if separated from their fellows and can easily switch allegiance to be adopted into a new herd; and the fithp have difficulty understanding the human sensibility which requires that culpability be limited to the individual, and thus tend to attribute the actions of any human to the group to which he or she belongs.

This is not a novel about the development of mutual understanding and learning to truly see the alien, however. Rather than use these differences to decentre anthropocentrism, Niven and Pournelle instead emphasise the monstrous nature of the fithp and contrast this to the values of courage and perseverance displayed by the human protagonists.[9] The fithp herd mentality includes an understanding of warfare in which fighting ends when one side surrenders to the other: to them, surrender is permanent and includes the entire herd. The herd that surrenders becomes absorbed into the victorious one, as slaves in the first generation but later as adopted members in the second, until there is finally no difference between those originally part of the herd and those who joined after a battle. Even once these rules have been explained to the humans, they refuse to respect this cultural difference: they regard the slaughter of an entire village based on the rebellion of a single individual within it as a war crime; they pride themselves on fooling the fithp by performing surrender without intending it to be permanent; and they deliberately misuse a fithp symbol that is meant to mark humanitarian aid facilities to hide a secret weapons project (a nuclear-bomb-powered spacecraft) that they eventually use to defeat the fithp. None of these actions is presented as duplicitous or culturally chauvinistic. The heroes of the novel are those military personnel who recognise immediately that any encounter with an alien species is going to be a violent one from which only one species might emerge victorious. From the moment the alien ship is spotted, those who counsel a peaceful approach and a desire for communication with these others are ridiculed as naïve at best, treasonous as worst. Human aggression is always heroic and justified, including the continued attack on the mothership after the fithp have told humans their weapon cannot destroy this ship: it can only 'harm us, kill females and children' (565). Nothing less than unconditional surrender of the alien other is sufficient for the heroes.

A significant role is given to a number of characters who become the President's 'threat team' – those advisors who presume the aliens to be hostile and brainstorm the specifics of this possible threat and how to respond to it – which is made up of sf writers, including transparent avatars of the authors themselves, Nat Reynolds (Niven) and Wade Curtis (Pournelle), and a deified leader Robert Anson (Heinlein). The one female member of this team, Sherry Atkinson,[10] is the only one who advocates negotiation with the aliens and she is always proved wrong by events.

The plot is a predictable Cold War thriller. The Americans consistently outpace the Soviets, and even the fithp think of the Earth in terms of Cold War politics, with the US and the USSR as the only political entities of relevance (although some of the action is set in Africa, where the fithp occupation is resisted by plucky, independent Afrikaners, and the Indian subcontinent is sunk when the fithp drop a meteorite on Earth, the 'footfall' of the title). The centrality of the sf writer characters to the novel's action is more than mere self-aggrandisement: it points to potential pitfalls in literary representation as a way to think about alien being, including that of animals. The sf writers are chosen as the most helpful advisors to the President based on the logic of wondering 'who else knows about aliens?' (108). And indeed in this world they prove to be helpful advisors, anticipating the very weapons the fithp use and coming up with effective ideas for defence against them.[11] An admiral, who eventually stages a *coup d'état* to prevent the less bellicose President from accepting a negotiated surrender instead of pressing on for complete victory, says that the sf writers are 'the only experts we have' (173).

Whatever this plot might say about Reagan-era politics – and it does say a considerable amount – what is pertinent in this context is the truncation of the imagination as regards other beings that is evident in Niven and Pournelle's characterisation of the fithp. The gestures toward thinking through the differences involved in herd species as compared to species, like primates, who form competitive social groups, are abandoned as soon as it is convenient for the thriller plot, and the insistence upon making the sf writers correct in all matters means that the fithp can only ever be conceived of through the values of human culture. When scenes are narrated from the fithp point of view they refer to the humans as 'prey', ignoring the fact that elephant-like herd animals would not be hunters, as well as contradicting their previous characterisation as a society that incorporates its defeated antagonists into its own herd. Like the aliens in 'The Discord Makers', Niven and Pournelle's fithp reveal most about human culture; like the image of the animal throughout human history, the elephant-like fithp are used as a screen onto which to project undesirable aspects of human behaviour. The human–animal boundary is further reinforced in the suggestions that the fithp's technology is not of their own making but instead is scavenged from a 'predecessor' culture whose visual appearance is a closely guarded secret (the implication is they were humanoid), and that hands and fingers are more effective technology-wielding digits than bifurcated trunks can ever be. This definition of the human via technology and the distanced relationship to the rest of the world it implies (Heidegger's notion of 'having' the world) is characterised by Derrida as part of 'a war against the animal' which is made literal in

Footfall. This violence toward animals is linked by Derrida to the culture of scientific rationalism so celebrated in this novel's story of human victory via militarised nuclear technology:

> that war is not just one means of applying technoscience to the animal in the absence of another possible or foreseeable means; no, that violence or war has until now been constitutive of the project or the very possibility of technoscientific knowledge within the process of humanization or of the appropriation of man by man, including its most highly developed ethical or religious forms. (*The Animal* 101)

It is unsurprising, then, that *Footfall* is much more interested in explicating its invented weapons than it is in understanding the alterity of fithp – or elephant – being.

Nonetheless, *Footfall* does have provocative connections to the material history of human and elephant cultural exchanges, although these insights emerge by way of the parallels between the novel's lack of interest in animal being and a similar lack of interest that has characterised much of this history. Most significantly, there is a terrestrial 'war' with animals over land, although this 'war' is initiated by human encroachment on elephant territory rather than vice versa (Wylie 180– 181). Under unstressed conditions, elephant social life is organised around matriarchal family units and has distinct but overlapping home ranges that associate into larger kinship groups without territorial aggression (Mitman 185). Yet as human occupation of elephant habitat or transformation of this land for human agricultural ends increases, elephants have been stressed for space which has resulted in the fragmentation of their social structure. Most remaining elephants are confined to wildlife preserves whose range is significantly less than the territory covered by free-ranging elephant groups of comparable size, which results in erosion of vegetation as the elephants require more food than grows within the area to which they are confined. Efforts to cull elephant populations have led to 'a marked increase in the frequency and savagery of elephant attacks against humans and other animals, and [ethologists] have concluded that decades of hunting, poaching, culling and habitat loss have resulted in a widespread trauma at both the individual and the collective levels' (Wylie 163). Thus, elephants have become more violent as a result of violent conflict with humans, producing a species somewhat closer to how Niven and Pournelle imagine the fithp. In a revealing moment near the novel's end, as he is contemplating whether the fithp will honour the new concept of negotiated rather than complete surrender, one of the human heroes ponders, '*we taught them conditional surrender. Have we also taught them to break their parole?*' (568). This moment of doubt is brief and is overwhelmed by a conclusion that otherwise revels in the triumph of human military might, but, nonetheless, this glimpse of some of the problematic aspects of human subjectivity are apparent, despite the novel's self-congratulatory tone.

Although *Footfall* might thus have little to offer in terms of greater understanding of animal being, it nonetheless provides significant insight into one of the ways animals have figured in the Western cultural imagination. This narration of anxieties and preconceptions can reveal as much about the human–animal boundary as can more conscious efforts to dismantle it. As the stories I discussed at the beginning of the chapter suggested, attempts to challenge or dismantle the human–animal boundary are often linked to an anxiety about the nature of the human subject which, as Derrida notes, simultaneously requires 'the denial of all rights to the animal, or render[s] radically *problematic* any declaration of animal rights' (88). Anne McCaffrey's *Decision at Doona* (1969) more explicitly engages with the idea of a specifically animal alien, balancing a concern with attempting to capture the alterity of non-human being with an interest in querying what makes the human subject function. The premise for *Decision at Doona* is the encounter between human colonists and cat-like Hrruban ones on the planet Doona, or Rrala as it is known in the Hrruban language. As chapters told from the point of view of each species reveal, both are surprised to find the other on what they thought was a planet without sentient species, and both are deeply invested in their own colony continuing. The Hrruban society is facing a crisis of ennui, its 'search for freedom from want and to remedy the inequalities of opportunity by the suppression of physical competition' having produced a culture without 'initiative, ambition and vitality' (3); the humans seek escape from an overcrowded planet in which it is the trip of a lifetime to be able to visit one of the Square Mile parks, longing for a society in which they can 'be free to run and yell and stride and – *feel*!' (12).

When the humans make first contact with the Hrruban they presume them to be an inferior species at a medieval level of technological development based on the lifestyle adopted by the Hrruban colonists. The Hrrubans' presence means the human colony will have to leave the planet based on their own ethical principle of Non-Cohabitation, an edict reached after a disastrous mass suicide of the Siwannese, an intelligent species who killed themselves in response to some action by a human colony that shared a planet with them. The humans do not know what provoked the Siwannese tragedy and the Principle of Non-Cohabitation embodies the extremity of their response: they cannot imagine harmony and cohabitation and so choose separation and isolation. The action of the novel takes place between the moment of initial contact when the human colonists conclude that they must leave the planet and the signing of a treaty, the decision at Doona, when Terran authorities are able to reach Doona and determine the colony's future. During the interim, the human colonists struggle with their intense desire to remain on the planet, trying to reconcile their own lust for open spaces with the appeal of their growing friendship with the Hrruban, and finally with their knowledge of humanity's troubled history of genocide which they explicitly note was a major consequence of the colonisation of Earth itself.

They resist the temptation of this 'easy solution' to the 'problems in dealing with minority groups' (38), and as the novel progresses they begin to understand their own society as a compromise that is, in some ways, not all that different. The severity of the Principle of Non-Cohabitation, one character theorises, is a consequence of Earth's own immediate history just before the Siwannese tragedy. Humanity passed through a period of the Amalgamation of 2010, described as 'bloodier than any previous pogrom', which produced a homogenised human species, leaving only 'ethnic surnames' (73) to signal a previously diverse population. Both Amalgamation as a way to deal with intraspecies difference, and the Principle of Non-Cohabitation as one to deal with interspecies difference, avoid rather than resolve the difficulty of how to live with another in mutual respect, sidestepping the complexity of the issue either by reducing the other to a mirror of oneself or else refusing the struggle altogether. The human characters on Doona recognise refusal as an inadequate response to the challenge of meeting another sentient species, particularly one that is considered an equal, which strikes at the heart of the dynamic the novel explores. Both the Hrruban (who have matter-transporting technology and a highly advanced level of technology on their home world) and the humans presume they are meeting an inferior species when they first encounter one another. This perception of their own superiority allows each to relax their guard and offer co-operative friendship, instead of allowing a paranoid insecurity to drive the interactions. The Hrruban and humans do prove to have much in common, not all of it flattering: both have allowed technological society to destroy all other species on their home planets, both have histories of aggressive conflict and both need the colony as a catalyst to revitalise a moribund culture. At the same time, however, both are also sincerely committed to new forms of sociality and thus to the shared colony on Doona, the experiment that is embarked upon in the novel's concluding chapter.

The connection between anxiety about relations with an alien species and the history of the Amalgamation – as well as other incidents in colonial history which are alluded to in the novel – reveals that *Decision at Doona* is concerned with a similar litany of human atrocities as that which concerns

Fast in 'The Large Ant'. Yet at the same time, McCaffrey is able to retain a dual focus on the Hrruban as both aliens who stand in for racialised others and beings linked to the cats they resemble, and hence to animals in general. Recall Adorno's argument that 'the possibility of pogroms is decided in the moment when the gaze of a fatally-wounded animal falls on a human being' who then defiantly repels this gaze with the mantra 'after all, it's only an animal' (105). The human–animal boundary functions as an alibi for the destruction of another who stands in the way of the gratification of one's own desires, a logic that is pertinent when applied to other species – emphasising the *only* in 'it's only an animal' – as well as to animalised humans. The history of human violence towards animals as well as colonised others is suggested by the importance of the animal species that form part of the terran colonial presence on Doona, species that are extinct on Earth and survive only through genetic recreation for such colonising efforts. During a discussion about the importance of not repeating a brutal colonial history, one character argues that the impetus for the Non-Cohabitation principle was 'the feeling that the greedy acquisition of more planets on which to spread the products of our then uncontrolled breeding was not the real answer to our problem. It was the knowledge that we have no right to take away from another species their own peculiar road toward self-fulfillment' (75). Although in the examples that follow this character implies that he is using 'species' in the way 'race' is used to differentiate *Homo sapiens* into distinct ethnic groups, at the same time the word and other aspects of the novel open it up to interpretation its more precise meaning as well. Humans are in conflict with other species for the world's resources, and our greed and overpopulation, among other factors, have stolen from such species a chance to develop unstunted by these contingencies.

Significant emphasis is put upon learning the Hrruban language and social customs, refusing an anthropocentrism that normalises human customs. The close friendship between a young Hrruban, Hrriss, and a terran, Todd, emphasises that despite cultural differences mutual ways of being in the world collectively can be achieved. Anthropocentrism is further disrupted by the section narrated from the Hrruban point of view which demonstrates that some of their senior officials see the humans as primitive, 'bareskinned beasts' (55) and a threat to the 'people' on the colony. The connection to cats in the Hrrubans' characterisation is pertinent given Western associations of cats with independence, egoism and the uncanny, associations which have often resulted in abusive treatment of cats. Cats are ideal models for aliens in a novel that wishes to disrupt hegemonic notions of human subjectivity and ethics, however, as they refuse 'to be absorbed into our worldview' (Fudge *Pets* 80). Like the best alien beings, cats have their own perspective on the world and continually remind us that they do not necessarily share our priorities. The novel's core value is the emphasis it places on '*listen*[ing] very hard' (245) to the other, an effort at imaginative connection which it suggests can overcome differences of culture and open a space for mutual respect and understanding,[12] for a new culture to emerge that is neither Hrruban nor human but something other entirely, something new which – like the molecular identities celebrated by Deleuze and Guattari – brings with it the possibility that the world might be otherwise. Derrida, too, suggests that he dreams of hearing what he calls a 'key' or 'tonality', a new note that will 'change the whole stave' (*The Animal* 63) of human subjectivity as it has been construed through the human–animal boundary, as well as modify the material relations among humans and other species:

> I was dreaming of inventing an unheard-of grammar and music in order to create a scene that was neither human, nor divine, nor animal, with a view to denouncing all discourses on the so-called animal, all the anthropo-theomorphic or anthropo-theocentric logics and axiomatics, philosophy, religions, politics, law, ethics, with a view to recognising in them animal strategies, precisely, in the human sense of the term, stratagems, ruses, and war machines, defensive or offensive manoeuvres, search operations, predatory, seductive, indeed exterminatory operations as part of a pitiless struggle between what are presumed to be species. (*The Animal* 64)

Despite its greater promise for rethinking ideological axioms, in many ways *Decision at Doona* is as naïve a work as *Footfall*, shifted only in ideological spectrum. Although the choice of cats as the models for the aliens is not without significance, at the same time little attention is given to the specificity of cat social organisation in the depiction of the Hrrubans. For example, they negotiate the world primarily through language and sight, as do the humans, rather than relying on embodied communication and tactile senses for some navigation, as do cat species; and differences in behaviour, such as nocturnal activity and diet, which one might expect in a species evolved from cats instead of primates, are not addressed. The narrative relies heavily on the charm of a precocious child for engendering affective ties between the two species, and its conclusion – which relies on this child's ability to master the Hrruban's formal dialect and associated diplomatic protocol in order to impress a civilian Hrruban audience and convince them of the worthiness of contact with humans – is as improbable as the heroics of sf writers in Niven and Pournelle's novel. Whereas Niven and Pournelle imagine utter and irreconcilable differences between species and thus total war, McCaffrey suggests an instinctual

harmony which implies – despite the many ground rules set out for the
new co-species Rrulan colony at the end – an ease of cohabitation and
mutual understanding. In contrast, Karen Traviss's *Wess'har War* series
(2004–2008) directly confronts the difficulties, contradictions and non-
innocence (to borrow a term from Donna Haraway) that are the material
context of the social relations we have with non-human species.

Consisting of six books – *City of Pearl* (2004), *Crossing the Line* (2004), *The
World Before* (2005), *Matriarch* (2006), *Ally* (2007) and *Judge* (2008) – the
series tells the story of Shan Frankland, an Environmental Hazard officer
sent to the planet Bezer'ej to recover a lost human colony that contains
the most complete genetic bank of Earth species. This resource is valuable
both because many of the species it preserves are now extinct and also
because the seed crops it encodes are ones whose genetics have not been
patented by agribusiness, and thus it represents *'the first time in over a century
that any man or woman can grow what they please without license or restriction'*
(*City* 256). Used to sorting out – her term – environmental exploitation on
Earth, Shan finds herself in the midst of a complicated nexus of environmental and moral conflicts. The human colony is tolerated but isolated,
watched over by an immortal warrior, Aras, a wess'har. He guards the
planet against possible repeat incursions from the nearby imperialist isenj,
who had once colonised the planet and nearly destroyed its local ecology
with pollution. The natives of the planet, bezeri, are sentient, aquatic
beings without space-faring capacity who are under wess'har protection.
Shan finds in the wess'har – and eventually in their parent species, the
eqbas – an uncompromising commitment to ecological justice. All species
are considered people, without hierarchy. The human–animal distinction
does not exist, and their intense devotion to the sanctity of all life and the
principle of ecological balance is matched only by their swift and lethal
action against any who violate these principles. The local word for humans
is *gethes*, carrion eaters.

More than any other text discussed in this chapter, Traviss's presents
the animal aliens as fully sentient beings whose cultures and lives are
taken as seriously within the text as are those of human characters. In
addition, the focus on environmentalism and a radical perspective that
might be aligned with that of deep ecology result in a novel that is equally
concerned with the relationships between human and other beings as it is
with the nature of the human. From this point of view, the novel might
be considered a work of ecopoetics as much as one of genre sf: both are
modes of worldbuilding that acknowledge a non-human perspective. Dana
Phillips has argued that ecocriticism aims to do more than merely interpret
works of literature from an ecological perspective, but further it 'represents
an attempt to improve behaviours and change minds well beyond the walls

of the academy' (37). He feels this is a goal in which it has largely failed because of its focus on 'the ever-receding and now-mythical past more than the real but troubled present, to say nothing of the possibly very grim future' (50). Traviss gives us a vivid picture of such a future, but at the same time she presents strategies – albeit at times harsh ones – that help us imagine how this world might be otherwise. The *Wess'har War* series is thus attuned to the utopian aims of ecocriticism because the characterisation of its alien animals gives us reason to embrace community with other species. Traviss's aliens exist for their own reasons, although they too must struggle with many of the same social difficulties as plague human culture.

Recall Derrida's arguments that the human–animal boundary founds metaphysics; that thinking about the animal is 'what philosophy has, essentially, had to deprive itself of' (*The Animal* 7); and that all discourse about animals might be categorised into texts signed by those who have 'no doubt seen, observed, analyzed, reflected on the animal, but who have never been *seen seen* by the animal' (13) versus those poets and prophets 'who admit to taking upon themselves the address that an animal addresses to them' (14). His concern, similar to Phillips' goals for ecocriticism, is how to bring these two sensibilities together so that what is thought and expressed by the poets and prophets can have some bearing on 'theoretical, philosophical, or juridical man' (14). The *Wess'har War* series seems to exemplify Acampora's contention, discussed in Chapter 3, that 'by continually immersing ourselves in concrete observation and then connecting our observations to vivid inner images, we enter into a conversation with the animal' (*Corporal Compassion* 36). Such conversation can form the ground for a changed social relation with them, as Traviss's work displays. The final volume includes the observation:

> Humans responded to inspiration rather than logic. And inspiration was talking to mesmerized kids about macaws that could speak an alien language, or getting humans to see that their species couldn't possibly be more special and deserving than an insect-sized bird that vanished in a blur of emerald light. Yes, humans' imagination could be captured. (277)

The series relentlessly refuses to let humans put their own lives ahead of those of other creatures, a concept that is most viscerally portrayed when Shan allows the Aras to execute one of her crew members because this scientist had dissected one of the berezi she found on the beach. Many of the human crew are outraged by this violation of the human–animal boundary and its distinction between those who can be murdered and those who can merely be killed, seeing the berezi's resemblance to jellyfish as sufficient reason to exculpate the scientist. Shan forcefully explains,

Let's rethink our attitude to species, shall we? This isn't roadkill. It's a child. Do you know what this is in human terms? You come across the scene of an accident. There's dead baby. So you pick up the body and take it away because you're *curious*. You don't report it, you don't try to contact the parents, you just take it, and slice it up for a few tests. Do you understand? (*City* 207)

This incident, in the series' first novel, is not understood by most of the human characters and perhaps not by many of its readers either. By the final book, the surviving characters have learned to embrace another way of understanding human subjectivity and interspecies relations. But those still on Earth, and perhaps many readers, still struggle to give up the comfort of human exceptionalism.

As Derrida insists, inspiring humans to think (and, as Traviss suggests, feel) differently about the human–animal boundary so that we no longer believe our species is 'more special and deserving' than others does not necessarily imply erasing all difference. Instead we must struggle to think through the 'multiple and heterogeneous border', recognising that this border 'has a history' (*The Animal* 31). Such a task is

a matter, on the contrary, of taking that difference into account within the whole differentiated field of experience and of a world of life forms, and of doing that without reducing this differentiated and multiple difference, in a conversely massive and homogenizing manner, to one between the human subject, on the one hand, and the nonsubject that is the animal in general, on the other, where the latter comes to be, in another sense, the nonsubject that is subjected to the human subject. (*The Animal* 126)

Crucial to this new logic is taking difference into account without inevitably creating a relation of subjugation as a consequence; this logic would 'complicate the simple distinction between *responsibility* and *reaction*, and all that follows from it' and hence would enable 'another thinking of life, of the living, within another relation of the living … to their own autokinesis and reactional automaticity, to death, to technics' (Derrida *The Animal* 126). As I have outlined earlier,[13] the distinction between reaction and response is related to a history of denying animals the capacity for communication and hence the faculty of consciousness. The changed relationship to technics that Derrida argues will be a consequence of this new logic of human–animal difference undermines the construction of the *Dasein* through a specific relationship to the world that is a 'having' of the world as discussed earlier.[14] Derrida's project of complicating the simple distinction between responsibility (which puts one in the realm of intersubjectivity, ethics and justice) and reaction (which is instinctual hence does not imply culpability) is premised on the understanding that without response, no change is possible as reaction can only reproduce the social formation as currently configured.

Working through the difficulties of this new logic and the material complications of the new world that emerges from this new grammar of social relations is part of the intellectual project of Traviss's series which continually both challenges and validates the wess'har axiom that all life must be regarded as absolutely equal. Through the human characters – and presumably the readers' – discomfort with this position, at times, the series shows the rifts in the easy conflation of multiplicity with homogeneity. Yet at the same time, the series insists the singular human–animal boundary is equally problematic. Some aspects of the series are suggestive of the logic of deep ecology, which positions humans as just one species among many and privileges the survival of the ecosystem over that of any particular species or any individual within any species.[15] Deep ecology shares with biopolitics a focus on the management of populations rather than individuals, accepting that certain deaths might be required for the better overall functioning of the entire ecosystem, just as neo-liberalist biopolitics works, as Foucault suggests, on a logic of 'power over "the" population as such, over men insofar as they are living beings … [which] consists in making live and letting die' (*Society* 247) – although in Foucault's analysis this sacrifice is for the greater sake over the functioning of the economy rather than that of the ecosystem. And like biopolitics, deep ecology, too, has its liberal underpinnings in its failure to question the structures of possessive individualism. Instead, it extends those structures to other species, expanding the range of individual self-interests that shape the social collective.[16]

The *Wess'har War* series stresses the need for multiple and heterogeneous structures of moral thought over easy axioms and singular categories in a number of ways. In the first three books, the bezeri are presented solely as victims: first of the isenj colonisation and its consequent pollution of their environment; and second of a neutron bomb set off by humans who are trying to destroy a parasite, c'naatat, and who inadvertently pollute the bezeri's environment once again. In the latter half of the series, however, two of the humans are transformed with c'naatat to live among the bezeri and they discover that in the species' distant past they hunted to extinction another sentient species, the birzula, who encroached upon – so their history says – bezeri hunting grounds. What is particularly damning is that the bezeri insist that they feel no remorse for this action; that it was justified by the birzula's inferiority. Following this, one of the human characters loses all sympathy for the bezeri and begins to refer to them as Nazis, while another argues 'we Cro-Magnons don't usually have a public guiltfest about the Neanderthals, either' (*Matriarch* 36). Yet when the bezeri are given a chance to move into a new habitat, they immediately begin hunting its dominant predator to extinction, perhaps implying that they are irredeemable.

Frequently the novel raises the question of humanity's toxic relationship to other life on our planet, often suggesting by direct comparison that we are no better than the species we see condemned by the wess'har rigid moral code. The overcrowded isenj planet, for example, is restored to balance through the military intervention of the eqbas who take drastic measures to reduce the isenj population in preparation to restore other species – all of whom have been made extinct by isenj overcrowding. The eqbas release a bioweapon which is tailored to genetic markers of the nations not co-operating with their environmental programme, killing upwards of 90% of the population in a plague of ebola-like symptoms. The suffering of individuals is horrible, but the planet as a whole is restored by this intervention. Given the specificity of the bioweapon, Shan notes that it is ethnic cleansing, but also that 'wess'har didn't care. Numbers were what mattered: they just reduced the number of isenj to the level that the global ecology could support. How and who didn't matter, no more than humans discriminated when they culled numerous animal populations' (*Judge* 115). Is this simply unsentimental, necessary ecological justice? Or should distinctions of ethnicity and location matter in the culling of isenj populations – or human ones and even animal ones? Thinking through such questions implies that perhaps they should matter in our 'management' of animal populations, among whom we typically do not make distinctions between species not to mention within species. In the context of our current global struggle for diminishing resources in a world perched at the edge of ecological collapse, struggling with climate change and avoiding the necessary changes that are required to Western consumption patterns in order to mitigate some of the worst effects of these problems, such questions are urgent.

Cooper argues that the Freudian concept of psychotic delirium, 'concerned with the breakdown and recreation of whole worlds' (20), is a more pertinent metaphor for the psychopathology of our present age than the dominant paradigm of neurotic fantasy. She uses this paradigm as 'a way of understanding the biotechnological project of reinventing life beyond the limit' (12), that is, the technological intervention into life itself that tries to remake life's productivity along the lines of capitalist modes of production, maximising the extraction of surplus value. But as Deleuze and Guattari have taught us, the energy of transformation and becoming opens up possibilities as well, and Cooper's metaphor might equally be taken to describe a psychotic break with reality as it is given, a reality that produces subjectivity through subjugation, using the image of animal aliens to create a whole world beyond the human–animal boundary. Such a world will not necessarily be a paradise of mutual, Eden-like harmony; instead, if we want to take seriously the prospect of a new logic of life and justice, we must think through its concrete specificity. Traviss presents us with a materialisation of what a world recreated on the principle of deep ecology might look like. Ethical choices made within the novel regarding the alien worlds continually invite comparison with Earth. Shan is willing to accept the violent purging of those who threaten the ecological order on isenj, but she initially feels reservations when the same logic is applied to Earth. She eventually decides 'Humans would have to live with the consequences of exploitation. It was simple. It was what she had always believed deep down' (*World* 318), but she – and the narrative – must leave Earth during the critical period of intervention as she is not able to bear witness to what she has concluded must be.

When the eqbas arrive on Earth, they determine 'the global population needs to be reduced to approximately one billion or fewer, zero growth to prevent further premature extinctions of other species, and to free up resources to reintroduce species whose habitats have been destroyed by human activity' (*Judge* 156–157); '*So, five or six billion had to go*', reflects the stunned but nonetheless accepting Australian Prime Minister,[17] a character who ends the series recognising that history will have to judge 'if I'm the saviour of the planet for letting the eqbas help us out with our environmental problems, or the worst monster in history for not fighting them while billions of humans died' (*Judge* 389–390). This is indeed a grim future, one that specifically refuses the escapism of typical sf scenarios of alien salvation. Although moral ambiguity and ethical heterogeneity remain watchwords in the series, the focus throughout is nonetheless also firmly on deflating human exceptionalism. Aras, the guardian of Bezer'ej and later Shan's partner, at one point erupts that what he most hates about humans is

> Your unshakable belief that you're *special*, that somehow all the callousness and careless violence that your kind hand out to each other and to other beings can be forgiven because you have this … this great human *spirit*. I have viewed your dramas and your literature, you see. I have lost count of the times that I have seen the humans spared by the aliens because, despite humanity's flaws, the alien admires their plucky *spirit* and ability to strive. Well, I *am* that alien, and I *don't* admire your spirit, and your capacity to strive is no more than greed. (*Crossing* 211, ellipses in original)

The parasite c'naatat is the device in the series that most effectively opens up the question of identity and kinship and which best represents its challenge to the human–animal boundary and the metaphysics of subjectivity which rest upon this boundary. The parasite is an organism that conveys immortality to its host, enabling one to heal from any wound, and transforming the body in various ways to adapt to new environments. It also retains and passes on the genetic traits of any host through which it has passed, and further conveys particularly vivid memories from one host to another, allowing it to be the basis for sharing both embodiment and experience. When a solider, Ade Bennett, is infected he finds his entire identity thrown into question and asks 'who am I?'; the response is 'Mostly human ... But a little isenj, a little bezeri, a little wess'har. A little of whatever host that c'naatat passed through' (World 1). This genetic conflation of distinct species categories, combined with the changed embodiment produced by the parasite, enables it to function as an apt metaphor for challenges to the human–animal boundary and the possibility for kinship that this boundary denies. A number of philosophers, including Derrida, posit the idea of a shared vulnerability as the basis for rethinking our relation to animals, a way of recognising that they can – do – make a moral call upon us to recognise them as fellow beings even if not beings identical to ourselves. This shared vulnerability – recognition of similar, mortal embodiment – becomes the basis for a new conception of subjectivity and a concomitant new human/non-human sociality.

Acampora's concept of symphysis is an example of this ethos. Arguing against the concept of human as *cogito* – separated from the world and needing to find some way to connect to it – he suggests instead that 'where we begin ... is always already caught up in the experience of being a live body thoroughly involved in a plethora of ecological and social interrelationships with other living bodies and people' (*Corporal Compassion* 5). By sharing physical embodiment with some of the alien, animal-like species via c'naatat, the human characters in the novels come to an understanding of personhood that exceeds their preconceived prejudices. As one of the infected works with the bezeri, for example, he 'thought of terrestrial octopuses opening jars and solving puzzles, and his solid view of the universe began to tilt and tear like a quake zone. He wondered if Earth's Squid had histories, and if he had simply never seen the obvious' (*Matriarch* 101). Some, like Shan, were predisposed to such an insight, suggesting that although c'naatat becomes a device through which this recognition is easier, the 'truth' of symphysis is beyond the genetic merging the parasite enables. For example, Shan is haunted by the image of a gorilla whom she encountered in a research lab while working on Earth; Shan did not know signing at the time, but now does and realises that the gorilla had been signalling to her, *'Please help me. Please help me. Please ...'* (*City* 9, ellipses in original). Based on this experience, she argues, 'every time I look at something that isn't human, I have to ask myself who's behind the eyes, not what' (*City* 237). Similarly, another character not infected with c'naatat comes to think of non-humans differently through his friendship with an ussissi, a species described as something like a meerkat: 'Eddie decided he would see animals differently in future, if he ever got home. Maybe weasels had something to tell him' (255).

Derrida argues that in the past 200 years, humans 'have been involved in an unprecedented transformation' (*The Animal* 24) which concerns 'an alteration that is at the same time more serious and less recognizable than a historical turning point in the relation to the animal, in the being-with shared by the human and by what the human calls the animal' (24), a transformation that is in part informed by 'the *unprecedented* proportions of this subjection of the animal' (25). Derrida characterises the present as 'a war … being waged between, on the one hand, those who violate not only animal life but even and also this sentiment of compassion, and, on the other hand, those who appeal for an irrefutable testimony to this pity' (*The Animal* 28–29). This war entails a new metaphysics and a new ethics, 'rethinking the very idea of right, of the history and concept of rights, which until now, in its very constitution, has presumed the subjection, without respect, of the animal' (*The Animal* 87). Traviss's series makes this war literal in its story of the military intervention of the eqbas, first on Umeh, the isenj homeworld, and then on Earth. The eqbas strategically distinguishes between those natives who sympathise with their ecological aims – those open to compassion in Derrida's terms, to symphysis in Acampora's – and those who refuse to acknowledge the need for change and to extend their sense of moral duty to other species; they then work 'to aid those who do [co-operate]. To reduce the population in those states that obstruct the process. And to then enable the remaining population to manage and sustain the restored environment' (*Matriarch* 70). They reject humans, *gethes*, who posit another standard of moral behaviour for their own species alone and insist, 'when the task force reaches Earth, we want to talk to those with *one* standard' (*Matriarch* 157).

The wess'har series thus seems to be an attempt to 'improve behaviours' and 'change minds', Phillips's ideals for ecocriticism. The fourth book, *Matriarch*, opens with an excerpt from news correspondent Eddie's journal: 'Recycling won't save the Earth, and neither will prayer. The Eqbas are coming. It might be a few decades away, but they're still coming, and I know them. They're very hospitable, they love their kids, and they can kill millions without losing a second's sleep' (1); he continues,

> And while they're at it, they want to restore Earth to a state of environmental balance. In brief: a lot of humans are fucked. Most of us, probably. They don't see us as special, you see. That's just our

view of the universe. It's not widely shared ... It all feels so far in the
future. But I know it's not. (2)

These sentiments, Eddie's reflections on an Earth that is twenty-five years
away in transit time, might equally apply to the reader's world, faced with
many of the same ills Traviss gives her Earth: biotech corporatisation of
life, mass extinctions, environmental crisis and vast inequities among
humans as well as between humans and other species.

Traviss does not provide any resolution to the issues she raises, but
according to Derrida, 'casting doubt on responsibility ... seems to me to be
... the unrescindable essence of ethics, decisions, and responsibility. All
firm knowledge, certainty, and assurance on this subject would suffice,
precisely, to confirm the very thing one wishes to disavow, namely, the
reactionality in the response' (*The Animal* 126). The novel shies away
from the full implications of its depiction of our 'grim future', deflecting
our attention from Earth at the moment of its transformation and ending
instead with the resolution of the three-way relationship between Shan,
Ade and Aras. This conclusion may reflect a retreat back into sentimental
notions of human exceptionalism that have otherwise been avoided in
the series. This focus on characters over philosophical issues perhaps
suggests something of the limitations of 'poetry' as a more open mode for
rethinking subjectivity than is philosophy, confronting us as it does with
our own lingering investment in human exceptionalism – our wish for the
alien to save us, our desire for a happy ending.

Yet at the same time, the novel also contributes to the posthuman
project as it has been defined by Barbara Herrnstein Smith:

> As 'posthumanists', we have begun to chart the costs and limits of
> the classic effort to maintain an essential species barrier and have
> sought to diminish those costs and to press against those limits in our
> own conceptual and other practices. The *telos* – aim or endpoint – of
> these developments is conceived here, however, not as the universal
> recognition of a single, comprehensive order of Nature or Being
> but, rather, as an increasingly rich and operative appreciation of
> our irreducibly multiple and variable, complexly valenced, infinitely
> reconfigurable relations with other animals, including each other.
> (166–167)

In *How We Became Posthuman*, N. Katherine Hayles, a critic perhaps better
known to sf readers, wrote:

> If my nightmare is a culture inhabited by posthumans who regard
> their bodies as fashion accessories rather than the ground of being, my
> dream is a version of the posthuman that embraces the possibilities

of information technologies without being seduced by fantasies of unlimited power and disembodied immortality, that recognizes and celebrates finitude as a condition of human being, and that understands human life is embedded in a material world of great complexity, one on which we depend for our continued survival. (5)

The resemblance is instructive. Both Hayles and Herrnstein Smith emphasise the possibilities for a transformed and enhanced human existence through escaping the limitations of subjectivity as conceived under liberal humanism, as well as the need to engage otherwise with non-humans (animal and possibly technological) in achieving this vision. These visions of posthumanism simultaneously, however, stress the need for more than a single order of being, of nature, of the human–animal boundary – just as Derrida does. The harsh vision of ecological justice in the *Wess'har War* series suggests that this deep-ecology-like perspective that refuses to recognise and work through difference is unlikely to lead to a better future, but instead will reproduce something as grim as the one the singular human–animal boundary has produced.

Just as robots, androids and cyborgs have been significant sf figures for working through Hayles's model of the posthuman, animal aliens are productive sites for thinking about Herrnstein Smith's. It is significant, though, that most of the texts discussed in this chapter imagine some future of war or conflict with alien animals, even if some resolve this into a co-operative relationship or others use the conflict as a point of critique of humanity's xenophobia. Among other things dramatised by sf animal aliens are the difficulties we face in working through 'our irreducibly multiple and variable, complexly valenced, infinitely reconfigurable relations with other animals'. Yet at the same time, the prevalence of these figures speaks to our continuing desire to find some way to connect with other life.

7. A Rope over an Abyss:
Humans as Animals

In *Thus Spoke Zarathustra*, Nietzsche defines humanity as 'a rope fastened between animal and overman – a rope over an abyss' (7). Although this abyss might seem to suggest the impossible gulf between human and animal being, another way of thinking about it is that it represents the risk we face if we try to cut ourselves off from animal being, to sever this necessary tie to our animal nature. As Ralph Acampora stresses, this 'rope is never cut by Nietzsche – rather, the braiding of its strands is only tightened and celebrated' ('Nietzsche' 6); Nietzsche sees the embrace of our animal being as potentially redemptive, the overman having the 'the courage and control to instinctually and artistically reappropriate – redeem and transvalue – ancestral animality from the prehistoric wild' (Acampora 'Nietzsche' 2). In the previous chapter, I looked at sf which explored the human–animal relations that emerge in sf that creates alien beings modelled on animals. In this chapter, my focus turns to sf which reverses this relationship, positing alien beings who perceive humans as animals rather than recognising in us fellow sentient beings. Like the texts discussed in the previous chapter, such works at times reinforce the human–animal boundary and at other times deflate its presumption of human superiority. The latter variety of texts are aligned with Nietzsche's own claim in *The Anti-Christ(ian)* that 'we oppose [that which suggests that] … man had been the great hidden purpose of the evolution of the animals. Man is by no means the crown of every creation: every living being stands beside him on the same stage of perfection' (580). Some of the reversal stories in this chapter celebrate precisely this insight.

These stories highlight the cultural specificity of human social arrangements – a common use of alien figures – and, more specifically, highlight the difficulty of judging sentience in another being whose perceptual world and cultural norms are different from one's own. Rieder highlights the way such stories are used to comment on colonial encounters in texts such as Stapledon's *Last and First Men* (1930), which he describes as 'an exercise in misrecognition based on … anatomical and cultural assumptions' (90): the aliens, intelligent micro-organisms, conclude that humankind are not intelligent beings because they die when pulled apart and do not respond to sunlight in the manner of the aliens. Placed within a context in which alien misrecognition of human sentience is directly connected to social arrangements in which the humans are treated as humans treat animals, such moments of reversal can prompt a reconsideration of our own assessment of other species. When J.M. Coetzee's Elizabeth Costello gives her lectures on animal welfare, she is challenged by her philosopher daughter-in-law who insists on the evident superiority of humankind. Costello is bothered by what she considers the arbitrary rules of the human–animal boundary, explaining that 'what I mind is what tends to come next. They have no consciousness *therefore*' (Coetzee 90). This 'therefore' justifies any use of the other, even killing it, for our ends. Her daughter-in-law insists it is not arbitrary, that

> human beings invent mathematics, they build telescopes, they do calculations, they construct machines, they press a button, and, bang, *Sojourner* lands on Mars, exactly as predicted. That is why rationality is not just, as your mother claims, a game. Reason provides us with real knowledge of the real world. It has been tested, and it works. (92)

John, Costello's son, concurs that 'it works' but goes on to ask, 'still, isn't there a position outside from which our doing our thinking and then sending out a Mars probe looks a lot like a squirrel doing its thinking and then dashing out and snatching a nut?' (92).

Leslie Stone's 'The Human Pets of Mars' (1936) explores what it feels like to be the squirrel whose purposeful activity is not recognised as such by the dominant species. The story opens with a strange gold ship hovering above the Washington Monument. From this ship emerge 'horrors' dubbed 'decapods', their 'ten tentacles … surmounted by a flabby sack-like body topped by a round soft head from which projected the tentacles, possessing a round rubbery toothless mouth and three lidless staring eyes' (730). Were such beings not clearly possessed of superior technology, they would no doubt be lifeforms – such as squid or octopi – which human culture would fail to perceive as sentient. Human scientists rush to try to communicate with these beings but their efforts are ignored, signalling that the decapods do not perceive humanoid figures as sentient any more than humans would normally recognise a squid as such. The decapods take up a number of specimens, 'men, women, youths; white and black, without discrimination' (732) and even some non-humans: a police officer with his horse, a girl with her kitten and a dog. Humans try to rescue the captives but their technology is no match for the decapods: 'the shells *simply bounced back!*' (733). The setting then shifts to Mars where the human captives awaken and quickly begin to assess the situation using their power of reason: given the lesser gravity and similar clues, they realise that they are on Mars, and that the decapods wore armour on Earth, hence their invulnerability to attack. Human powers of reason are also used to interpret the demands that the decapods make of their new pets, determining, for example, that a 'high piping tone from the monster' signifies 'come here!' When one subject, Brett, attempts to 'teach the monster that he, likewise, was a thinking creature' (739), he soon realises that the task is impossible: 'having an intelligence of a vastly different order than that of Man, the decapods were unable to conceive the fact that an Earth-man was a thinking entity. Possibly to them Man was no more than a new type of animal' (740).

The story concerns the struggles of its human protagonists to survive their experience as pets: their antics to make the decapods notice them and take seriously their desires are treated as the cute entreaties of mindless animals. They are treated kindly but are never allowed to express their own agency – they eat when fed, walk at a pace set by the leash and are able to spend time with one another only when their owners congregate in a public, park-like area. Thus the story provides details which might cause us to question the ways in which we integrate pets into human lifestyles, encouraging us to see the various ways in which they strive to get our attention or disobey our rules not as the instinctual behaviour of inferior beings, but as an assertion of preference for a different way to spend time or use space asserted by a fellow sentient being. The focus in 'The Human Pets of Mars' quickly shifts, however, to a heroic adventure story common to many contemporary pulp stories, recounting the ways in which the humans – specifically the heroic male, Brett Rand – learn about the decapods' technology and thereby find a way to escape their captivity and return to Earth. The main motivation for the escape is that the human creatures are sickening from some deficit in Martian food: the kitten and horse die first (although the dog is saved), followed shortly by a young girl. Despite their many differences from humankind, the decapods are socially organised into heterosexual couples who practice a sexual division of labour and thus Brett is able to learn about their technology by successfully insisting one day that he accompany the Mister to work rather than remain at home with the Missis. Brett and another white man are able to discern how to operate decapods' technology and, *assisted* by a black man, they rescue the women and children – and some inferior, less manly and less able white men – and return to Earth.

Crucially, 'The Human Pets of Mars' keeps the category of 'animal' intact; that is, it does not challenge the logic by which some creatures are considered sentient beings whose existence must be respected in the colonial encounters of first-contact sf, while others are merely part of the landscape, exotic fauna who might be used equally by the indigenous or alien sentient beings. Although a female captive, Dell, exclaims 'when we *do* get home, I'm going to start a movement to release every pet in the land!' now that she knows what it is like to be 'a dumb brute thrown in with creatures whose language is not its language, who make their will its will' (762), this line of enquiry is quickly abandoned as another crisis – decapods attack during their voyage home – takes centre stage. Overall, the story stresses the categorical misrecognition that places humans in the exploitable class of pets. Their ability to almost instantaneously master decapod technology – so much so that they defeat the pursuing ship and save the Earth from any future visits by the species – calls attention to the evident superiority of these 'human pets' over not only more ordinary pets but also over the animal-like decapods. The story is similarly invested in the superiority of heroic white men over women and 'mulatto' and 'negro' (770) men and children. Only Brett remains strong throughout the story and his triumphant plan to exploit the technology of the decapod ship upon his return to Earth gets the story's last word. Yet, at the same time, when asked about her career plans, Dell, now Mrs Rand, does repeat her plan to free all the pets. Leslie Stone is one of few female sf writers successful in pulps of the 1930s, which might give us reason to see more ambiguity in 'The Human Pets of Mars' than its heroic narrative suggests. Although the plot of the story asserts the superiority of men over women and of human ingenuity over that of all other species, the plight of animal pets on Earth is not neglected in the story's otherwise conventional conclusion. Reading somewhat against the grain, we might see in this reminder of the parallels between the human pets and our pets, as well as, in the championing of their cause by a female character, a hint of priorities other than those endorsed by the formula of technophilic adventure fiction which the story otherwise replicates.

Gordon Dickson's 'Dolphin's Way' (1964) similarly plays with the conventions of sf narrative to deny his readers the expected conclusion in a way that draws attention to animal being as something analogous to human being. Protagonist Malcolm Sinclair works at Dolphin's Way research station where he worries that his research funding will be cut by administrator Corwin Brayt. The station researches dolphin communication using wild dolphins who choose to come to the centre rather than captive animals. Mal is committed to his work with dolphins, in part, due to his theory that 'there is some sort of interstellar civilization' that is 'waiting for the people of Earth to qualify themselves before making contact', the criterion of acceptability being 'learning to communicate with an alien culture' (101) rather than some feat of technological prowess. Research has been stalled by the 'environmental barrier' (102) which is an expression of the difference between communication and understanding. Humans and dolphins are able to 'agree on denotation of an auditory or other symbol, but not on connotation' (103) because they live in different environments and are differently embodied. Thus, Mal explains,

> My notion of 'powerful' is relative to the fact I'm six feet tall, weigh a hundred and seventy-five pounds and can lift my own weight against the force of gravity. Castor's [a dolphin] is relative to the fact that he is seven feet long, can speed up to forty miles an hour through the water, and as far as he knows weighs nothing, since his four hundred pounds of body-weight are balanced out by the equal weight of the water he displaces ... My mental abstraction of 'ocean' is not his, and our ideas of what a current is may coincide, or be literally worlds apart in meaning. (104)

Mal asserts that both the dolphins and he are trying but so far no way has been found to bridge this gap. In part, he is convinced that the dolphins are trying – that is, are recognising humans as fellow sentient creatures and attempting to find a way to think enough like us to reach him – because despite their capacity to kill humans easily and the fact that even in research activity 'men have caught and killed dolphins', 'no dolphin has ever been known to attack a human being' (105).

The visit of Jane Wilson, reporter for *Background Monthly*, to the station serves as an occasion for Mal to explain his research. He overtly rejects readings of dolphin behaviour toward humans as an instinctive recognition of human superiority. Later, musing on the differences between dolphin and human culture further, he notes their lack of 'visible impulse to war, to murder, to hatred and unkindness' (108) and begins to long for dolphin being while quoting to them from Matthew Arnold's 'The Forsaken Merman'. He realises the dolphins 'had been matching his speech largely in the inaudible range while he was quoting' (109) and begins to hear their vocalisations as an invocation to come away with them. Improvising dolphin embodiment through a snorkel and tying his lower legs together, Mal makes a breakthrough, realising the problem has been a human insistence on communicating 'by sound alone' instead of the 'rich ... symphony or orchestra' that is dolphin communication by sound, movement and touch, 'all of it in reference to the ocean conditions surrounding them at the moment' (113). This progress comes too late however: first, Mal is told that his research funding is cut and thus his work is at an end; next, Jane reveals that she is not really from *Background Monthly* but instead is a representative of the interstellar civilisation about which Mal hypothesised. Her observation of successful interspecies communication has made further research irrelevant, but it turns out that

she is there not to witness human success in transcending the environmental barrier and communicating with another species, but rather the
dolphin's. Jane regretfully tells Mal that her people and humans are 'not
going to be getting together ... ever' (116) and leaves with the dolphins,
who, it seems, had also been long awaiting 'visitors from the stars' (117).

Dickson's story thus neatly reverse the human expectation that we
are the dominant species on the planet and further offers a critique of
humanity's relations with other species as the reason why humans are
not the chosen species from the alien point of view. This decision and its
focus on the violence of human's past relationships with other species
reveals a significant pattern regarding the appearance of animals in sf,
one that also sheds light on the relationship between our material history
with animal others and the representations of aliens in the sf imagination.
As I suggested in the previous chapter regarding the prevalence of war
scenarios in alien contact stories, the sf imagination is structured by
a dialectical tension between our desire to communicate with a non-
human sentience and our fear of otherness as something that necessarily
threatens the self and hence must be destroyed. Depictions of aliens at
times strives for the I–Thou relationship which acknowledges the other as
a living subject fully as complex as oneself, but at others fall into the I–It
relationship which objectifies the other. Dickson's focus on the material
history of humankind's relationship with dolphins and the dolphins'
superior ability to continue to conceive of the humans as subjects points to
something of a guilty conscience on humanity's part in relation to these
questions of alterity, which are so central to sf. We both long for and fear
the idea of contact with an alien other because we know the history of
our own failures in relation to other species here on Earth. The anxiety
in this story about humanity being left behind in the interstellar progress
of civilised species is thus the other side of the same coin of Stone's story
and its reversal that let humans – if briefly – experience something of the
disenfranchisement we regularly visit upon other species, even those we
care for such as pets.

André Vilares Morgado's 'A Night on the Edge of Empire' (1996) offers
yet another perspective. The story tells of the avian Cultural Ambassador
from the Croap'tic, CandidSong, and his 'protobrachiant servant' (79)
Chirptic – a primate species. The Ambassador is overwhelmed by the
stressful Earth astroport with its myriad humans rushing about 'waving
packs of forms as if they had no other goal in life but to circulate this
way' and confused by the air-traffic controllers' picket signs that seem to
him to read 'MORE WORK FOR THE HUMID CIRCUITS, DOWN WITH
STONEWARE!' (79). He is disoriented on this planet where 'evolution has
suffered random rules', it being 'the only known planet where brachiants

are sophonts with full legal rights. Sophonts and aggressive, to top it all' (80). Chirptic, an 'almost sophont species', is fitted with a 'gnostic amplifier' that enables him to function as an aide to CandidSong, who would otherwise be unable to manage all the paperwork demanded by terrestrial Customs, having only 'two vestigial fingers' (81). From the moment they arrive on Earth, CandidSong is treated like an animal and Chirptic like a sentient being: he is asked if his animal has 'fleas' and if it has 'disinfected its feathers' (81), but Chirptic explains that he is 'the domestic animal' and that his 'mentation only exists due to direct integration with the prefrontal lobes of my Beloved Master' (82). Chirptic is confused by the humans' hostile attitude, which CandidSong explains stems from 'somatic complexes' on the part of a species that cannot face the fact that 'there isn't in the known Galaxy any other mammary species who has been through the same evolutionary process' (83). Attacked by a group of pro-human activists whose T-shirts proclaim 'DOWN WITH GODZILLA! KING-KONG LIVES!', they are separated and an uncomprehending Chirptic is told, 'you're free pal! Ethnic oppression is over', while CandidSong ponders, 'they have separated him from his *fingers*. But *why*? *Why*??' (86). As he stretches his neck to 'sing a song about peace, love and reconciliation between all species' (86) they kill him, crying out 'Death to all mammary gland oppressors! Victory to the opposable thumb' (87). The story ends with Chirptic in a state of shock, abandoned in 'an incomprehensible world made of luminous forms, odours and sound lacking all semantic sense' (87) in the absence of his gnostic amplifier.

Morgado's story is quite obviously intended as a humorous spoof in many ways, from its erotic nightclub supposedly marketed toward 'exotics', that is, bird-like aliens, whose slogan 'CHICKS CHICKS CHICKS CHICKS' (85) is meant literally, to its premise that a brachiant companion is necessary due to the excess of paperwork that is characteristic of human culture. At the same time, however, it also points to more serious aspects of the human–animal boundary as it is articulated through the pet bond, not only in the familiar violence and chauvinism which characterises its humans, but also in the fate it projects for Chirptic. In this instance, what is literalised through the figure of the gnostic amplifier is the dependence that has been bred into many domestic animals who – after thousands of years of domestication and, at least since the Victorian period, a regime of breeding for specific morphology that is not always conducive to the animal's health – are not able to survive without human support. Freeing such animals from human 'domination', then, is another cruelty rather than a rescue, but this fact does not mean that we cannot consider the specific configuration of the human–pet relationship and potentially modify it to be more respectful of the animal's agency. As Braidotti suggests, the kinds of animal welfare activism which see animals as furry people whose rights can be made equivalent to those already existent for humans 'denies the specificity of animals altogether. The point is to see the inter-*relation* human/animal as constitutive of the identity of *each*' (108). Thus, as I have been arguing, humans become posthuman as their relationship with animals changes.

The history of the animal welfare movement is itself deeply entwined with the rise of pet culture. Keith Thomas dates the practice of pet-keeping to the sixteenth century (181), while Karen Raber suggest that 'love of pets has probably always existed; but pet love was *invented* as a social and cultural force in the seventeenth and eighteenth centuries – both the excessive love of people for their pets and the assumption that human affections were returned by the pet in question' (87), although she does point out that this concept was satirised as much as it was celebrated. Pet-keeping and animal welfare both emerged as specifically middle-class concerns, and from the beginning 'suppress[ion] of dangerous elements of human society' (Ritvo 131) was one of the central missions of British animal protectionists, which also emphasised the tendency toward cruelty in immigrant cultures (127). In fact, fears of the working classes are so evident in early RSPCA documents that testimony emphasises the depravity of the torturers more than the suffering of animals: neighbours were encouraged to report on one another, and one member went so far as to argue that legislation against cruelty was now required because a gentlemen can no longer 'correct' or punish acts of the lower classes he witnesses, as was possible under previous social relations (Ritvo 147). Specific targets for action also ensured that the working classes were selectively prosecuted: livestock and working horses cared for by the working classes were the original beneficiaries of any protective legislation, it being presumed that middle-class pets did not need such external shield, and the practice of using fines as a penalty meant those less affluent found the punishment more onerous (Ritvo 137); finally, gentlemanly men-of-science were presumed to be above depraved acts of cruelty and hence animals used for experiment were excluded from early legislative protections (Ritvo 160). Berger associates the unprecedented number of pets found in twentieth-century society with its capitalist social organisation and its 'withdrawal into the private small family unit, decorated or furnished with mementoes from the outside world, which is such a distinguishing feature of consumer societies' (12). Animals were bound up, too, in assumptions about class identity. The editor of the *Spectator*, R.H. Hutton, a member of royal commission looking into vivisection in 1874, argued that dogs and cats should be exempted from vivisectionist experimentation because 'in the course of domestication, such animals had acquired the same heightened sensitivities that distinguished civilized men from barbarous tribes' (White 68).

Pets were entwined with class in the emphasis placed on pedigrees and bloodlines for species such as dogs, horses and cats, as well as the rise of a show culture which evaluated individual animals based on their proximity to a conformation standard set for the breed. Such prize animals were important to Victorian social hierarchies in two ways: first their own lineage reflected and endorsed an analogous concern with human heritage that unpinned the class system; second, 'qualities were valued only because they were unusual or difficult to produce' which thereby enabled them 'to symbolize the power to manipulate and the power to purchase' (Ritvo 106). The conflation of pet culture and class bias is one of the objects of satire in Thomas Disch's *The Puppies of Terra*, a novel which tells, in imitation eighteenth-century picaresque style, of the life and adventures of White Fang, also known as Ben White, and his transition from being a prized pet to a 'dingo', one of the rebel humans who resists the Masters' domination of Earth and its inhabitants. The novel also bears similarities to Virginia Woolf's 'biography' of Elizabeth Barrett Browning's eponymous spaniel *Flush*, a novel that uses the dog's point of view and his longing for the freedom of his sexual and otherwise embodied life before he became a lap dog to critique the stifling sexual proprieties of the Victorian culture in which Browning lived. Disch, too, uses the contrast between White Fang's life under the aesthetic and cultural guidance of the Masters with the freedom enabled by a life beyond the constraint of the Leash to explore aspects of human cultural formations and the nature of the animal that is 'man'.

White Fang opens by telling us how he came to be a 'dingo', representative of the free humans of Earth, when he began life as a pampered pet of the Masters, alien beings who came to the planet sometime around 1970. They 'can be said to be a pure electromagnetic phenomenon – formed of a "substance" that cannot be called either "matter" or "energy" but which nonetheless displays a *potentiality* for either' (24). When they arrived the Masters took over all electro-magnetic technologies, including media broadcasts, and adopted most of the humans as pets, keeping them in splendid homes made from a technology that moulds matter into any shape which then behaves as a solid object but is really only one molecule thick. The kennels in which these pet humans live are spaces of leisure:

> human labor became obsolete as the Masters – in themselves, a virtually unlimited power supply – stayed on and took things over, setting automatons to do the dirty work, freeing man from the drudgery of the commonplace that had been his perennial complaint.

Freeing, at least, those who would accept such freedom – who would, in short, agree to become pets. (64)

In this ideal space humans are free to pursue art or athletics, although the latter is preferred based on a feeling that the first generation of pets had gone in a bit too much for intellectual refinement. As White Fang explains, for the new generation 'the important thing, as we saw it, was not to be witty and cultivated and bright, but to be *sincere*' (46).

The ironies that structure the book are multiple. White Fang takes his name from Jack London's novel about a wild wolf-dog becoming civilised; it is the companion novel to London's *The Call of the Wild* (1903) about a tamed and pampered pet dog, Buck, who is forced to return to the wilderness after he is kidnapped and sold as a sled dog. Buck learns to survive in the harsh Yukon environment and eventually goes wild, becoming the alpha leader of a wolf pack. In *White Fang* (1906), in contrast, the dog protagonist is a mixture of wolf and dog who begins life as part of a wolf pack and is later raised by Natives who take in the pup and his mixed wolf/dog mother. His adventures take him further from the wilderness and closer to human civilisation, moving from the Native encampment to a white settlement's dog fighting ring and finally to the loving and domestic home of a gold hunter who tames him and relocates him from the frontier Yukon to domesticated California, where he ends the novel in middle-class, patriarchal bliss, surrounded by his puppies. Given what Disch's White Fang says about the trajectory of his life at the beginning of the novel – that he has moved from the civilised but stifling status of a pet to the independent status of freed man living off the land – we might expect Buck to be a more appropriate literary model. The name White Fang thus can signify a reversal of our usual expectations of civilised and savage, thereby suggesting the Masters who enslave humans are the uncivilised ones. Yet from the opening paragraph, the narrative continually signals that although White Fang presents his narrative as one of consciousness-raising – he comes to experience himself as a free man – he more strongly feels nostalgia for his time as a pet. His first statement is,

> My name is White Fang, though of course that is not really my name. My name is really Dennis White, now. I like the old name better; it is more in keeping with the image I have of myself. But perhaps such an attitude is just a hangover from the time I was a pet. (9)

He goes on to say that 'some people would say that once you've been a pet, once you've grown used to the Leash, you're never quite human again – in the sense of being free' (9), but he never actively endorses this position himself, recalling instead that 'it *is* more fun to be Leashed' (9).

The language of dog names and the use of terms such as kennel, leash and pet are the product of a novel-within-the-novel, *A Dog's Life*, written by White Fang's father, Tennyson White. This novel is told entirely from a dog's point of view – 'a *real* dog, a canine of the Industrial Revolution' (19–20) and its publication made such terms, which had previously been used pejoratively, into emblems of pride for human pets. It also popularises the moniker 'Dingoes' for the wild humans who rebelled against the Masters and fled the Leash or else were considered too old or otherwise inferior at the time when the Masters arrived and thus were not accepted into the kennels. *A Dog's Life* was conceived during a period in which Tennyson believed he was shortly to die of leukaemia because although treatment for this disease is within the Masters' power, 'it was considered *unsporting* to tamper with the basic genetic materials, as any permanent cure would have required' (19). Although White Fang spends most of his life believing that his father was killed by the Dingoes, he learns when he is twenty and himself falls into the Dingoes' hands that his father faked his own death in order to join the Dingoes, whom he had secretly supported all along. Far from being a rallying call for pet identity, *A Dog's Life* was 'a time-bomb disguised as an Easter egg and planted right in the middle of the Masters' basket; it was a Trojan horse; it was a slow-working acid that nibbled at the minds of the pets ... For men, in the last analysis, are not meant to be domestic animals' (141). The book inspired many to see what they had considered a paradise with new eyes and thus flee the Masters' influence; 'those who didn't (and sadly, these were by far the majority) stayed with the Masters and incorporated the monstrous satire of *A Dog's Life* into the fabric of their daily lives. They became dogs' (141).

Despite this assertion, however, which White Fang recounts near the end of his tale, most of the novel describes his blissful – but unproductive and monotonous – life as a pet. A large aspect of pet identity is investment in a class system of bloodlines similar to the ranking of purebred animals, and White Fang is proud of his heritage as son of the most famous literary figure in pet history. He tells us 'now, of course, I realize that that kind of talk is undemocratic and subversive, but then my tender mind, depraved by the false values of the Mastery, was flattered by such a compliment' (40). He recalls with enthusiasm his time spent at Swan Lake kennel in which everyday activity was turned into a continual dance accompanied by music spontaneously created by a technology that responded to movement: 'there was nothing *wasted*. I think that's the important thing. Not a word or thought or glance between two persons but that there was a deeper meaning to it' (46). Even in his re-educated state, White Fang laments 'it was paradise – and it is quite, quite gone' (56). Yet much of the dog life is also intellectually insipid: his brother Pluto fancies himself a poet and writes pretentious and impenetrable prose usually accompanied by rituals that are a miscellany of religious ceremony and popular culture prattle. Although he believes himself to be perfectly fulfilled in his pet life, White Fang nevertheless recalls that during the first evening he spends with his wife outside of the influence of the Leash – she has begged their Master to give the a brief opportunity to 'know what wilderness tastes like' (58) – he finds 'though we had known each other intimately for years, I had never felt quite this urgently desirous of Julie' (60). This brief experiment with freedom becomes extended when unusual sunspot activity temporarily 'knock[s] the Masters out of commission' (75) and all of mankind must get by without their authority until the Masters heal and return.

Yet at the same time, conditions are perhaps even worse when White Fang – now reverting to his birth name, Ben – spends time with the Dingoes. At first he and his family are captured while trying to find their way back to the Masters. In a farcical series of coincidences that even characters within the novel identify as ludicrous, White Fang parachutes from a plane and lands in a facility in which Dingoes have imprisoned pets. Because he is wearing a major's overcoat for warmth, he is mistaken for a major whose inspection was imminently expected and manages to parlay this misrecognition into control of the camp for a brief period. He inspects the conditions in which the pets are held, finding them dismal – justified by the command staff based on the logic that 'There're only pets, after all. It's not as if … I mean, they aren't like *us*. They don't quite seem … what is the word … *human*? They know their place, and they keep in it' (88, ellipses in original). He is able to reunite with his half-brother and a mother he has rarely seen since childhood, and together they use a performance of the story of Salome and John the Baptist – a pastiche of biblical, theatrical, popular culture and invented sources – to enable the pets to escape and return to the recently restored Masters. White Fang seems to find greater fault in these human commanders than in the Masters, even as he recounts this narrative in his changed state – although he does qualify at the beginning of the text that he cannot 'tell the story of [his] life as a pet without using a pet's language, without adopting [a pet's] attitudes' (9–10). When a guard complains 'everyone has to work – that's life' while castigating the laziness of pets who refuse to do the manual labour necessary to produce their food, White Fang replies 'well, *workers* – of course *they* have to work. But perhaps the pets – the goddamned pets, I should say – have an attitude more like our own, Doctor. Perhaps they think of themselves – however misguidedly – as officers and gentlemen' (102). Despite their rhetoric of freedom, equality and the dignity of human labour, the Dingoes are at least equally banal and exploitative as the Masters.

Further contradictions abound. White Fang describes the experience of the Leash as the feeling of 'the tides of knowledge that sweep through the mind; the sense of being in communion with the most transcendental forces, of being a spoke from the hub about which the universe is spinning; the total *certainty* that it affords; the ecstasy and the consuming love' (24). Yet this certainty and feeling of acceptance can also be understood as a refusal of responsibility, a bad faith retreat from the burden of being free, as Sartre describes it. Like religion, it is an opiate that exempts humans from the difficult struggle that is life. Tennyson sarcastically tells his son, 'Your Master takes care of everything for you and leaves you so perfectly free. Except that you can't taste anything from the good-and-evil tree, why there's nothing that isn't allowed you' (134). White Fang, in turn, is disillusioned by what he sees as an absence of justice in some of his father's revolutionary choices and equally sarcastically asks if his father is fighting the revolution 'just so you can feel guilty about it' (135). Tennyson counters, 'dirty hands is one of the prices you pay in becoming a man again' and that he is fighting because 'guilt and sweat and black bread are all part of being human. Domestic animals are always bred to the point that they become helpless in the state of nature. The Masters have been breeding men' (135). Yet there is little evidence that, left to this state of nature and the responsibility to accept the burden of freedom, humans can accomplish much of note. Tennyson's second novel, *The Life of Man*, is intended to 'forge an army from the unorganized mass of apathetic Dingoes who had never left Earth' by 'show[ing]the Dingoes what they were: an amorphous mass of discontent, without program or purpose; a race that had taken the first step towards it own extinction' (142). The book repeats scenes 'from the first novel ... *verbatim*, but now its pleasantries have become horrors. Allegory gives way to the brutal, damning realism' and White Fang tells us that, as he reads, 'every word of it seemed an accusation aimed directly at me' (140). Yet this book is never as successful as *A Dog's Life* and Tennyson finds he must invent a mythology based on electricity to motivate the masses of Dingoes.

The Puppies of Terra thus seems to be trapped between two alternatives, neither of which is very appealing. On the one hand, it potentially suggests that an identity as a pet is what the human species is best suited for, a narrow and unflattering assessment; on the other, that Dingo-organised civilisation has little to recommend it, based as it is on superstition and brutality. In the final scenes of the novel, White Fang contemplates his surroundings and feels that he 'belonged to the Earth' and that his 'spirit' is 'dilated with happiness' (148). At this moment of fulfilment, he feels the Master's Leash return and is told that the Master had heard him calling. White Fang insists that he did not call but just felt happy. As he is

deliberating about whether to return to a Leashed life, he is distracted by
the sight of a frog, caught within the jaws of a water snake and desperately
trying to escape with its front legs, even as its hind ones are digested.
He tells us 'the Leash bade me not to look at this thing, and, truly I did
not want to. It was so horrible, but I could not help myself' (149), and he
finds that contemplating this sight drives the Master away. His father later
queries him about his feelings toward the frog, to which White Fang replies
'It was ugly. I felt ... disgusted' (152, ellipses in original). His father seizes
upon this feeling of disgust as the weapon humanity can use to finally
free themselves from the Masters, and proceeds to subject White Fang to
a series of horrifying images – the culminating one a picture of someone
with Elephantiasis – and to record White Fang's mental state and project
it into the ether, thereby driving the Masters away. White Fang tells us of
this experience that 'the people in the pictures were beyond the reach of
medicine. Beyond the reach, even, of sympathy' (155), and the novel ends
'The Masters had left Earth. They couldn't stand the barking' (159).

To a degree, *The Puppies of Terra* is not concerned with questions of the
human–animal boundary or the moral issues that are raised by the motif
of reversing the power dynamic of the species relationship and placing
humans in the position of pets. Rather, in proper Swiftian[1] fashion, 'the
notion of *inhumanity* operates as a third term generated by the human–
animal distinction' (Armstrong *What Animals Mean* 23). The motif of
animality works to show that humans are more beastly even than the
beasts, not redeeming the denigration of the animal that occurs via the
human–animal boundary but instead using this imagery to conduct an
even harsher critique of humanity's failure to achieve humane status. Read
within the context of HAS, however, we can see that this very critique of
human subjectivity is not as removed from an ethical reconsideration of
the human–animal boundary as it might appear on the surface. It is not
insignificant that the two final images used to mark the failure of White
Fang's compassion and thus produce the Master's withdrawal from the
human race are both images that are linked to animals: White Fang is
unable to have compassion for that which is different from himself, seeing
only ugliness rather than suffering in the frog's dilemma; the very name
Elephantiasis for the disease lymphatic filariasis marks the way in which
human culture denies compassion for the animal, labelling a human
deformity via a name that suggests the normal appearance of another
species, thereby situating that species as inherently abnormal. Disch's novel
reveals much about how animals are integrated into human cultures – and
the limitations of this model of intersubjectivity for humans – although
it does not explicitly comment on the subjectivity of the animals and the
damage done to them. The metaphor of pets is doubly significant here, for

'pet keeping ... [can be] another way to hide from ourselves the real violence between humans and animals beneath an image of sensibility, or even a means to deflect us from awareness of the violence between ourselves and others in an age of class conflict and global domination' (Kete 15).

This symbolic use of animal imagery is common in satirical fiction and, within sf, is frequently linked to fears about degeneration as a consequence of humanity's self-destructive tendencies. Rieder argues that sf written after WWI tends to articulate its vision of catastrophe through 'hyperbole, where the decline of imperial power debouches into the decline of civilization or of the human species itself' (143). This propensity is further transformed into anxious visions which show the human species replaced by another as the dominant intelligence on the planet. Isaac Asimov's 'No Connection' (1948) is a particularly interesting example of such a story: its protagonist, Ralph, is described as 'a typical American of his times' (226) and although details of his physiology – he 'would have topped two and half yards' had he 'stood erect' and masses nearly 'a quarter of a ton' (226) – make it clear that Ralph is not human, other details of his life seem so blandly middle American that it is easy to miss this point. Ralph is working on research regarding the 'reconstruction of the Primate Primeval' (227), a figure that, his son insists, 'looks just like an Eekah' (228), reputedly intelligent inhabitants from the another land who have recently arrived via air machines. As the story unfolds we learn that Ralph is part of a civilisation of bear, their name is Gurrows, who have only recently discovered that there are other continents on their world and inhabitants of these continents who do not resemble bear. These Eekahs have arrived as 'political refugees' (232), a category that makes no sense to the Gurrows because the Eekahs are not guilty of any crime, as the Gurrows understand it, but merely of 'disagree[ing] with their Administrator on principles of policy' (237). Gurrow society is collectively organised around units called 'groupings'; they define jobs as 'regular work, the fruits of which adhere to others in addition to the worker himself' (232) and divide jobs into two classes: 'Voluntary Jobs' which people do by natural inclination and 'Community Jobs', 'annoying but unavoidable' work that is done by 'lot or rotation' (233). All work contributions are regarded as equal in stature, and no one is compensated more than any other or lives in any more luxurious conditions.

When the Eekahs arrive on the 'new' American continent, they kill five Gurrows with 'an instrument that expelled metal pellets at high sped by means of a controlled explosive chemical reaction' (238), but the Gurrows decide not to brand the Eekahs as criminals because they accept as mitigating circumstances the fact that the Eekahs 'did not realize we were intelligent beings' (238). The more the Gurrows learn of Eekah civilisation, the more concerned they become: Eekahs 'kill one another periodically for obscure reasons'; live in 'huge conglomerate societies – yet find it impossible to allow for the presence of one another'; are 'gregarious without being social' and politically organised under the domination of 'a few, who are in turn dominated by their queer need for security which they confuse with an Eekah word called "power" which, apparently, means the prevailing of one's own will over the sum of the will of the community' (241). Most of the plot concerns Ralph's desire to visit the Eekah refugees to see if they offer any support for his theory that 'Primate Primeval was an intelligent creature with a developed civilization' (235). He is puzzled by the fact that sites of Primate Primeval culture are always found in areas that give 'strange and impossible' fossil dates, evidence that the reader is easily able to discern suggests that a nuclear war destroyed human culture and contaminated certain parts of the globe with radiation. The story ends with Ralph insisting that there is 'No connection! No connection!' (249) among 'a dead creature that must have aspired to heights' (his Primate Primeval), 'a living creature of erratic habits' (the Eekahs), and 'a sordid present of explosives and neutron bombardments' (249) now that the Eekahs know of the existence of North America and regard it as 'a new land of opportunity' – more precisely, 'a new and empty land' (247). The reader, however, cannot doubt the connections.

The colonial structure of Asimov's story links it not only with sf tales of human–animal reversal but also with the colonial imagery apparent in many sf animal texts, discussed in Chapter 5. Another common motif in sf texts which position humans as animals is the zoo, an institution similarly allied with imperialism. Zoos and menageries have long been associated with displays of imperial power from at least the era of the Roman Empire. Like the reversal stories of pets, imagery of zoos in sf is frequently used to demonstrate the error of alien perceptions when they presume that humans are specimens suitable for zoos rather than recognise that we are sentient beings. A typical story in this vein is Laurence Manning's 'The Call of the Mech Men' which recounts the adventures of two men imprisoned in a zoo by the Mech Men who presume that organic beings cannot be sentient. Unlike Stone's 'The Human Pets of Mars', these men find no reason to empathise with the animals who share their fate and in fact decide to eat some rabbits who are housed with them in order to demonstrate to their captors that they are not herbivores and hence, they believe, ensure they will be properly fed in the future. Despite the lack of a common language between humans and Mech Men, when one man writes, 'I AM INTELLIGENT AND HUMAN. CAN YOU UNDERSTAND THIS?' (371), the Mech Men swiftly conclude that 'graphite markings on wood pulp seem useless, but positive must represent thoughts' (377) and proper communication is established in short order. The humans are soon happily sharing histories with the Mech Men, an exchange that only momentarily wobbles when the Mech Men realise that the humans use machines rather than vice versa.

The story takes little opportunity to comment on the ways zoos limit the opportunities for successful communication among species, a frequent topic in HAS. Early menageries and zoos were not concerned with animal subjectivity but were merely an opportunity to display the power of imperial conquest and its exotic booty; although modern zoos justify their existence in large part based on a rationale of conservation of endangered animal species and education of the public regarding animals, this surface often hides a brutal relationship to animals that is involved in the procurement of zoo specimens: young animals are preferred as they more easily adjust to human contact and this often means killing the mother in order to obtain the specimen (Ritvo 246). Some Victorian-era zoos displayed exotic animals and exotic people side by side, an apt demonstration of the conflation of colonial racism and the human–animal boundary; the last such exhibit was organised in 1931 with group a natives from New Caledonia, who disappointed their audience by being too similar to Europeans – learning European languages, dressing in modern styles and otherwise assimilating – and thus failing to fit the expected stereotypes of the savage (Rothfels 141). Rothfels contends that such exhibits of natives were doomed as soon as 'people in the shows began to talk back', unlike the animals who could be silenced, maintaining that 'this enforced "silence" is perhaps the defining feature of the modern zoo' (12). Berger goes so far as to suggest that the artificial and impoverished environment of the zoo produces animals who are not 'real' animals in their temperament and behaviour: such 'animals', isolated from each other and without interaction between species, have become utterly dependent upon their keepers. Consequently most of their responses have been changed. What was central to their interest has been replaced by a 'passive waiting for a series of arbitrary outside interventions' (23). Acampora notes a similar transformation on the somatic level, produced by the 'seriously deleterious effects' of caging which are 'most visible morally from the existential viewpoint of somaesthetic transaction or orientation. The jailhoused bodies of individual animals prevent a full and healthy range of corporal expression' (*Corporal Compassion* 99).

Such contexts expose as all the more improbable the fantasy of human captives being able to demonstrate intelligence to alien beings or remain sufficiently healthy, mentally and physically, to escape. Further, they remind us of our own failures in assessing the intelligence or other capacities of captive animals whom we observe in unnatural, stressful and disheartening circumstances. Carol Emshwiller's 'Animal' (1968) uses the zoo reversal fantasy to raise some of these issues. The story tells of the captivity of an unnamed being referred to as only 'the animal' found 'in the deepest part of the forest' (84). He reacts poorly to his captivity, refusing to eat – although 'this was expected' (84) – and spending much of his time watching out the window of his cage. Incongruities between the story's descriptions – for example, one 'keeper of a particular sensitivity' offers the animal 'both a grilled cheese sandwich and a hamburger' (85) in order to tempt him to eat – and our expectations of caged animals alert the reader to the humanoid form of this animal. It becomes increasingly apparent that this animal is a man who is no different from those who observe him other than the ways he is infantilised and robbed of agency by his status as animal. He is treated with kindness but nonetheless still resists his captivity and eventually escapes. Emshwiller skilfully uses the story to demonstrate the disservice humans do to animals, even those whom we regard with affection and treat with kindness, when we erase their subjectivity and substitute instead a projection of our fantasies about animal being. One woman in particular continually visits the animal and offers him treats, but it is clear that her behaviour is as motivated by her own desire for returned affection as it is by concern for his well-being. The dominance that adheres to this relationship is represented by the 'silver chain ... with which to lead him to breakfast, lunch and dinner' (92) that she has made.

The animal becomes a successful artist [2] and attends 'cocktail parties in his honor' but then returns 'to his cage without complaint' (91). The more successful the animal's art, the more anxious become his keepers about its possible influence on the townspeople. Various experts begin to study his behaviour and the townspeople's attitudes toward him. Although 'the animal himself has expressed the view that he would like to be considered as an individual as well as an animal' (93), in the symposium that is organised on the matter he 'will preside as chairman, though he will have no real say in the proceedings' (93). Before the symposium occurs, the animal 'walked away into the deepest part of the forest' (94); the townspeople miss the animal and 'sometimes call out silently toward the forest, come and write us your animal opinions. Sit in our park. Adorn our cocktail parties' (94) but to no avail. The story concludes with them hoping that the genetic traits of offspring they attribute to the animal – a series of rapes that occurred during his earlier escape – will 'in some future time, be a part of us all' (95). In the conclusion, the animal becomes as much a symbol of the rebellious spirit of art – and the alternative perspective on hegemonic morals that it can provide – as an image of the experience of animal subjectivity under the stultifying conditions of zoo imprisonment.

Yet the two motifs are related. The outsider perspective of the artist articulates another way for the townspeople to be in the world, a different set of values that would organise their experience and potentially allow them to reconfigure what it means to be in their community. Similarly, rethinking our relationship with animal others and finding a way of living with them that does not impose upon them the sensory and cognitive restrictions of zoos can also imply another way of configuring what it means to be human when 'human' is no longer produced through the subjugation of 'animal'. Acampora argues that such changed sociality is transformative: 'the task before us is not one of transsubstantively becoming-other (indeed impossible) but of articulating our already familiar experiences of *being-with* others' (*Corporal Compassion* 120). Haraway suggests something similar in her idea of companion species which she insists is not simply a new term for animals who are integrated into human sociality, but rather a term that refers equally to the human and animal participants in a companion species relationship, both of whom are transformed by it. She further contends that 'resistance to human exceptionalism *requires* resistance to humanization of our partners' (*When Species Meet* 52) and thus that we need to find ways to integrate animal beings into social relations that do not fantasise them as children or other imitation humans. Emshwiller's story refuses to gratify the townspeople's desire for the animal to serve their affective needs as an image of sexual prowess or symbol of primitive energy. Instead, he remains an individual who cannot be reduced to a mere exemplar of what the townspeople construct as 'animal' being, and the townspeople have no access to the difference his perspective embodies because they refuse to open themselves up to being transformed by the encounter with the animal. Their attempts to fit him into their preconceived categories are damaging both to the animal's own experience and to the townspeople's opportunities for transformation. Haraway argues that a practice such as dog-training approached from the point of view of companion species enables both partners to 'learn to pay attention to each other in a way that changes who and what they become together' (*When Species Meet* 208). In 'The Animal' there is no companion species relationship remaking both partners, but its absence is presented as a loss and a failure.

Emshwiller's more recent novel *The Mount* (2002) provides such a vision. Its structure is similar to that of Disch's *Puppies of Terra*: alien beings superior to humans have settled on Earth and integrated humans into their social networks as domestic animals. Rather than pets, however, the humans in Emshwiller's novel are working animals, serving as mounts for the alien Hoots, whose legs are too weak to support them in Earth gravity. Another crucial difference is that Emshwiller's aliens have crashed on Earth and are unable to return to their own planet. The story focuses on the experience of Charley, an adolescent boy who has been chosen as the mount for his Little Master, 'The-Future-Ruler-of-Us-All, His Excellent Excellency' (20). Charley is at first invested in his identity as a mount, proud to be part of an elite lineage of Seattles, the strain of mounts preferred for endurance and muscular physique. He is proud of his physical conformation and has internalised the class values of the breeding system, continually evaluating other humans he sees in terms of their appearance, viewing as inferior the Tennessee mounts who are bred for speed and refusing even to acknowledge the existence of the non-pedigreed 'nothings' who result from unsanctioned breeding. The hoot relationship with the mounts is both instrumental and affective: mounts are disciplined into obedience by poling (a high-tech cattle prod), kept in paddocks and allowed no autonomy, but at the same time fondness can develop between particular mounts and their riders, training involves positive reinforcement through pats and treats and the Hoots' rhetoric continually emphasises the need to be kind to their mounts. Humans exist in a limbo status between working animals and pets, and some individuals are treated more kindly within this continuum than are others. At the beginning of the novel Charley identifies strongly with the Hoots and his life as a mount, using his Hoot name, Smiley, and speaking with pride of his pedigree and training even though one of his earliest memories is of his mother being poled and scarred when she tried to prevent him being taken from her.

Before we get to Charley's story, however, the first chapter of the novel establishes that relations are often tense between species. It is the address of a Hoot to her mount, whom we later learn is Beauty, his mount name, or Heron, his human name, Charley's father and leader of the free human resistance. This rider outlines the Hoot understanding of the relationship and presents her reasons as to why it should be harmonious, arguing 'in fact we're built for you and you for us' (1). She highlights the benefits of obedience – 'We'll pat you if you do things fast enough and don't play hard to catch' – and laments the human failure to appreciate this co-operative partnership – 'you still call us aliens in spite of the fact that we've been on your world for generations' (1). Yet as her narrative continues, aspects of the domination that Tuan argues is one half of the pet dialectic begin to overshadow the affection. She tells him 'We prefer that there be no fight left and no ideas' (3) and reminds him why, although humans can talk and humans and Hoots could easily converse with one another, this is prevented by the training regime: 'Silence is important for many reasons. Your kind has a tendency to have ideas' (12). *The Mount* comments more directly on the analogous situation of animals: the mounts' enforced silence is like that of zoo animals; the dialectic of dominance and affection is used to produce a stunted 'pet' subjectivity; and the fragmentation of intraspecies social bonds that disrupts Charley's family parallels the way domesticated animals are isolated from their own species and trapped within a cultivated dependency on humans for their physical and social needs.[3]

The novel is structured as a bildungsroman in which Charley matures into an adult perspective and comes to have a more critical view of human–Hoot relations. The typical pattern of the bildungsroman novel emphasises a conflict between the protagonist's values and those of society, usually prompting some kind of journey in which the protagonist is jarred from his/her familiar home. While on the journey, the protagonist struggles with the gap between his/her needs and desires and the values of the dominant social order, with the resolution finding some way to reconcile the protagonist to his or her place within this social order – now seen in a new light. At first, Charley is fully integrated into Hoot society and its evaluation of interspecies relations. He feels no identification with the rebelling, wild humans, exclaiming, 'they [the Hoots] care about us so much! How can my kind turn against them!' (29), and concurring that such rebels bring disasters upon themselves, 'disaster, like the Hoots have always told us and told us. There's nothing we could ever do to hurt them. They're smarter than we are, they grow the food, and they have all the tools and weapons' (31). Charley finds himself ejected from this protected existence when a rebel attack destroys the Hoot village where he lives. Unlike most of the other mounts who embrace their new freedom, Charley clings to his Hoot life by finding and rescuing his Little Master amid the chaos. Both are taken in by the wild humans, largely because of the authority of Charley's father, although Little Master's presence is resented by most. Charley is originally alienated from his father and unreceptive to his father's attempts to communicate the importance of the rebellion to him, an exchange complicated by the fact that years of being a martial mount, wearing spikes in his cheeks and a bit, have damaged Heron's ability to talk at all. His fragmented '"Wouldn't you like ..." Another stop. "Your own life?" Stop. "Not be ridden? Not told? Where? Forced? Wherever they! *They*"' (44, ellipses in original) does not move Charley, who still identifies with the values of Hoot society, telling the reader 'I just can't get used to seeing all of us Sams and Sues walking around with no Hoots on them. They look like half-people' (51).[4]

The novel is not simply the story of Charley's coming to revolutionary consciousness, however. Instead, both he and Little Master are engaged in the journey to maturity, separated from the habitual practices and taken-for-granted assumptions their culture trains in them both. As they find their place within the rebel encampment and struggle with their feelings about the free humans they meet and with the violence these rebels enact on Hoots, both Charley and Little Master find that 'the more things that happen, the more I don't know which side I'm on' (87). They learn from their symbiotic relationship: Little Master cannot walk far without Charley, but similarly Charley is dependent upon Little Master's superior hearing and vision to navigate in the often dangerous world. Little Master learns that he cannot endanger Charley by using violence to ensure obedience because, as Charley tells him, 'you have to remember, if I'm not safe, you're not either. If I'm not safe, you're as good as dead' (71). Charley similarly realises that 'I've never been without Little Master. And a good thing, too, or I'd be choked to death. Without him, maybe dead a lot of times' (115). Little Master also learns greater autonomy during his time with the rebels, working with Charley to train himself to walk and achieving a state in which, although he is still limited in range given the harshness of Earth gravity for his physique, he is able to walk further than any other Hoot. Eventually Charley's father comes to see that violence against the Hoots is not a viable route to a better society, realising that 'the Hoots are here to stay' (148): they cannot return to their own home even if they wanted to, and their extremely strong arms and ability to incapacitate humans with their voices (the origin of the name Hoot) mean that finding a way to live co-operatively with them is the only path forward. At the same time, however, Hoots need to realise that living co-operatively does not mean subjugating humans to their will. The humans have built technologies that can damage Hoot settlements and so only the path of mutual co-operation will ensure a better society for all. Heron sees an ideal of this in Charley's relationship with Little Master, suggesting that *'The way you and Little Master are together! That's entirely new. Hoots talk of kindness and caring, but you two have come to it. Your relationship is not mount to host but friend to friend'* (193).

The novel ends with Charley and Little Master returning to Hoot society where Little Master asserts his role as Present, no longer Future, Leader-of-Us-All. The current Hoot leader attempts to accommodate the human rebellion by offering limited autonomy, but Little Master refuses such concessions as inadequate. He tells Charley,

> I was there with your father, too, remember? I listened. He didn't convince you, but he convinced me. He was right about false freedoms. He wanted to open the doors of all the land, not just the doors of the snacks, but it's going to be hard to tell when and if they surrender. (204)

They settle for nothing less than the transformation of the Hoot social order. Thus, unlike the typical bildungsroman in which the protagonist is

reconciled to the social order, Emshwiller's novel ends with the transformation of the social order, looking toward a new co-operative relationship
between Hoots and humans in which true friendship rather than species
hierarchy structures the exchange. Humans will help Hoots as they choose
but they will not be owned as mounts, and humans will work with Hoots
to develop technologies that will assist the Hoots in walking and thus
remove their need to exploit human labour. The conclusion is careful
to insist that the lack of exploitation and the greater space for autonomy
and mutual respect does not imply that the two species should just exist
independently of one another. Charley and Little Master reaffirm their
mutual reliance. Little Master tells him, in front of an assembled group of
humans and Hoots, 'without you, I'm only half. Even though I can walk
on my own, I'm still just a part. You're just half, too, you know, can't hear,
can't smell, can't see all the way around' (204). In the future, both species
will 'imprint each other' (227) and create a new society that is truly one
of companion species, both irrevocably changed by the new culture that
is neither human nor Hoot but what the two species produce – and are
– together.

The Mount suggests ways in which the sf imagination can inspire us
to new relationships with the species with whom we already share this
planet. Like the Hoots, most are not going away – although the rapid
extinction rate offers a direr picture of this relationship than the one
in Emshwiller's novel. Yet there is still time to ensure opportunities for
sharing the planet with such creatures, finding ways to acknowledge our
and their needs for space and other resources, and thus to open ourselves
to the possibility of a companion species relationship in which we too are
made otherwise. The most evident analogy established by the reversal is to
our relationship with domesticated animals, upon whom we depend in a
variety of ways, some more exploitative than others. We depend upon pet
animals for affection and companionship, and constructing a way of living
that relationship that is more respectful of their species-specific needs is
one of the potentialities suggested by Emshwiller's novel. Yet we also exist
in dependent relationship with animals domesticated as food sources,[5] a
much more complex exchange that cannot easily be resolved by ideals of
friendship. The spirit of Emshwiller's vision can nonetheless be brought to
these relations as well, acknowledging our dependence on them and thus
our obligations to them as beings whose lives are sacrificed for human
ones. Haraway argues that

> In eating we are most inside the differential relationalities that
> make us who and what we are and that materialize what we must
> do if response and regard are to have any meaning personally and

politically. There is no way to eat and not to kill, no way to eat and not to become with other mortal beings to whom we are accountable, no way to pretend innocence and transcendence or a final peace. Because eating and killing cannot be hygienically separated does *not* mean that just any way of eating and killing is fine, merely a matter of taste and culture. Multispecies human and nonhuman ways of living and dying are at stake in practices of eating. (*When Species Meet* 295)

As the texts discussed in this chapter reveal, sf visions of human–animal reversal can help us think through such complex ethical entanglements as we strive to make a posthuman future that respects the multispecies world in which we live.

8. The Modern Epimetheus:
Animals and/as Technology

The story of Prometheus is well known to most sf readers, with the fire that Prometheus steals from the gods standing in multiply for civilisation, science and technology, and the light of knowledge more generally – all things taken to mark the birth of humanity. In some versions of this legend, Prometheus is contrasted with his foolish brother Epimetheus, who is given the task of distributing positive traits to the animals. Lacking foresight, Epimetheus has run out of gifts when he reaches humans; in compensation Prometheus steals fire for humanity, giving humans a trait until then associated with the gods alone. Fire or technics thus sets humanity apart from the rest of the natural world, a separation that is generally taken to indicate the superiority of humankind, particularly as Prometheus is depicted as more intelligent than Epimetheus. Derrida's recounting of this myth emphasises that Prometheus steals fire 'in order to make up for the forgetfulness or tardiness of Epimetheus, who had perfectly equipped all breeds of animals but left "man naked"' (*The Animal* 20), later linking this story to a Lacanian notion of lack in which humanity is defined by 'an imperfection, because of an originary lack or defect in man, who has, in sum, received speech and technics only inasmuch as he lacks something' (122). Rather than seeing technology as a sign of human superiority, then, we might reconfigure this story to focus upon humanity's greater vulnerability and reliance on external prostheses. Such a 'modern' reading of the story would focus on Epimetheus's gifts and acknowledge Prometheus's compensatory gift of technology as that which has created the human–animal boundary, and thus has had deleterious effects for humans and animals.

Science and particularly the rise of a modern culture of experimental laboratory practice is one of the primary intersections of human and animal life in modern Western cultures. Animals are an important but often invisible presence in the very constitution of scientific knowledge and thus also central to the conditions informing the emergence of the industrialised, scientifically oriented Western society that gave birth to sf.[1] Galen, whose theories created the tradition of Western medicine, frequently gained anatomical knowledge from the dissection of animals killed in the Roman arena (Kalof 'Introduction' 15), and Albertus Magnus, one of the most important figures in the medieval period, used animal experiments to test the legitimacy of knowledge inherited from Aristotle[2] (Resl 23). Part of this experimental culture tries to understand the moral and legal accountability of animals, and of humans toward animals, and thus many experiments have been interested in assessing the human–animal boundary. Albertus Magnus observed in animals 'human' abilities such as learning, art, speech and so on (De Leemans and Klemm 164), yet these observations did not disincline him from continued experimentation on animals. This moral dilemma continues to inform a research culture in which animals are deemed sufficiently like humans such that results of animal clinical trials will reveal likely outcomes for human patients, yet simultaneously sufficiently unlike humans such that the suffering and death of these animals is not a moral question. The development of Robert Boyle's air pump – an invention whose rigorous testing required reproducible results and their verification by 'neutral' observers, and which is commonly regarded as the emergence of modern experimental scientific practice[3] – demonstrated the creation of vacuum by suffocating small animals for many audiences.

When animals are made prominent in laboratory sites in sf, it is most often the negative consequences of their incorporation into culture that are narrated: these animals become subjects, which allows the sf narratives to supplement, in the Derridean sense, the official discourse of science which recounts their experience only as objects. The marvels of human engineering are less celebrated by the engineered, such as the 'talking intelligent dog' briefly encountered by protagonist Mae in Geoff Ryman's *Air* (2004) who *'asked* to be put back as a dog' (321). Even less invasive experiments, those designed to learn something about the animal's intelligence or behaviour rather than to use its body as a resource for human medicine, offer alienating and frightening encounters for the animal, as Coetzee's Elizabeth Costello points out. Further, such exchanges limit what the animal can be in a laboratory setting and also what human–animal interactions might occur. Discussing an experiment in which bananas are placed out of a primate's reach in order to test his problem-solving abilities, Costello notes how absurd this ordeal must be from the animal's point of view:

> The bananas are there to make one thing, to spur one to the limits of one's thinking. But what must one think? One thinks: Why is he starving me? One thinks: What have I done? Why has he stopped liking me? One thinks: Why does he not want these crates any more? But none of these is the right thought. Even a more complicated thought – for instance: What is wrong with him, what misconception

does he have of me, that leads him to believe it is easier for me to reach a banana hanging from a wire than to pick up a banana from the floor? – is wrong. The right thought to think is: How does one use the crates to reach the bananas? (72–73)

As Costello goes on to note, this bizarre assessment is not only illogical and cruel from the animal's point of view, but it further produces the animal as the sort of subject

driven to think the less interesting thought. From the purity of speculation (Why do men behave like this?) he is relentlessly propelled toward lower, practical, instrumental reason (How does one use this to get that?) and thus towards acceptance of himself as primarily an organism with an appetite that needs to be satisfied. (73)

Ursula Le Guin's 'Mazes' (1975) uses the point of view of an alien experimented upon by humans to make this argument. Unlike the reversal fantasies discussed in the previous chapter in which humans 'wrongly' treated like animals are able either to convey their true capacity to their captors or else escape and return to Earth, the intelligent narrator of this story is trapped in the laboratory environment which increasingly dulls its mental and social capacities. The story opens with the statement, 'I have tried hard to use my wits and keep up my courage, but I know now that I will not be able to withstand the torture any longer' (69–70). To this captive, 'the alien's cruelty is refined, yet irrational. If it intended all along to starve me, why not simply withhold food?', a practice less disorienting than the provision of 'mountains of food, all the greenbud leaves I could possibly want … [but because not fresh] the element that makes them digestible to us was gone, and one might as well eat gravel' (70). The narrator laments the human inability to perceive intelligence in another being, observing that 'we are both maze-builders: surely it would be quite easy to learn to talk together! If that were what the alien wanted. But it is not' (71), going on to explain how mazes are a meanings of embodied, communicative dance for its species. Faced with a complicated maze that will enable expression of the Eighth Maluvian, '[noble] statement of our being', the captive 'work[s] hard at the problem of that maze, planning all night long, re-imagining the lines and spaces, the feints and pauses, the erratic, unfamiliar, and yet beautiful course of the True Run' (72), a performance to which the human observer is blind as he or she is looking for intelligence to be expressed only via taking the shortest route through the maze.[4] The narrator struggles to reconcile its sense that the alien (human) being is intelligent but yet fails to communicate or perceive communication, coming to the conclusion that the tester is 'a solitary creature, totally self-absorbed …[which] would go far to explain its cruelty' (73).

Unlike the human in the story, who continues to perceive intelligence only through performances that mirror its own being, the narrator comes to realise that the tester may be communicating *labially*, a possibility it is willing to concede even though it finds this 'a limited and unhandy language for one so well provided with hands, feet, limbs, flexible spine, and all' (73). Yet this insight is not sufficient to bridge the species gap. As the human moves on to another method of testing that involves electric shocks for wrong choices, the narrator becomes more and more despondent, no longer trying to communicate verbally or in its tactile language of dance, explaining that the narrative we are reading is danced 'of course, in my mind' and that it 'simply crouched there, silent' (75). The story ends with the narrator convinced that the alien species, humans, is 'grossly cruel' (75) and that communication was impossible. Although the human said 'it was sick of torturing me, and wanted me to help it', the narrator's responses go unacknowledged because the human 'did not understand. It has never understood' (76). Like the Le Guin stories discussed in Chapter 3, this one comments on the difficulties of interspecies communication and indicts humans for our blindness to the intelligence and communicative capacities of species who express these in ways other than our own. At the same time, the story builds on the critique of laboratory culture articulated by Costello, suggesting that the very structure of science and its ways of engaging animals produce conditions under which it is impossible for us to see their intelligence, even were we to look for it. As the narrator's increasing despondency suggests, caged laboratory animals quickly lose the will to connect with human experimenters whose presence frequently brings pain. They are not, therefore, occupied for long with the questions set for them to solve by mazes or other trials, but instead 'the question that truly occupies' the primate Costello discusses, 'as it occupies the rat and the cat and every other animal trapped in the hell of the laboratory or the zoo, is: Where is home, and how do I get there?' (Coetzee 75).

William Kotzwinkle's *Doctor Rat* (1971) similarly explores the experimental laboratory from the animal's point of view, in this case that of a laboratory rat who introduces himself as Doctor Rat, explaining that 'it's only right I be given some mark of distinction other than the tattoo on the inside of my ear' (1) because he has been a resident at the laboratory for so long he has learned as much as its students. Doctor Rat identifies entirely with the scientific discourse that grounds the operation of the laboratory, insisting that this role is 'helping my fellow rats to understand the important role they play in global affairs' (3). At the same time, however, the novel frequently draws attention to the suffering of the animals as Doctor Rat describes the procedures in clinical detail that both mimics the language of the methods section of a scientific article and narrates the experience of the test subject, whose existence as a living being rather than merely as another part of the apparatus is glossed over in official scientific discourse. Doctor Rat rallies the rats to take pride in the great enterprise of knowledge creation in which they play a part. Yet, the more he describes experiments, the more the novel's satire emerges, reproducing critiques made by animal-welfare activists regarding things such as the wastefulness of repeating lethal experiments simply for the sake of training students in already-established knowledge. Doctor Rat's dual address to the reader and to the animals he tries to motivate draws attention to the lack of concern for animal suffering that is commonplace in laboratory practice through his dismissive tone which, given his identi- fication with the scientific establishment, stands in for the researchers' attitudes. He chastises a rat for not 'showing the scientific attitude at all' when she complains about the 'hole in [her] stomach' cut to observe her 'embryonic ratlings develop' (15). Similarly, he laments the escape of rabbits 'who were to be boiled alive tomorrow' because it will 'set the government heat-stroke study back terribly. We've got to *continue* verifying facts that were established a hundred years ago. Such verification is essential to national defense' (163).

The narrative shifts between Doctor Rat's explanations of the necessity of the laboratory practice and a rebellion among exploited animals that begins in a stockyard and spreads across the animal world, eventually manifesting in Doctor Rat's laboratory. Doctor Rat is, of course, a loyalist who attempts to thwart the rebels. His responses are used to reiterate the common rationales used to explain the necessity and legitimacy of animal experimentation. The satire is heavy-handed at times, such as Doctor Rat's fervent insistence that 'just because we haven't yet determined the deep significance of stitching two rats together does not mean we won't eventually find out' (35). Doctor Rat's narrative is punctuated with references to the journal articles that publish the results of the particular experiments that he describes in disturbing detail, but these more legitimised descriptions of the purpose of the research are constantly in tension with his anecdotal comments, such as this one which follows a long description of the death of a beagle in a gas chamber: 'If we could understand these differences in resistance to the deadly fumes, we might succeed in producing a better shoe polish for the army. Of course, it will require a great many more beagles, but we've got them, my friends, and the Pentagon's got the funds' (42). Yet the official discourse is equally dismissive of animal suffering, even though it uses abstractions to minimise the affective content, such as this 'excerpt' from a Johns Hopkins study of a cat: 'when her tail was grasped between the jaws of a large surgical clamp and compressed sufficiently to produce a bruise she cried loudly and attempted to escape

... during the 139 days of survival she was subjected, every two or three days, to a variety of noxious stimuli ...' (46, ellipses in original). Other interwoven chapters stress the suffering of animals in other domesticated contexts: the overcrowded battery hens; cattle and pigs moving through slaughterhouse processing lines, fearful and aware; animals in zoos who regard themselves as inmates; whales who have been 'hunted, and their home ... turned into a gigantic toilet' (88). In each instance, as in Le Guin's 'Mazes', the animal narratives indicate attempts to communicate with or seek compassion from the humans, attempts which are ignored – or rather, are not even perceived as such in order to be dismissed.

The novel's conclusion is a harsh condemnation of human cruelty that rivals Swift's misanthropic conclusion to *Gulliver's Travels* (1726) in intensity. The spirit of the revolution has spread to animals across the globe, and they are commonly drawn to a central gathering site where they believe a new interspecies order will emerge. They are convinced that 'man will come too. He will realize that we are all one creature, and he will stop killing us. His realization will be sudden and wonderful' (114). As the gathered animals wait for 'man' to take his place among them, representatives of the US government (who seem to stand in for humanity) discuss the benefits of using the gathering as an opportunity for 'selective harvesting' of herds to achieve 'a dynamic balance of the animal population' (172), as well as the bonus of a chance to test 'new machinery under battlefield conditions' (173). Humans thus arrive at the gathering where the peacefully assembled animals are thrilled that 'the meeting is complete! We'll surge together with man. We'll know the wonderful moments of all hearts beating as one!' (181). Inevitably, their 'gesture of receiving' (181) is met with hails of gunfire and other artillery, and the ensuing descriptions – like earlier ones of laboratory practice – emphasise the animals' disorientation and suffering. The military's glee in the massive slaughter that follows is equally dismissive of animal life and revolutionary consciousness. One general boasts, 'Those pantywaists at Harvard and MIT who protested chemical agents should see what happens when you let a revolution get ahead of you ... I regret a few noncombatants got smoked out. So we killed a few rabbits and some cats. What can I tell you? All these gooks are alike, if you ask me' (187–188). The final word is from Doctor Rat, who finds that he is now the only non-human animal left on Earth. He must leave the laboratory that can no longer serve its purpose without subjects upon whom to experiment and comments that 'the Final Solution gives you a sort of lonely feeling' (215).

The end of the novel thus extends its critique to the ways in which the human–animal boundary has been and continues to be used against certain humans – the Vietnamese (in a conflict contemporary with the novel's publication) and most egregiously those killed during the Holocaust. Yet the earlier portions of the novel which emphasise animal suffering in various human institutions are equally important. The point is that such oppressions overlap and mutually reinforce one another, producing a human subjectivity that requires the expulsion of the animal and thus is incapable of entering in the vision of animal unity proffered by the novel's animal rebellion. This sort of human is Heidegger's *Dasein*, a status of being in which 'man is not simply regarded as part of the world within which he appears and which he makes up in part. Man also stands over against the world. This standing-over-against is a *"having"* of world' (Derrida *The Animal* 152). Part of Heidegger's conception of the animal being poor-in-world is that the animal does not have access to the unconcealing of nature that is the characteristic of technology[5]; it is thus not surprising that the laboratory and scientific method features so strongly in Kotzwinkle's novel, as the set-apart attitude of the impartial scientific investigation is closely related to Heidegger's *Dasein*. Heidegger sees the animal as being deprived of the access to the world which might enable technology, but *Doctor Rat* offers the reversed perspective. Here, it is humans rather than animals who are lacking, failing to receive gifts from Epimetheus and thus requiring technological prosthetics to compensate, thereby producing a way of being-in-the-world that forever cuts them off from fellow creatures. Further, this fetishisation of technology results in the culture that is destroying the world for all species through warfare and polluting industry. As the novel makes clear through Doctor Rat's descriptions of specific experiments, contemporary weapons technology and contemporary manufacturing processes that produce pollution are both traceable directly to experiments on laboratories such as the one in which he lives. This is the unacknowledged dark side of his proud identification with the glories produced by participating in the culture of modern, experimental science.

Just as laboratory conditions produce a reduced notion of animal being, allowing expression to only a fraction of what that animal's subjectivity might be, so too does modern science produce an impoverished version of nature as a whole because 'the part of nature under scrutiny, that nature which can be examined in laboratory conditions under control of the scientist, comes to represent *all* nature for him' (Noske 55). Paul White stresses that animals in Victorian Britain stopped being seen as full organisms in early experimental practice but instead were 'deconstituted and reassembled as components of scientific instruments' (63) as part of a culture that 'transmuted animal subjects into working parts of the experimental apparatus' (65). In many examples of animals in sf texts, the animal subject becomes a product, a technological intervention, a cyborg being that challenges taxonomic divisions among humans, animals and machines. H.G. Wells's *The Island of Doctor Moreau* (1896) is the foundational text in this tradition. Armstrong argues that the novel enacts

> the radical separation of epistemological authority from emotional response, best represented by the scientific requirement for disengagement with affect in the pursuit of empirical objectivity ... [and] the discrediting of the Enlightenment and Romantic valorization of sympathy and sentiment, which will henceforth be banished to the undervalued domains of popular and feminine culture. (92–93)

These linked epistemological moves are instructive for our understanding of the relationship between animals and technology in the emergent culture of science. The novel demonstrates that foundational assumptions of science as a practice that objectifies and 'tames' nature and inextricably all those (non-whites, women, the working classes, as well as animals) who are associated with the body and nature. Thus, the connection Kotzwinkle suggests between militarism, the exploitation of animals in the laboratory and the attacks upon civilian populations in Vietnam are anticipated in the culture of scientific rationalism that Wells dissects.[6]

Brian Aldiss's *Moreau's Other Island* (1980) similarly explores such synergies, telling the story from the point of view of Calvert Madle Roberts, Under-Secretary of State, who is stranded on Mortimer Dart's Moreau-like island during WWIII.[7] Like Prendick in the original novel, Roberts is shocked to discover the monstrosities produced by Dart's research and further by Dart's own grotesque appearance, a consequence of exposure to thalidomide during gestation.[8] Aldiss's novel corresponds to Wells's in many ways – the Beast People of the island have developed a cult of worship around the Master, Dart/Moreau, and chant songs that reflect this training in the proper aspiration to human morphology; Roberts/Prendick, the interloper, sympathises with the experimental subjects and feels increasingly alienated from the doctor's agenda; the social order that structures the island eventually collapses and the Beast People rebel, ending the experimental regime – but it also reverses Wells's novel in significant ways. Most specifically, the Beast People on Dart's island are not animals changed toward human form through surgery, but instead are humans upon whom Dark uses 'only drugs, to change the foetus in the womb' (63), producing birth defects such as flipper-like appendages that caricature animal embodiment. Wells's novel was animated by a concern with degeneration. Moreau argued that he was trying to 'burn out all the animal' in his experimental subjects, but was disappointed to find that the creatures always regress. Thus, like Frankenstein, Moreau turns against his created beings when their material reality does not match his aspirations and he 'turn[s] them out when [he] begin[s] to feel the beast in them' (59) because he can 'see into their very souls, and see there nothing but the souls of beasts' (59). Moreau's goal is to be able to change minds as well as bodies, hypothesising that 'in our growing science of hypnotism we find the promise of a possibility of replacing old inherent instincts by new suggestions, grafting upon or replacing the inherited fixed ideas' (54).

Moreau begins with animal subjects and finds that, despite his abstract ideals about a purified culture, he cannot 'burn out' the animal or supplant 'old inherent instincts' toward carnivorous predation and the like. Yet part of Moreau's error, as Wells is all to clearly aware, is that he exempts humans from the category of animality. When Prendick complains that there is no 'application' to justify the pain Moreau inflicts, Moreau responds that Prendick's perspective is too 'materialist' (54) and contends that

> it is just this question of pain that parts us. So long as visible or audible pain turns you sick, so long as your own pains drive you, so long as pain underlines your propositions about sin, so long, I tell you, you are an animal, thinking a little less obscurely what an animal feels. (54)

Moreau thus reinforces a metaphysics of subjectivity derived from the human–animal boundary, and his easy dismissal of the suffering of others is bound up with the values associated with this construction of subjectivity, the distanced relationship to the world that is characteristic of Heidegger's *Dasein* and of the abstract, scientific attitude which Moreau exemplifies. The novel critiques such a conception of human identity through the contrast between Moreau and Prendick, who at the novel's conclusion finds himself similarly reverting to a beast-like state as he lives alone with the Beast People during the period between the destruction of Moreau's laboratory and Prendick's rescue and return to civilisation. This vision is not one of positive embrace of animal being, however, but rather uses the close connection between humans and animals to satirise humanity. When he returns to civilisation, Prendick finds himself – like Gulliver – unable to 'persuade myself that the men and women I met were not also another, still passably human, Beast People, animals half-wrought into the outward image of human souls; and that they would presently begin to revert, to show first this bestial mark and then that' (102). Ironically, or perhaps, fittingly, the very practice of vivisection – and it is for excesses in such procedures and the resultant scandal that Moreau retreated to the island in the first place – may in fact provoke this so-called bestial aspect of humanity to emerge. Contemporary anti-vivisectionist advocates argued that 'the performance and witnessing of vivisection, increasingly common in medical education by the 1870s, eroded human sympathy and unleashed brutal passions, with practitioners undergoing a process of zoomorphism in the laboratory as bestial instincts were unleashed through the repeated and prolonged infliction of pain on helpless creatures' (White 70).

On one level, Aldiss's novel is even more removed from a concern with animal being since his Beast People are modified humans rather than animals. Like Prendick, Roberts is concerned with the consequences of the experimental programme, but his apprehensions have to do with control of the technology rather than the suffering that its discovery entails. As a senior member of the White House staff, Roberts is quick to see that 'what [Dart] was doing might possibly be of value to the world', but he concludes at the same time that 'he must immediately be prevented from doing it' because 'all knowledge was valuable; only in the wrong hands was it destructive, and Dart's were decidedly wrong hands' (66). However, the more time Roberts spends with Dart and with the Beast People, the more he begins to realise that there is no difference between the war efforts he supports and the megalomaniac attitudes he sees promulgated by Dart, and the more he begins to develop a sense of compassion and connection to other living things and thus to see that they do offer another and less destructive way of construing subjectivity. By the time Roberts is confronted with the fact that Dart's funding comes from the US government – and hence his own threats to 'expose' the operation are futile – he is no longer willing to endorse the research programme, even if its results are kept in the 'right' hands. Roberts plans to expose not only Dart but the entire government for its financing of such radical research once he returns to his office where he will have access to the secret files on this and similar projects 'subsidised by the tax-payer, … [that] had to be kept secret from him because of their dreadful nature' (108). The true site of horror, Roberts realises, is not the island's research laboratory but rather the file in which 'lived Moreau's other island, a doppelganger of the real island, a tidy little utopia docketed into paragraphs and subheads. It would make dry legal sense. It would be an abstract. And there would be neatly entered figures, with all columns carefully balanced by accountants once a year' (145).

Although the beings in Aldiss's novel are not animals, the human–animal boundary is nonetheless integral to the novel's themes. The separation of mind from body in Descartes's *cogito*, which is also the separation of human being from animal being, is accomplished by a similar abstraction from sensual material reality, the calculative, rationalised version of subjectivity which produces a culture of Moreau's other islands. Thinking about being – life and death – through such abstractions is what enables the sort of calculations about acceptable causalities and

the like that produce the rational absurdities of military logic. Dart and
his supporters partake of a similar logic, and Roberts comes to regret his
own complicity in such systems: 'in a flash of terror, I saw myself back
in Washington, turning up the Moreau file, issuing my blanket condem-
nations – only to find my own rubber-stamp signature on the original
authorisation ...' (149, ellipses in original). Coetzee stresses in *Elizabeth
Costello* that our shared vulnerability with animals, the fact that both we
and they will experience death, is both a ground for connection to other
species and an opportunity to rethink aspects of human subjectivity. Our
common material embodiment as animal beings, the aspect of human
existence that Moreau tries to deny through testing 'the plasticity of living
forms' (Wells *Moreau* 53), should be valued for its ability to draw us back
from the power of abstraction, from this other island:

> The knowledge we have is not abstract – 'all human beings are
> mortal, I am a human being, therefore I am mortal' – but embodied.
> For a moment we *are* that knowledge. We live the impossible: we live
> beyond our death, look back on it, yet look back as only a dead self
> can. (Coetzee 77)

Wolfe further reminds us that humans are 'always radically other ... in
our subjection to and constitution in the materiality and technicity of a
language that is always on the scene before we are, as a precondition of our
subjectivity' ('Introduction' 27). The technological mastery and abstract
reason emblematised by Dart and the government which funds him are
misrecognitions of the nature of human being and endorse a destructive
relationship to life in general. They emerge from a laboratory culture of
instrumental relations and thus are an example of the sort of calculative
'firm knowledge, certainty, and assurance' (Derrida *The Animal* 126) which
Derrida suggests marks the failure of ethics.

A similar critique is suggested by Aldiss's novel. Dart's work is ultimately
aimed at the production of gnome-like creatures called SRSRs, the Stand-
by Replacement Sub-Race, who are 'immune to certain radiations lethal
to us, gestate in only seven months, mature early, bulk less, consume less
food, less oxygen. All telling plus-factors in the sort of catastrophe scenario
they are designed for' (153). The SRSRs are deemed necessary because the
cost of winning the war will be high and 'a world of want is going to result'
(154). The SRSRs can

> take over the enormous tasks of reconstruction. They are already
> receiving indoctrination in Co-Allied aims. They will be less
> vulnerable to radiation than the rest of us, will propagate faster, will
> consume less supplies because of their smaller bulk. They are, in fact,
> our survival kit for the future; they may even replace us. And even if

the picture isn't as gloomy as I have painted it, then we'll find other uses for them. Waste not, want not. The SRSRs would be ideal as crews for spaceships. (154)

Moreau's Other Island, like *Doctor Rat*, connects the instrumental attitude demonstrated toward other species in laboratory practice with an embrace of military technology and an ambition for conquest that threatens all life on Earth. The SRSRs function, as do animals, as both an analogue for human being and a distinctly different and 'inferior' category of being that might be subjected to dangerous conditions, their lives subordinated to human ends. The opening and closing sections of the novel offer a perspective on human activity that emerges from the ocean's depths, associated with animal consciousness. This perspective is beyond the petty struggles of human warfare and represents a state of being that will persist beyond the time of 'man'. In the opening chapter, this voice notes 'their actions were full of sound and fury. They had just launched themselves into a global war which threatened to lay waste much of the land area, besides bringing about their own extinction' (8), and in the concluding chapter it contrasts human reason with human instinct, suggesting *'until humanity comes to an armistice between these yin-yang factors, there is no armistice possible on Earth. The bombs will fall'* (174).

Unlike Wells, Aldiss does not present this risk as an outcome of human degeneration: instead, it is reason that *'invented the twenty-four hour clock'* which represents the threat, while instinct, *'which keeps to its own Great Time'* (174), suggests a less damaging connection to animality and the abiding presence of this voice. Yet the novel does not transcend the human–animal boundary entirely. Its conclusion laments the destructive qualities of human being, but still feels that the only hope for the future lies with humanity and the question of whether its *'instinct for survival would impel it to find a way to permanent peace. Otherwise, all would be lost. For the ocean was ultimately no more enduring than Instinct alone, or unaided Reason'* (174). Kotzwinkle's novel combined a critique of militarised instrumental reason with a concern for animal being and the suffering of human and animal subjects in the world it produces. Aldiss's focus remains on humanity, offering a critique of its failings and the spectre that it will destroy life on Earth through nuclear war, but his concern is limited, in the final analysis, to fearing the inevitable end to human life that such a tragedy would imply. *The Island of Doctor Moreau* links its critique of human subjectivity to institutions of science and their instrumentalised attitude towards living beings; similarly *Moreau's Other Island* connects problematic aspects of human culture to government institutions and their rationalised abstraction of a concrete, material world into paragraphs and subheadings, columns and calculations. They share a common concern with the operation of the human–animal boundary to secure an ethical distinction between those who might be treated as expendable and those whose subjectivity must be respected, and further with the prospect that such a model of human subjectivity dooms humanity, a concern more distantly – and slightly differently – shared by Wells in his frequent exploration of evolutionary themes and their implication that *Homo sapiens*, too, is a species that will evolve into and be displaced by other life. Kotzwinkle and Aldiss, however, connect their concern with the value of the human to metaphysical rather than morphological features, thereby aligning their themes with the scholars such as Hayles and Haraway, who suggest that enabling possibilities are attached to the cultural and philosophical 'evolution' of the human into another mode of construing subjectivity, a posthumanism that renounces anthropocentrism.

The technological manipulation of other species into forms that might be called post-animal – created beings who function as laboratory tools such as knock-out gene mice, animal species adjusted by genetic pharming techniques so that they produce substances useful for humans, and similar biotechnological artefacts – also find their way into sf depictions of animals and technology. Such biotechnological modifications can be used to demonstrate that the human–animal boundary is permeable, such as Bruce McAllister's 'The Girl Who Loved Animals' (1988), about a woman who serves as a surrogate for an extinct gorilla foetus. McAllister makes clear that the surrogate mother, Lissy, is as much a victim of the modernist social order that has caused extinctions as are the animal species, most of whom survive only as media records. Lissy has few financial or other prospects beyond the surrogacy contract, but she makes clear that her own motivation is, as the story's title notes, her love of animals: her desire to connect with another species that might love her back. She is the victim of an abusive relationship and her surrogacy symbolises her protest against a culture in which social relationships have all but disappeared, substituted by technological interfaces that allow humans to escape from the damaged world they have produced and retreat into more pleasing VR simulations. McAllister's depiction of this world that has squeezed out animal being through 'the toxics, the new diseases, the land-use policies' (90) highlights both the consequences for animal subjects and what humans lose through the production of a planet that leaves no space for life other than our own.

F. Paul Wilson's *Sims* (2003) similarly focuses on legal issues surrounding the ethical standing of beings who transgress the human–animal boundary. The novel begins with a 'chilling' Author's Note that warns it is set 'just around the corner, timewise, in your town, your country, your world', going on to somewhat paradoxically announce that the novel 'may seem like science fiction, but it isn't' because 'someone somewhere is altering a chimpanzee's genome to make it more human. *Right now*'. The novel is concerned with the human–animal boundary being challenged and potentially rewritten by the techniques of genetic engineering more strongly than it is concerned with animal being and the nature of the relationship between human and animal subjects. *Sims* thus shares the perspective of biotechnology critic Jeremy Rifkin who, in a project with biologist Stuart Newman, created a series of laboratory protocols to create a human/mouse chimera named Humouse™. These protocols were submitted to the US Patent Office in 1997 'in an attempt to force the legislative hand of the federal government on the question of patenting of human life' (Rader 128). Such work draws attention to the biological links between humans and other species and invites ethical scrutiny of the practices of genetic engineering which create beings, many of whose lives are filled with suffering such as the first knock-gene animal being, OncoMouse™ – made famous by Haraway's analysis.[9] At the same time, the anxieties surrounding the application of genetic engineering techniques specifically to human life reinforces rather than challenges the human–animal boundary. Such work does point to the complexities of this boundary and enable us to think about the perplexing ethics required for the material world of multispecies relations in which we live.

Sims is about a struggle over the legal status of the genetically modified chimpanzees, sims, who form the bulk of the manual labour force in this future. A certain group of sims who work at a golf club have asked lawyer, Patrick, to help them unionise: 'They weren't asking for wages, not for anything material, they just wanted a little personal continuity in their lives ... the right to keep certain close-knit groups of sims from being broken up ... allowed to live together and work together ... as a make-shift family of sorts ...' (19, ellipses in original). As Patrick begins to work on the sims' case, he is drawn into a conspiracy, a thriller plot that gradually reveals a secret of the sims' origin. The possibility that sim labour organisation is a diversion turns upon the identity of the mysterious Zero, who funds Patrick's legal work, and upon the reason for the rift between brothers Mercer and Ellis Sinclair, the inventors of the laboratory protocols that produce the sims (and the owners of all sims who are leased to their employers). Patrick combines forces with Romy, an animal-welfare advocate who investigates abusive uses of sims in contexts such as prostitution, which enables a number of scenes in the novel to provide a rich background picture of how sims are integrated into human social existence in exploitative ways, mistreatments often shared by animals, such as the use of sims in baiting entertainments. The sims are given a voice in the novel as well, characterised as gentle and simple folk

whose ambitions do not extend beyond wanting more humane treatment
while they keep 'their place'; they uncomfortably resemble caricatures of
'faithful' slaves in antebellum Southern literature.

The sims are treated as if they fall clearly on the animal side of the
human–animal boundary. They can be protected from certain kinds of
abuse, as can many animals under animal welfare legislation, but their
status as owned beings who have no right to self determination is never
questioned. This is notwithstanding the fact that, as Zero points out,
sims are chimpanzees who have some human genes spliced into them
to increase their intelligence and utility for labour, and hence are more
properly understood as human–animal chimera rather than strictly as
animals. Although the sims' disenfranchisement is emphasised from
the first pages of the novel – and many scenes critique acts of discrimination routinely practiced against them – the trajectory of the novel moves
steadily toward a greater concern with their potential human qualities,
beginning with a search for a sim who has been impregnated by a human
– prompting Patrick to insist that their legal status must be changed from
Pan Sinclairis to *Homo simians* (287) – and culminating in the revelation
that they are not chimpanzees who have been more 'highly' evolved by
the addition of human DNA, but rather humans who have been 'devolved'
via chimpanzee DNA. Zero is the original test subject whose linguistic
skills and intelligence proved to be 'not only far above sim average but
above human average as well' (412). All other sims were derived from
his genetic material, but he was to have been destroyed because his too-
human appearance would never be acceptable to the public.

As in Kotzwinkle's and Aldiss's novels, the real enemy is the US
military who funded the sim research, looking for a way to produce near-
human super soldiers who might more readily be sacrificed in battle. Thus,
questions of labour politics and of animal welfare are abandoned in the
novel's conclusion. The 'good' Sinclair brother – who ceased participation
in the corporation as soon as he learned the truth of the sims' origin,
and who has remained silent only to protect his family from government
violence – confesses that the dream of an intermediary between human
and animal is illusive, the 'Quixotic quest to develop a true chimp-
origin sim to replace the human-origin sim in circulation' having proved
'impossible' (473). The conclusion thus evades resolving the complicated
issues it earlier raised both about the existence of a problematic third
term between what is conceived of as a binary division between human
and animal, and also about the ethical status of beings such as the sims.
Further, the horror the novel attempts to evoke based on the revelation
that sims are 'really' human is even more conservative in its automatic
presumption that the abuses that have been documented throughout

become more heinous in retrospect when one realises the suffering beings were once genetically human. *Sims* fails to engage the challenging ethical questions it provokes, but it is nonetheless instructive in its performance of contemporary anxieties about labour, the human–animal boundary and the prospects for military research in an era of biopolitics. Few of its passages are set within the laboratory itself and therefore, although the novel shares a concern with *Doctor Rat* and *Moreau's Other Island* about the intersections of scientific research and military application, it does not directly link its themes to a critique of the instrumental attitude toward animals (and often people) that permeates the culture of science.

None of these novels effectively address the thorny moral question of how to balance concern for animal welfare with the potential benefits – to humans but sometimes to other species as well – that emerge from laboratory practice on animal bodies. *Doctor Rat* in particular emphasises only the futility of research depicted as tortuous, done to confirm what is already known and perhaps even, the novel suggests, to indulge the sadism of the scientist. *Moreau's Other Island* critiques specific research agendas (and, in the final analysis, the sort of world such priorities imply), but leaves aside the more troublesome question of whether (and when) research using animals as test subjects might be justified; *Sims* is merely a conspiracy thriller. In contrast, Haraway's thinking on these matters is careful to resist the seductive appeal of easy binaries and a tendency to condemn all animal research as exploitative. She argues that the research practice itself is not 'the enemy', but rather a failure to see that laboratory animals are 'somebody as well as something, just as we humans are both subject and object all the time' (*When Species Meet* 76). In her view, laboratory research that involves animal subjects is an inescapable part of the material, multispecies world in which we live, and our transformative efforts should resist a culture of science in which such interactions are based on 'unidirectional relations of use, ruled by practices of calculation and self-sure of hierarchy' (71). She calls instead for a laboratory culture of what she terms 'nonmimetic sharing' (75): that acknowledges the animals' suffering for research as suffering and requires us 'to recognize copresence in relations of use' (76). We must struggle with the material, ethical choices of laboratory practice which includes at times killing animals, instead of retreating into a calculative morality in which experimental science is either 'good' (in which case, the experience of animals under its regimes is irrelevant) or 'bad' (and hence never justified, no matter the medical benefits for humans and non-humans alike).

Haraway's invocation of 'nonmimetic sharing' requires a vision of laboratory practice that goes beyond mere sympathy for the animals that is evident in some of the texts discussed in this chapter, and she links her ideal of another kind of laboratory culture in which 'mattering is always inside connections that demand and enable response, not bare calculations or ranking' (70–71), a new vision of ethics similar to Derrida's. Thus, minimising cruelty or rejecting 'unnecessary' research that simply reproduces the known are laudable efforts to reduce animal suffering, but they are not enough. They do not take us beyond a predetermined human–animal boundary in which it is always possible to argue that a sufficient benefit to human health and welfare automatically justifies animal suffering, an automaticity that emerges from the persisting hierarchy between human and animal that underpins such welfare advocacy. Part of what shapes Haraway's vision is her sense that we are all, human and animal, living in a world of 'webbed existences, multiple beings in relationship' (72) in which animals as well as humans stand to benefit from the knowledge gained by experiment. She suggests that rather than regarding laboratory animals as simply instruments (as does traditional science) or – the mere reverse – as victims, we should instead understand them as 'significantly unfree partners' (72) in the shared production of knowledge. Animals may be unwilling partners in such research, but they are not mute and passive equipment entirely subject to the experimenters' will. Instead they can and do express agency in laboratory situations, agency that could – if acknowledged as such and taken seriously – move research practice in new and unanticipated directions. Beginning from the premise that animal lives matter as well, we could envision a laboratory practice that is less wasteful of animal lives, less nonchalant about their suffering, more willing to extend the benefits of research to improving animal as well as human lives and more willing to allow humans as well as animals to be experimental test subjects. If this last suggestion shocks some readers, this reaction is testament to the continued power of the human–animal boundary to structure the horizon of our understandings of subjectivity and ethics. Haraway does not feel a simple moratorium on killing is realistic or sufficient, but neither does she suggest that once we admit that animals are subjects and nonetheless continue to kill them that any sort of killing goes. Instead, she argues, 'it is a misstep to pretend to live outside killing … the misstep of forgetting the ecologies of all mortal beings, who live in and through the use of one another's bodies' (79); thus, she contends, 'it is not killing that gets us into exterminism, but making beings killable' (80), that is, refusing to take responsibility for the killing and suffering we cause by positing a moral system in which such sacrifices are not morally relevant.

Haraway adds necessary complexity to our thinking about these matters, but does not suggest a clear path forward. She does not deny that experimental practice often causes pain and killing, and is aware that even under transformed conditions this will remain. She insists that 'these practices should never leave their practitioners in moral comfort, sure of their righteousness' (75), but the idea that the same practices might simply go on within a new framework seems frustratingly inadequate. Yet this frustration is precisely the point, the reality of the multispecies, material, contingent world of mutual obligation and competition in which we live. In advocating for a more caring and responsible laboratory practice, Haraway insists that we remember that we cannot achieve a position of innocence, that 'none of this makes the word *wicked* go away' (82). At the same time, however, she believes we need to balance the 'wicked' of laboratory practice with the 'wicked' of other suffering – both human and animal – through disease, environmental degradation and other conditions that laboratory practice at times aims to ameliorate. This means thinking about laboratory practice and laboratory agents – human and animal – in more complex terms, and evaluating research practice in terms of their ability to contribute toward a more just world for all beings. Justifications for research require rationales that balance human and animal needs in setting priorities for research, require experimental design that enables the test subjects to live their lives as fully as possible within the parameters of the experiment and require taking seriously the question of whether the research will benefit animals as well as humans.[10]

Companion-species approaches to laboratory practice '*must* actually engage in cosmopolitics, articulating bodies to some bodies and not others, nourishing some worlds and not others, and bearing the mortal consequences. Respect is *respecere* – looking back, holding in regard, understanding that meeting the look of the other is a condition of having face oneself' (Haraway *When Species Meet* 88). The contingent world of shared suffering and, at times, necessary killing is much more difficult to negotiate than the comfortable world of the human–animal boundary in which animals are regarded as only objects (and hence we do not have to question any of our laboratory practices); but it is also more difficult to negotiate than the equally comfortable reversal in which regarding animals as subjects automatically requires an end to all laboratory practice (thereby denying the benefits science has brought to some animals and some humans, and failing to distinguish among experiments and among animals). If regarding animals as unequal partners does not take us far enough in entangling some of the knots of our entwined experience – and I do think Haraway's formulations tend to minimise the massively unequal power relations between humans and animals which structure all our interactions with other species most especially in the laboratory – this position nonetheless offers a direction forward. Companion species, recall, is an ideal of both species transformed by the interactions: thus the humans who approach their research from this new perspective of taking seriously the animal as a subject and seeing the killing and pain caused by their work as wicked, if perhaps also necessary, will not be the same humans as those involved in current laboratory culture. Whether or not posthuman laboratories will transform this interspecies space remains to be seen.

Haraway points specifically to sf as a tool that enables us to think about – and hence bring into being through practice – a laboratory culture based not on instrumental relations between humans and animals, but grounded in a relation of companion species, which recognises that the other deserves caring and compassion, and is a partner, if often an unequal one, in a shared enterprise:

> our debt is just opening up to speculative and so possible material, affective, practical reworlding in the concrete and detailed situation of here, in this tradition of research, not everywhere all the time. This 'here' might be quite big, even global, if abstractions are really well built and full of grappling hooks for connections. Maybe sf worlding – speculative fiction and speculative fact – is the language I need. (*When Species Meet* 93)

Olaf Stapledon's *Sirius* (1944) offers one example of how such sf worlding can cultivate our understanding of a laboratory subject as a companion being with an emotional and intellectual life as fully complex as, if different from, our own. The novel tells the life story of a created dog named Sirius, who is given speech and enhanced cognitive capabilities through the combination of selective breeding and a series of surgeries. Perhaps more importantly, his creator, Trelone, raises Sirius as part of a human family, feeling that 'it was very important to bring him up not as a pet but as a person, as an individual who would in due season live an active and independent life' (21). Sirius is educated alongside Trelone's daughter, Plaxy, and they develop a life-long bond that changes them both into companion species in Haraway's terms, both human and non-human becoming something other in the exchange: Sirius is clearly more than an 'ordinary' dog given the modifications to this body and his humanised socialisation, but Plaxy is equally something other than an 'ordinary' girl as a result of her long interaction with Sirius. When she is an adult, Plaxy explains 'I am not just a girl. I am different from all the other girls. I am Plaxy. And Plaxy is half of Sirius-Plaxy, needing the other half. And the other half needs me' (171). Yet, although both Plaxy and Sirius are changed by their interactions, they are confronted with the incompatibility between their subjectivity and the dominant culture in which they must live, a conflict which propels the novel to its tragic end. Plaxy in particular struggles against her love for Sirius and desire to have a life with him, and impulses that she ascribes not to herself but to 'the female human animal' (10). She continually insists that she is more than this reaction, striving for the intersubjective response that she associated with the pronoun 'I' and is the part of her that can embrace life with Sirius. Yet because humans are social animals and the society in which Sirius and Plaxy find themselves is unwilling to extend its concept of subjectivity to Sirius, the two are isolated and their connection suffers from this pressure.

The story is told by Robert, who becomes Plaxy's partner by its end, displacing Sirius in her heart and her life. Robert had known Sirius and Plaxy in their youth and thus he is not shocked to encounter the thinking and speaking dog: he is shocked, however, to discover the extent of Plaxy and Sirius's relationship, which is physical as well as emotional. But he is careful 'not to betray my revulsion' (169) as he correctly perceives that he will have better success policing Plaxy back into a conforming middle-class morality with kindness than with condemnation. Robert sees himself as rescuing Plaxy from a depraved existence with Sirius, but he also comes to respect that Sirius, too, realises the futility of their love and encourages Robert to take his place for her sake. The novel traces the inevitable separation of Plaxy and Sirius, in large part because miscegenation across the species line is a violation of taboo too powerful to be countered. Yet before this anticipated conclusion, the novel raises questions about interspecies relations and challenges both the moral order that requires the separation between humans and animals and the nature of human subjectivity and sociality that is erected on this foundation. Although Sirius and Plaxy both aver the requirement that they cannot live as lovers within contemporary British society, they never allow that this prohibition is anything other than arbitrary convention. When Sirius concedes, for example, that they both need sexual partners of their own species, he realises that Plaxy, 'being human, and a girl and in England, and middle class, ... can't *merely* have lovers and an illegitimate litter ... [but] must have a husband' (146). Yet this concession to necessity is a pragmatic one, not a capitulation to this moral order. Although Robert, and perhaps many readers, view Sirius and Plaxy's relationship as an aberration, the novel does not resolve its moral dilemmas so simply.

Dogs' capacity for social relations is elaborated throughout the text and is frequently contrasted with human failure to allow a place for Sirius within our social community. Trelone works on a number of species in his initial experiments, but he ultimately settles upon dogs because they 'excelled in social awareness', although he acknowledges that at present 'the dog's sociality involved, in relation to man, abject servility' (16). Trelone believes that raising Sirius as a social equal will compensate for this problem, although he stresses that 'one could not treat a puppy precisely as a baby without violating its nature. Its bodily organization was too different from the baby's' (19). Stapledon skilfully characterises Sirius's youth by acknowledging the ways in which he and Plaxy learn together, while at the same time paying attention to the specific capacities that differentiate the species as well. Yet these differences never serve as grounds for a hierarchy: Plaxy has better eyesight and excels at tasks which required manual dexterity, while Sirius is frustrated by the lesser functionality of his mouth for manipulating objects;[11] Sirius gains mobility much more quickly than Plaxy and his superior sense of smell enables him to perceive aspects of reality Plaxy misses. Plaxy and Sirius are also characterised as true companion species, both learning ways of being in the world that neither would have developed had they not been raised together as social equals – although Plaxy's tendency to navigate via smell does 'outrage the family's notions of propriety' (22–23). Trelone believes that 'a dog with human intelligence, brought up to respect itself, would probably not be servile at all, and might quite well develop a superhuman gift for true social relations' (20), and this does prove the case during Sirius's youth.

Yet as Sirius ages, experiences more of the human social world and bears the brunt of its prejudice, his capacity for sociality is thwarted and begins to transform into resentment. In this way, *Sirius* draws upon the familiar tale of *Frankenstein* and its creature's failure to find a place in the human social world. Like the creature, Sirius finds that his isolation and the unwarranted rejection he experiences cause him to reassess his admiration for humans and even his desire to be part of their society.[12] He observes that

> since [humans] thought he was 'only an animal', they often gave themselves away badly in his presence. When they were observed by others of their kind, they maintained the accepted standard of conduct, and were indignant if they caught anyone falling short of that standard; but when they thought they were not being watched, they would commit the very same offences themselves. (83)

He experiences abuse at the hands of humans who believe him incapable of reporting such malice and is shocked when he travels to London and sees the vast social and economic inequities among humans. On more than one occasion, humans try to shoot him, but it is only his own violent retaliation against them that is considered a crime. He increasingly comes to feel 'stifled by the surrounding herd of the grotesque super-simians who had conquered the Earth, moulded the canine species as they trimmed their hedges, and produced his unique self' (103) and concludes that the world's ills are 'all due to man's horrible selfishness ... *Homo sapiens* was an imperfectly socialized species, as its own shrewder specimens, for instance

H.G. Wells, had pointed out' (104). Sirius develops the gift for 'true social relations' that Trelone anticipated, but unfortunately finds most of the human species lacking in a similar capacity for sociality, particularly in relation to subjectivities that are not identical to their own. Losing respect for humans, Sirius retreats into the wilderness, lamenting, 'What a species to rule a planet! And so obtuse about everything that wasn't human! So incapable of realizing imaginatively any *other* kind of spirit than the human!' (106).

In another parallel with Frankenstein's creature, Sirius is without community; he realises 'there is no place for me in man's world, and there is no other world for me. There is no place for me anywhere in the universe', to which Plaxy responds, 'wherever I am there is always a place for you. I'm your home, your footing in the world. And I'm – your wife, your dear constant bitch' (184). Yet, just as Frankenstein refused to create a female companion for his creature because he saw their race as competitors for possession of the planet, not as fellow beings with whom we might share it, so too does Plaxy's society refuse to allow a space for Sirius. He is subject to increasing harassment as rumours about Plaxy and him begin to spread, including mutilation of the livestock for whom Sirius serves as shepherd, reflecting the disrespectful attitude to other life that Sirius concludes is the essence of human existence. Despite their differences in embodiment, Sirius comes to believe that all sentient creatures share a potentiality that he calls 'spirit', that quality he castigates humans for failing to recognise in any species but their own. He is frustrated by his work as a shepherd because although he manages the herd and thus does 'a man's work', nonetheless such manual labour 'does deaden the mind. And the mind – is *me*. I'm not human, but I'm also not canine. Fundamentally I'm just the sort of thing you are yourself. I have a canine clothing, just as you have a human clothing, but *I* – I am ... a spirit, just as you are' (77).

Sirius comes to believe that his particular subjectivity – possessing spirit as do humans but also possessing a greater capacity for sociality – gives him unique insight that could serve as the foundation for a better world. He explains that he needs to do more than simply care for the sheep because

> I feel I have my *own* active contribution to make to – well to human understanding. I can't be just a passive subject for experiments, or at best a tenth-rate research worker. There's something I *must* get clear in my own mind, and when I have got it clear, then I must get it across somehow to mankind. (91)

Sirius's epiphany is that 'if you serve the spirit you can't serve any other master' and that, since the spirit demands 'love and intelligence and strong creative action in its service', serving the spirit enables a perception of all living beings as fellow subjects, not as objects. Such an insight enables Sirius to experience 'love of the sheep as individuals to be made the most of, not *merely* as mutton ... but as individual vessels of the spirit. *That* spirit – love, intelligence, and creating – is precisely what "the spirit" is' (144). Sirius thus offers a vision of a future world of interspecies relation that delivers on the promise Haraway sees in the practice she calls 'sf worlding', a community open to 'possible material, affective, practical reworlding' (Haraway *When Species Meet* 93). Were humans as capable of perceiving the spirit and thus of sharing the planet with beings radically other than ourselves, this world would have had room for Sirius and for his relationship with Plaxy. Instead, the novel ends with Sirius's death: he is shot by a mob of humans who hunt him after he repeats the trajectory of Frankenstein's creature and turns against a humanity who spurned him – in Sirius's case committing the taboo not only of killing a human but also feeding from the corpse. Sirius knowingly goes to his death, recognising that this world will never have a space for him. In the novel's final pages, Plaxy reflects that Sirius had 'epitomized in his whole life and in his death something universal, something that is common to all awakening spirits on earth, and in the farthest galaxies' (187). Sirius leaves an artistic work, a musical composition that humans can perceive as beautiful but which embodies choices that no human composer would make. The music is a materialisation of Sirius's capacity to see the world otherwise, a concrete artefact of the potentiality of alterity. Plaxy says this music is illuminated by 'a brilliance which Sirius had called "colour"' (187), a quality neither human nor canine 'had ever clearly seen, the light that never was on land or sea, and yet is glimpsed by the quickened mind everywhere' (188).

Although *Sirius* ends in tragedy, the hope remains that this quality of spirit that human, canine and other beings share will continue to grow in sentient beings who may find new ways to form community. Like the posthuman subject who anticipates a state of becoming that opens up new possibilities for subjectivity and sociality, Sirius is a 'postanimal' – a non-human sentient being who is presented as an 'awakening spirit' by the novel's conclusion, an anticipation of better things to come. A non-instrumental relationship with the other – one capable of recognising difference without collapsing into a subject/object binary; one capable of perceiving that at times interspecies relationships involve killing but that sheep can be loved nonetheless as *more than* mutton – is the key to this possible new world. James T. Tiptree Jr. arrives at a similar, if perhaps more pessimistic, conclusion in her story 'The Psychologist Who Wouldn't Do Awful Things to Rats' (1976), a story which reveals the dehumanising effects of instrumental laboratory regimes for their human perpetrators.[13]

Tilly, the story's protagonist, struggles in his job as a researcher because he cannot discipline himself into thinking of the laboratory rats as objects. As he walks through the space, he cannot help but notice their 'packed' cages and 'bloody heads', and feels disappointed by the gap between his fascination with 'the intricate interrelated delicacies of living matter' (673) and the actual protocols he is allowed to investigate. At a disastrous meeting with the supervisor of his grant, he is unable successfully to rationalise the research he wants to do regarding rat emotion and learning into some direct application that immediately serves humans.

Tiptree stresses other gaps: between the language of experimental science and the social life Tilly perceives in the rats; between the long-term behaviourial research he wants to conduct and the short-term protocols dominant in this setting; between Tilly's observations of the rats as social beings, and the horrific procedures to which their bodies are subjected in experimental practice; in short, between Tilly's desire for 'some kind of understanding, helpful attitude toward the organism, toward life' and the actual investigations he sees about him, characterised by hostile and rather redundant work: 'Testing animals to destruction' (678). Like Sirius, Tilly longs for another model of interspecies relations, one that would enable other emergent behaviours to come to the fore. The story relentlessly confronts the reader with the very different social order that is Tilly's reality: the laboratory animals starved over the holidays as no one wants to come in to feed and water them; the shipment of stray cats from the pound destined for experiments, one of whom has 'a red collar' (679); the dietary restrictions that produce malnourished and anxious rats; the seemingly endless killings as rats are sacrificed and transformed into data in spreadsheets; the 'cage of baby rabbits with their eyes epoxyed shut' (681). Against this culture, he realises, 'his tiny, doomed effort to ... what? To live amicably and observantly with another species?' (681, ellipses in the original) begins to seem crazy, even to him. The contradictions of this denial of sociality do seem to drive Tilly crazy, in the sense of producing a break with consensual reality, a consensus that denies subjectivity to all species but humans and thus one he cannot endorse. Ordered to kill all his rats and begin a new research project, he is tormented by their 'trustfully expectant' (682) response to his approach and begins to fantasise about a reversed species hierarchy: 'Jones having his brain reamed by a Dachshund pup. A kitten in a surgical smock shaving Sheila' (682). He finally motivates himself to disregard the animals' pain by recalling that people 'didn't think my people's pain mattered either, in the death camps a generation back. It's all the same, endless agonies going up unheard from helpless things' (683). In failing to feel empathy with animal life, Tilly risks his ability to feel empathy with life at all.

Tilly has a dream of an animal being he calls the Rat King who offers him a vision of united human and animal being, the recognition that 'I am an animal, too!' (684). This vision gives him a peaceful sense of unity with other beings, but a voice that he characterises as 'his human voice' (686) calls him back with the knowledge 'only it isn't real' (687). As he feels the animal presence recede, he is left trapped 'in a clockwork Cartesian world in which nothing will mean anything forever' (687). And in this loss of connection to animal being, Tilly loses his compassion for others – human and animal alike – as well as his fascination with the living, complex, continually becoming quality of life itself. He emerges from the dream and now sees the animals with hatred, and is thus able to quickly kills his test subjects and to plan his new research project – using 'electrodes that will make an animal increase the intensity of whatever it's doing. Like say, *running*' (688) – to secretly manipulate race horses and make his fortune. The drastic reversal of the story's conclusion is jarring and its implications extreme. Yet considered in the context of massive species extinctions caused largely by human activity and of contemporary technoscience which has created and patented living beings as laboratory tools, this utter alienation from and contempt for other species does not seem so implausible. The genius of Tiptree's work is that she suggests all the more strongly than does Stapledon the tremendous costs to human being and culture of a human subjectivity that cannot imagine a way of living amicably, at the very least, with another species.

Conclusion

'Other Fashionings of Life':
Science Fiction, Human–Animal Studies
and the Future of Subjectivity

Frank Schatzing's huge, best-selling novel *The Swarm* (2004, English translation 2006) at first seems to be about animal revolt against human domination, and its multiply plotted tale echoes scenarios of earlier sf. Scientists, ethologists and animal-rights activists across the globe notice that the planet seems to have turned against human occupation: the weather system disasters associated with climate change are exacerbated by new forms of marine life that seem to attack and destroy human installations such as offshore oil derricks, and new forms of species regularly consumed by humans transmit a fatal virus. Whales and dolphins being observed by human researchers seem to return the scrutiny, and eventually attack boats of human tourists and fishermen. Pro-environmental groups war with pro-industry groups in seeking to explain this changed behaviour, while protagonists of various disciplinary backgrounds haphazardly assembled into a crisis-response team debate the possibilities of animal sentience and consciousness. The seemingly unrelated incidents begin to look like a conspiracy, a sense that 'the world is changing ... closing ranks against us. Somewhere something has been decided, and we weren't part of it. Humanity wasn't there' (313). What is particularly frightening is that this is more than just the revenge of a single species but instead betrays 'Alliances. Strategies' (394) among species, as well as an ability to grasp long-term relations of cause and effect and conduct attacks which always demonstrate that 'somewhere along the line, [humans are] always to blame' (398).

The human characters in Schatzing's novel can be roughly grouped into two kinds: those who acknowledge their culpability in environmental and other crises, strive to respect the being of other species and look for co-operative ways to resolve their difficulties; and those (conflated with caricatures of right-wing, Christian Americans) who see these crises as a terrorist conspiracy against the hegemony of the West, refuse to acknowledge that other beings might read the world differently than do we and insist that the only possible outcome is destruction of the enemy. In many ways, the novel is the story of the conflict between these two tendencies in human responses more than one of a conflict between humans and other species, and thus as in many of the sf works discussed in this book the role of animals is to offer a way to think about the construction of human subjectivity, ethics and culture. *Swarm* encapsulates the recurrent patterns in sf representations of animals: the identification of a metaphysics of subjectivity that excludes animals at the root of many of humanity's problems; a concern with environmental destruction and the loss of a liveable world for humans and other creatures; a recurrence of war with fellow creatures, human and non-human; the threat of human annihilation and a vision – sometimes fearful, sometimes optimistic – about another species replacing us as the dominant form of life; themes of isolation, loneliness and alienation that are encapsulated in humans' relationships with other species. My exploration of animals in sf texts has found a continual dialectic between texts which reproduce the known history of the human–animal boundary and those which open up possibilities for what Haraway has called 'other fashioning of life' (*Primate Visions* 4), a capacity she associates with the power of fiction.

Swarm eventually reveals that the marine animals who appear to be in revolt are in fact animals treated as technology by another sentient life form on the planet, a single-celled organism that is so different from human life – living in a different environment, collectively organised rather than individualistic, able to move in and out of group conglomerates without loss of sentience or life – that it might as well be thought of as alien. The progressively minded characters conclude that 'we're going to have to get used to the notion that we're not the only smart species on this planet' (493) and work to find a way to communicate with the 'aliens' they name the Yrr. One of the book's protagonists has spent the summer before these events 'reading visionary writers like Thomas More, Jonathan Swift or H.G. Wells' (18). These writers, who have all been associated with sf, are also known for their satirical writing and their advocacy of other possible worlds, based on transformed social relations and hence the ability to transcend the limitations of human cultures so incisively critiqued by works such as *Utopia* (1516), *Gulliver's Travels* (1726) and *War of the Worlds* (1898). *Swarm* has similar ambition, revealed in passages that rail against a society in which 'people knew less about reality than they did about its substitutes. Children in America drew six-legged chickens because drumsticks came in packs of six, while adults drank milk from a carton, and recoiled at the sight of an udder' (228). Like many of the sf texts discussed in this book, the novel associates animal being with new possibilities, with hope and openness for another way of conceiving humanity and creating the world and with the utopian impulse for a future that might be otherwise than the present. Early in the novel, two characters who eventually become key to the crisis team, SETI researcher Crowe and whale researcher Anawak, realise a deep connection between animals and aliens in the human imagination, that 'they were doing much the same thing, listening for signals and hoping for answers. They both had a deep-seated longing for the company of intelligent beings other than humans' (36).

Yet simultaneously Schatzing's novel demonstrates the failure of this quest, our inability to escape the molar patterns of fixed human and animal identity and embrace a new mode of becoming in which neither human nor animal is given in advance. The Yrr prove to be sufficiently unlike humans that they live in harmony with other marine species and do not destroy the ecosystem as do humans, but sufficiently like humans that their solution to the problem humans represent is to annihilate humans as troublesome vermin. They also use various marine species as tools in their attack on humanity, demonstrating an instrumental attitude toward them consistent with the instrumental attitude toward other species that has characterised most of the history of human–animal relations. Thus while Schatzing is able to imagine the Yrr as a collective intelligence whose perceptions and values would differ from those of individualist humans, he fails to present them as beings capable of transcending the human–animal boundary and its demarcation of 'real' subjects from the rest of objectified life. *Swarm* exemplifies all that is most enabling and all that is most limiting about the intersection of the sf imagination with representations of animals. As the texts explored throughout this book have demonstrated, animals are linked to the various ways that sf has explored alterity (women, the colonial other, aliens, androids and other artificial beings) and often these sf animals help us to see connections between the discourse of animality and the material history of disenfranchisement of both human and animal others, at times reinforcing this ideology and at other times critiquing its logic. Like *Swarm*, many of these sf texts use the trope of alterity to imagine new ways of being, specifically foregrounding new ways of relating to other species, as well as dramatising the tremendous costs of continuing to construe human subjectivity through the exclusion of the animal.

The conclusion of *Swarm* shows the most important antagonists to be not the Yrr but rather those humans – mainly highly placed members of the American administration – that refuse to recognise the need for change. The novel enacts one of the major crises of the twenty-first century in which environmental crisis, climate change, massive species extinctions and increasing inequities between the global North and South are the heritage of more than two centuries of capitalist expansion and other human activity. One of the key differences between the Yrr, who came to consciousness 'at the beginning of the Jurassic Era' (755), and humans is that the Yrr have genetic memory. Thus, the massive changes to the planet that have been the consequence of the last two centuries of human activity[1] are something that the Yrr would expect humans, as intelligent beings, to perceive. Since humans have demonstrated that we do not have this capacity that 'would save us from our own stupidity', the Yrr conclude 'trying to get along with humans is a pipedream … it's the reason they've decided to mobilise against us' (757). Those people willing to change the ways in which humans relate to other life on the planet struggle to convince the Yrr that humans can and will change, but the forces working against them are not direct agents of the Yrr but rather other humans who are unwilling to face the consequences of such change for those humans privileged by the current patterns of social organisation.[2] The real danger is humans who cannot recognise that 'life is interconnected' (775) or, more specifically, the problem is a biopolitical attitude that reduces life to something that can be governed and which takes its abstractions for the whole of concrete, material reality:

> All mankind is trapped within a waking dream of a world that doesn't exist. We live in an imaginary cosmos of taxonomic tables and norms, incapable of perceiving nature as it really is. Unable to comprehend how everything is interwoven, interlinked and irretrievably connected, we grade it and rank it, and set ourselves at the head. To make sense of things, we need symbols and idols, and we pronounce them real. We invent hierarchies and graduations that distort time and place. We have to see things in order to comprehend them, but in the act of picturing them we fail to understand. (847)

The humans who hope for a better future are victorious in the novel's conclusion and they assure the reader that humanity has learned its lesson about respecting others and seeing a world filled with living subjects, that 'nothing is the way it used to be' (875). Humans have recognised that 'the health of our psyche may depend on the existence of other animal species' and that 'if we continue to damage the Earth and destroy the diversity of nature, we'll be destroying a complex system that we can't explain, let alone replace' (880). Yet, as the inconsistencies that plague the novel reveal, such insight is more easily stated than enacted, and even the novel's final words are tinged with irony as the chapter's narrator repeats 'nothing is as it was. Although, come to think of it, I haven't stopped smoking. We all need continuity of some kind, don't you think?' (881). The question of whether hostilities with the Yrr have been resolved, or simply suspended temporarily, remains unanswered.

As the texts discussed in this book have demonstrated, fiction has the capacity to show open-ended and heterogeneous responses to the complexities of animals in/and human life. It can stage the problems that confront us in rich, concrete detail and thus potentially enable its readers to perceive the world and other species in new ways, to deterritorialise, in Deleuze and Guattari's terms, our habitual response to other species based on the importance of the human–animal boundary to human subjectivity, and to reterritorialise our intersubjective relations in new and promising configurations. Fiction can also reflect and reveal the anxieties and preoccupations that trouble the current social configuration, allowing us to perceive them in new detail and understand their connections to other aspects of human existence more fully. Sf in particular is useful for thinking about the contemporary difficulties of human–animal exchanges given its ongoing interest in rethinking human subjectivity which, as HAS scholarship has established, requires rethinking the human–animal boundary. Such interrogations offer hope for a changed social world for all species which is urgently needed. Sf reveals our desire to communicate with another being, while the insights of HAS herald an opportunity to form bonds with 'real' aliens with whom we share the planet, at the same time that both discourses warn us that we must make such changes quickly, before all other animals become extinct. Both sf and HAS share the goal of imagining the world and social relations otherwise. Animals, both like us and different in their experience of our shared world, both homely and uncanny, offer a productive way for thinking about other modalities of being, other modes of perception and other ways of being in the world – in reality as much as in fiction. Foucault argues that 'establishing the intelligibility of reality consists in showing its possibilities' (*Birth* 34). Sf is a fruitful way of making alternative realities intelligible.

Building on Claude Lévi-Strauss's observation that animals are good to think with, Lorraine Daston and Gregg Mitman emphasise that they interpret 'thinking with' to mean thinking alongside. They suggest 'thinking with animals can take the form of an intense yearning to transcend the confines of self and species, to understand from the inside or even to become an animal' (7). Ursula Le Guin's story 'Buffalo Gals, Won't You Come Out Tonight' builds on this fantasy, telling of a girl who falls from the sky, losing an eye in the fall. She is taken in by Coyote, a version of the trickster figure found in many Native American legends, who calls her 'Gal' after the chorus of the song from which the story gets its title. The loss of an eye immediately puts the Gal in a different world, but at first this is an impediment more than an aid as her partial vision and lack of depth perception mean she is estranged from her familiar world. At one point the Gal confronts Coyote with the tremendous gap between her previous experience of consensual reality and the world of Coyote and the other animals she encounters after her rescue. When she tells Coyote that she does not understand 'why you all look like people'; Coyote sensibly replies, 'We are people'. The Gal persists, 'I mean, people like me, humans', to which Coyote points out 'resemblance is in the eye' (35). In typical trickster fashion, Coyote teaches the Gal that the two kinds of people are not 'humans and animals', as her common sense experience might suggest, but instead 'the first people, and then the others' or, more pragmatically, 'us' and 'them' (36). Coyote thus turns the joke about there being only two kinds of people – the kind who say there are two kinds of people, and the kind who do not – into a more philosophical insight about a tendency to ground subjectivity based on exclusion of the animal, on two kinds, versus a new kind of subjectivity that does not need to define itself through opposition. The Gal realises that her struggle is to figure out 'where she belonged' (39) because one is not allowed to pass between worlds.

The Gal is able to see two different worlds with two different eyes when she substitutes a piece of coal for the missing one, this fantastical eye standing in for another experience of the world. She realises that as long as she sees the animals as people, she does not see the world of humans, the world of 'the metal places, the glass places' that the animals call 'holes' that are separated from their reality by 'walls' (42), from the one from which she came. When the Gal looks at such a hole, she momentarily sees evidence of human civilisation, but then it fades from her sight, 'leaving nothing – a hole in the world, a burned place like a cigarette burn' (46). The animals explain that a shared world between human and animal that was lost produced this bifurcation: 'when we lived together it was all one place ... but now the other, the new people, they live apart. And their places are so heavy. They weight down on our place, they press on it, draw it, suck it, eat it, eat holes in it, crowd it out' (49). They worry that in the future there will be only one place again, but it will be a human place only with 'none of us here' (50). In the end the Gal must go back to her own people, but the hope is that she will 'keep [her] eye', and thus will remember animals and their being 'in [her] dreams, in [her] ideas' (60). This story uses techniques of fantasy rather than sf as no rational explanation is offered for the Gal's experiences in another realm. Yet the story nonetheless epitomises an insight that informs much of the scientific work on animal cognition and communication. Animals do live in a materially different world from the one humans inhabit, in part because their perceptual machinery of sight (and other senses) is different from our own (and, beyond this, the human tendency to express understanding through metaphors of vision is not reflective of the dominant sensory experience of many species). Le Guin's story thus points to an important way that sf and HAS might instruct one another: scientific research in ethology could become the basis of future hard sf extrapolation, and the sf imagination can help concretise the lifeworlds of other species as we learn more about their perception and cognition. Both can make the animals' realities more intelligible to humans.

Andre Norton's *Beast Master* novels, *The Beast Master* (1959) and *Lord of Thunder* (1962), similarly explore the desire to understand the animal 'from the inside' and to capture something of the experience of what it is like to be another animal.[3] Like Le Guin's story, the series takes its inspiration from Native American epistemology and its more respectful relationship to animal autonomy and greater willingness to acknowledge kinship with animals. The series similarly imagines an affective and co-operative relationship between humans and animals created to serve human needs. Protagonist Hosteen Storm is a Native American Commando in the service of Earth Force in their war against the Xik. Storm works with specially bred animals, his Beast Master team, with whom he is in telepathic communication: a dune cat, Surra; two meerkats, Ho and Hing; and an eagle, Baku. The very title, Beast *Master*, indicates the privilege given to Storm's contributions to the team. He is in command, but the novels stress that the relationship is a co-operative and affective one, not one of domination. At one point, for example, Storm finds himself wishing

> he could have coaxed Surra to serve as an additional drover, but the big cat had disappeared on her own errand in the rain and the Terran knew she was going to hole up somewhere out of the wet. Since he had given her no definite orders she would follow her own instincts. (*Beast Master* 91)

The relationship between Storm and his team is shown to be one of mutual care, protectiveness and respect; although Storm is the leader, he does listen to the animals and the entire point of the telepathic team seems to be that the animals are able to perceive things that humans cannot. This structure suggests something of a blended culture between humans and animals, a companion-species relationship.

Storm's identity as Native American is often invoked to describe the special relationship he feels with his team. For example, he is more strongly attuned to smell than are other humans, something that connects him both to the animals and to his own childhood which seems to have been spent in a pre-colonial Native culture, despite the larger context of space-faring and other signs of 'progress'. An optimistic reading might see this characterisation of Storm as an endorsement of a quite different socioeconomic relationship with animals characteristic of North

American Native cultures, and thus as a possible model for a transformed society. More cynically, we might see in Storm merely a stereotype of the noble savage and thus dismiss his connection to the animals as a sort of primitivism. *Lord of Thunder* suggests something of the former in its endorsement of a less alienated relationship with non-human life that is characteristic of Storm's cultural identity:

> An Amerindian had an ancient tie with nature and the forces of nature, which was his strength, just as other races had come to rely more and more on machines. It was upon such framework that his whole education had been based, his sympathies centered. So, both inborn and special conditioning had made of him a man aloof from, and suspicious of, machines. One had to be anti-tech to be a Beast Master. (132)

In many ways, however, the traditional human–animal hierarchy is not challenged by the series. When Storm is called upon to save an alien native, for example, he 'was loath to risk Surra, but he must give Gorgol a chance. With his hands resting lightly on the dune cat's shoulders, his thumbs touching the bases of her large sensitive ears, Storm thought his order. Find the Norbie – bring him back –' (*Beast Master* 132). The conclusion of *Lord of Thunder* shows Storm finding his remaining human family and being reunited with them; although the animals remain part of his social relations, there is the sense that he has found a more important community when he is restored to human family. Nonetheless, the series insists that the animals are also part of this community and thus enacts a less alienated way of interacting with other species, even if we continue to expect them to serve our ends.

Yet stories such as the Beast Master series, despite the ways that they reinforce the human–animal boundary, also open up our thinking through the evident desire they demonstrate to be like an animal, to think with the animal. Matthew Calarco argues that 'becoming-animal and challenging anthropocentrism is not a matter, as Heidegger seems to think is the case with Rilke and Nietzsche, of imitating or identifying with animals. Rather, it is a matter of being transformed by an encounter with nonhuman perspectives' (42). Many of sf's animals operate in this way, enabling human protagonists to see their world and themselves in a new way once they have been confronted with the animal's perspective, its subjectivity. Derrida launches his discussion of animal being and the metaphysics of human subjectivity when he sees his cat looking at him and asks '*who I am* – and who I am (following) at the moment when, caught naked, in silence, by the gaze of an animal' (*The Animal* 3). This encounter with the gaze of the other changes what it means to know oneself, and such knowledge is potentially revolutionary if one allows oneself to be, as Derrida suggests, naked – to experience the encounter without quickly falling back on molar categories of identity and the easy ethical calculation of the human–animal boundary which shields the human from potential critique. The possibility comes from acknowledging that the cat, too, has 'a moral existence' (9).

Clifford Simak's series of short stories collected in *City* (1952) strives to be just such an encounter, an aim that is accomplished as much through the 'editorial' framing of the collection as through the stories themselves. These eight interconnected tales recount the disappearance of humans from what proves to be a group of parallel worlds and their replacement by a civilisation of sentient, talking dogs. The stories are presented in a collection that includes an editorial introduction to the sequence as well as introductions to each tale, written by a scholar from this future civili- sation who treats them as legends about a mythological creature, Man, albeit acknowledging that 'There still are others who believe that Man and Dog may have risen together as two co-operating animals, may have been complementary in the development of a culture, but that at some distant point in time they reached the parting of the ways' (7). The early stories, 'City' and 'Huddling Place', recount the gradual disappearance of concentrated human settlement in cities as humans become dependent upon technology and inclined to live isolated in private homes, revealing 'a deepening instinct to stay among the scenes and possessions which in their mind have become associated with contentment and graciousness of life' (59). The second tale tells of humanity's loss of the insights promised by a new philosophy developed by Juwain – a Martian who, significantly, is described as having a 'furry hand' (51) – as a consequence of the inability of physician Webster to leave his home and travel to treat Juwain's illness. These tales set the stage for 'Census', the third story in which the dogs appear. They have been created by a Webster descendent in an attempt to compensate for the loss of the Juwain philosophy. What humanity needs, these early tales repeat, is an encounter with a non-human perspective, Martian or canine. Humans have become trapped in a moribund pattern of thinking just as they have become trapped in isolated homes, and only an encounter with a non-human perspective can save them.

Yet as the next stories demonstrate, humans seem incapable of allowing themselves to be transformed by this encounter. The first person outside the Webster family to encounter a talking dog tells this dog, Nathaniel, that 'Men may not always be the way they are today. They may change. And, if they do, you have to carry on; you have to take the dream and keep it going. You'll have to pretend that you are men' (101). Humans are thereby revealed to be so wedded to their ideology of human superiority that they insist that this particular model of subjectivity and its goals must become the guiding dream for any sentient species. The next two stories, 'Desertion' and 'Paradise', tell of the experiences of Captain Fowler and his dog Towser on Jupiter, where they have been transformed by a technology that turns them into the form of indigenous Lopers, able to survive the harsh conditions on the planet. As the editorial notes on this tale point out, 'It is Towser, not the human, who is first ready to accept the situation which develops; Towser, not the human, who is the first to understand' (102). The experience as a Loper provides Fowler with an opportunity to experience the world from a non-human perspective and he finds the event transformative. He pities his previous existence using only 'unseeing human eyes. Poor eyes. Eyes that could not see the beauty of the clouds, that could not see through the storm', trapped within a subjectivity that produced 'Men who walked alone, in terrible loneliness, talking with their tongue like Boy Scouts wigwagging out their messages, unable to reach out and touch one another's mind as he could reach out and touch Towser's mind. Shut off forever from that personal, intimate contact with other living things' (115). Fowler compels himself to return to human embodiment so that he might report on this 'paradise', and finds he is thwarted by another Webster who sees him as 'the greatest threat mankind's ever faced', because once humans are made aware of Loper existence 'all the humans would be Lopers' and 'the human race would disappear' (129). Clinging to the notion of human exceptionalism is so important to Webster that he misses the opportunity for humanity to achieve its 'greatest advancement' (129), the ideal he continually evokes, as he cannot *concede* that another state of existence might be preferable to human, although his description of the threat Fowler represents demonstrates that Webster can *conceive* of this alternative.

'Paradise' also reveals the insight offered by the Juwain philosophy, which has been completed by a 'mutant' named Joe, part of a population of evolved humans who live isolated from the rest of humanity. This philosophy, if embraced, would enable humanity to take the leap Webster envisions, but like Fowler's paradise of Loper-becoming it would require humanity to embrace change:

> The Juwain philosophy provides an ability to sense the viewpoint of another. It won't necessarily make you agree with that viewpoint, but it does make you recognize it. You not only know what the other fellow is talking about, but how he feels about it. With Juwain's philosophy you have to accept the validity of another man's ideas and knowledge, not just the words he says, but the thought back of the words. (135)

Webster resists this, too, and in fact initially responds with genociuai hatred for the mutants who have promulgated this capacity by creating kaleidoscopes that transform the perspective of any humans who use them according to the precepts of the Juwain philosophy. The next two tales, 'Hobbies' and 'Aesop', turn their attention to the far distant future and the flourishing of a dog society[4] that has arisen in the wake of most of humanity's departure to embrace Loper existence. These final tales fulfil the promise of the editorial framing of the first, showing that dog civilisation is so different from human that the early tales can now be read only as mythology, describing, as they do, things such as the city, 'an impossible structure, not only from the economic standpoint, but from the sociological and psychological as well' (9), and the existence of 'another concept which the reader will find entirely at odds with his way of life, and which may violate his very thinking, ... the idea of war and of killing' (10). These stories contrast the dogs' social order with that created by humans, ultimately concluding that the dogs' dreams for the future *'Maybe even better than the dreams of man, for they held none of the ruthlessness that the human race had planned, aimed at none of the mechanistic brutality the human race had spawned'* (168).

The dogs are assisted by a race of robots, also created by man, who have been trained to serve as the dogs' hands, supervised by Jenkins, a Webster family robot who first appears in the second tale and whose longevity provides a unifying perspective. The dogs are creating 'a civilization based on the brotherhood of animals—on the psychic understanding and perhaps eventual communication and intercourse with interlocking worlds' (183), a programme they promote through educating predator species regarding the sinfulness of killing and through the provision of feeding stations to take the place of hunting. In the first story, another Webster descendent uses the city of Geneva's defence mechanisms to lock all those humans remaining on Earth within the city to ensure that the dogs 'have their chance ... to try for success where the human race had failed'; humans must be removed from the equation to ensure that 'a new pattern – a new way of thought and life – a new approach to the age-old social problem' is not 'tainted by the stale breath of man's thinking' (187). In the next, a peaceful civilisation of animals is disrupted by the re-emergence of killing for sport, a problem caused by the descendents of some human children who were playing outside the city when the lockdown happened. Jenkins concludes that humanity can never fit into this new utopian dog society: 'Once I thought that Man might have got started on the wrong road ... might have taken the wrong turning. But I see that I was wrong. There's one road and one road alone that Man may travel – the bow and arrow road ... For a man will invent a bow and arrow, no matter what you do' (211). Fortuitously, at the same moment that humanity's inescapable violence is discovered, Jenkins also discovers that some of the parallel worlds are occupied by malevolent creatures called cobblies, creatures defined by their hatred and desire to annihilate other beings. Jenkins takes the remaining humans and lives with them in the cobbly world, a place where 'the old blood-lust of Man, the craving to be different and to be stronger, to impose his will by things of his devising – things that make his arm stronger than any other arm or paw, to make his teeth sink deeper than any natural fang, to reach and hunt across the distances that are beyond his own arm's reach' (219), will be a benefit rather than a bane.

The final tale 'The Simple Way' is even more pessimistic: Jenkins returns to an even further future dog world, announcing that he has been living alone on the cobbly world for the past 4000 years. The dogs are threatened by a rising civilisation of technology-using ants, the heritage of an experiment by one of the mutants millennia ago. The ants are compelling the robots to build structures, structures that threaten to take over the entire world and eliminate all the space and other resources needed by the dogs and other animals. The ants function as a doppelganger for humans: a species that lives in groups, is driven by accumulation and technology and refuses to acknowledge the validity of any perspective but their own. Jenkins recalls that the humans had a way of solving their problems with ants, and so he travels to the underground caverns of Geneva where he is able to consult with a surviving Webster who has entered permanent stasis. Jenkins hopes to find some way to reconcile the ants' imperialist projects with the dogs' and other creatures' needs. The solution to dealing with ants, he is told to his great shock, is to poison them. The entire sequence concludes with Jenkins returning to the dogs and making plans to migrate to another of the parallel worlds, judging 'better that one should lose a world than go back to killing' (252). *City* is unable to imagine a way out of the human–animal boundary that has structured our encounter with other species. The collection effectively conveys what is wrong with human subjectivity constructed on this foundation and demonstrates on an apocalyptic scale those consequences for humans and other species. It struggles, however, to imagine another world.[5]

Simak's stories illustrate what Matthew Calarco has called, describing Nietzsche's animal philosophy, 'an "overcoming" of the human' as the most promising way to contest the network of institutions and knowledges linking 'humanism, anthropocentrism, and nihilism' (41). In a foreword to the collection written in 1976, Simak reflects on the creation of the stories and confesses that *City* was written 'out of disillusionment' that 'man, in his madness for power, would stop at nothing' (1). Despite the deep pessimism of the collection's trajectory, Simak also implies a quality of hopefulness in its demonstration of the 'overcoming' of the human: he tells us that the stories were not a protest but

> a seeking after a fantasy world that would serve as a counterbalance to the brutality through which the world was passing. Perhaps, deep inside myself, I was trying to create a world in which I and other disillusioned people could, for a moment, take refuge from the world in which we lived. (2)

Although the stories themselves suggest that the only way to 'overcome' the human is by eliminating the species and starting again with the dogs, the readers' desire to live in a world that resembles the dogs' world suggests the possibility that human subjectivity, construed otherwise, could find a way out of the nexus of humanism, anthropocentrism and nihilism that produced the culture Simak rejects. Haraway offered the cyborg as an image that 'can suggest a way out of the maze of dualisms in which we have explained our bodies and our tools to ourselves' ('Cyborg' 181). The sf animals analysed in this book suggest that animals – and a corresponding sense that the human could be otherwise by becoming-animal – offer another powerful image for thinking about human subjectivity, ethics, alterity and our relationship to the rest of the world. As Haraway insists throughout her work, the power of thinking with these figures is that they are 'creatures of imagined possibility and creatures of fierce and ordinary reality' (*When Species Meet* 4). Posthuman theory, like sf, has spent considerable effort thinking about the experience of technoculture and our relationship with machines. In *The Companion Species Manifesto* (2003), Haraway proposes that we now turn equal attention to our relationships with other organic species, suggesting that dogs might offer more promise than do cyborgs for creating 'livable politics and ontologies in current life worlds' (4). Simak's *City* and its cyborg-dogs are one contribution to this project, asking us to think imaginatively about the 'fantasy' society the dogs represent, but also about our ordinary reality of encounters with other species, too often epitomised by the poison 'solution'. *City* demonstrates that this way of construing human subjectivity clearly does not enable 'livable politics' and thus prompts us to embrace change more readily than can his humans.

Braidotti asserts that becoming-other, a mode of posthumanism, is about the mutation of cultural values as well as the mutation of bodies:

> This mutation is bio-genetic as well as ethical: it redefines what it means to be human through nomadic practices of transpositions of differences in the sense of practices of the not-One, of affinities and viral contaminations, interdependence and non-entropic economies of desire. It is in some ways an evolutionary move, but not in a narrow Darwinian sense and not in a hierarchical model. It rather moves

towards the construction of possible and hence sustainable futures by enforcing the notion of intra-species and intra-generational justice. (274)

Sheri Tepper is a writer whose work has always been committed to questions of social justice, and she has increasingly focused on intraspecies encounters. With Braidotti, she shares a commitment to transforming the human subject through exchanges and affinities with other beings, a practice Braidotti calls 'transpositions', a term that, in genetics, refers to the changes that occur when a sequence of DNA moves from one part of the genome to another and in so moving changes its function.[6] Transposition means that 'genetics information is contained in the sequence of the elements, which in turn means that the function and the organization of the genetic elements are mutable and interdependent' (6) rather than the fixed expression of an isolated DNA 'truth'. Braidotti's notion of transpositions is committed to an understanding of becoming as 'non-linear, but not chaotic; nomadic, yet accountable and committed; creative but also cognitively valid' (5). Tepper shares Braidotti's commitment to constructions of subjectivity that acknowledge interdependence and multiplicity, and to the centrality of intraspecies and intragenerational justice in ethics, but at the same time Tepper's commitment to fixed categories of 'right' and 'wrong' – right being the capacity to recognise other species as fellow creatures; wrong being the reliance on anthropo-centric knowledge – means that she fails to embrace the radical alterity captured by Braidotti's notion of transpositions.[7] Thus Tepper engages the content but not the process of becoming-other, as she suggests that there is a preferable, more inclusive subjectivity at which one could 'arrive', rather than recognising the need for accountable and committed, yet never fixed, subjectivity.

The Family Tree (1997) epitomises this problem. It tells two stories that eventually converge: one, set in the present, concerns police officer Dora Henry's investigation of the murder of a scientist, Dr Winston. Although he seems to have no enemies, the more Dora pursues the investigation the more she learns there is something secretive about his research into improved livestock animals. The world in which Dora lives is meanwhile being radically transformed by a type of vegetation that is taking over: destroying highways, preventing the operation of most motor vehicles and even painlessly absorbing back into constituent elements excess children from families who have overbred. Although many humans are injured in confrontations with this 'weed', Dora treats it respectfully and talks to it, and she is rewarded by the plant's willingness to engage with her as a fellow sentient subject. The second story is about a struggle for imperial power in a far future time in which a variety of different tribes, each with distinctive languages and customs, must work together in order to thwart a plan by the Emperor's nephew to seize the throne and institute a much harsher sovereign order. This group of allies eventually learn from the mysterious and robed Brothers of St Weel, who control access to a time-travel device, that the conspiracy is much bigger than originally suspected, prompting them to a travel into the past in order to stop one of the Order who has turned against the co-operative alliance. As another Brother explains, this criminal, the Woput, has decided 'that we … our tribe was almost extinct because your people … your tribes had become so numerous. If you had died out long ago, our people would have survived. So, he went back in time to kill off the other tribes' (290, ellipses in original).

The two plots converge when the future protagonists travel back into the past to stop the Woput, who turns out to be the murderer Dora seeks. Dr Winston was killed because he had been augmenting the intelligence of animals and then smuggling the talking creatures out of the laboratory and into safe houses where they can thrive outside human control. When Dora first meets the group sent back to stop him, the reader discovers that the various tribes of people are in fact various species of animals: monkeys, pigs, racoons, dogs, cats, cockatoos, otters and more. This future society has a version of the human–animal boundary, the distinction they make between *persons* who are intelligent and *creatures* who are not, but their enactment of this boundary does not justify all kinds of exploitation, as is often the case with the human–animal boundary: creatures can be eaten, but they must nonetheless be treated with kindness and respect while they live. As is typical in sf that uses the trope of human–animal reversal, Dora must adjust her perceptions to see all these beings as people (a shift that, given her sensibilities, is not difficult for her to achieve), while the people from the future must accept that humans, whom they call umminhi in their time, are people rather than creatures in Dora's time. Accepting that humans are more than beasts of burden proves more challenging for them than did the reverse for Dora: 'I had never believed umminhi could think. It was hard to admit that these two were thinking, but I made myself accept it by thinking of them as ponjic persons in umminhi masks' (319). It does not take long for the group to discern that the Brothers are the descendants of humans, the few who have survived an apocalypse, who disguise their appearance so that it is not evident they share embodiment with the voiceless umminhi.

The various crises are resolved through a somewhat convoluted plot: humans learn to live more respectfully with the environment through the influence of the tree; the possibility for the sentient animals to evolve from Dr Winston's protégés is preserved; and Dora is able to skip ahead into the future and live in this more harmonious world with her new friends. There she discovers that the umminhi are not in fact humans who have degenerated to a pre-sentient state, but rather they are part of a guild of those committed to the flourishing of all life who

> took a vow of silence, a vow to atone to the creatures of the world by serving and assisting them. They set up libraries to preserve knowledge. They took an oath to protect diversity, to go naked and silent, to be beasts of burden, to suffer what creatures had suffered at human hands, in order to atone ... (465, ellipses in original)

In the time in which Dora finds herself at the novel's conclusion, after 3000 years of such servitude, the umminhi conclude that the debt has been paid and they remove their harnesses, reveal that they can speak and join the society of all species as another tribe. The emperor's nephew is killed, a necessity the emperor says he regrets and feels guilty about. This nephew 'felt it was more important to be true to his nature than to create a peaceful world' and thus the 'only one way to stop him eating people ... was to kill him' (477). *The Family Tree*, like Simak's *City*, suggests that the only way to embrace a new subjectivity of becoming, one that allows for the personhood of all species and the production of a world based on values other than hierarchy, is via the elimination of those humans judged too rigid to escape their molar being. The novel's title refers to the realisation that umminhi, too, are part of the tribes of people, that they cannot be regarded as 'merely creatures, prunable twigs from the family tree' (465). Yet this is precisely what the emperor enacts at the novel's end, regretting that his nephew 'was not merely a person who had gone wrong. He was family' (478) – but insisting on the necessity of pruning him nonetheless.

Another Tepper novel, *The Companions* (2003), explores similar concerns about human overpopulation, our instrumental attitude toward other species and looming mass extinctions with somewhat more nuance. The novel's main protagonist, Jewel Delis, is an animal conservationist on a future Earth in which the right-wing lobby IGO-HFO (In God's Image, Humans First and Only) has succeeded in outlawing animal life based on the logic that 'animals had no right to exist anywhere on Earth – or on any other human occupied planet – because all space, air, water was needed for the one creature made in God's image' (29). Jewel and her fellow arkists have been working to breed and preserve species that would otherwise become extinct and to install them on planets deemed not to have resources worthy of exploitation. Human occupation of colony planets is always linked to the extraction of resources, and the overpopulation crisis on Earth is linked to the peculiar economies of this colonial arrangement: birth rates are kept high to ensure an adequate workforce for expansion, but prices for living space are kept out of reach for those no longer economically productive. A Law of Return supported by politicians who benefit financially from the colonial corporations grants any human the right to return to Earth in old age; it is the only human-occupied planet where the means of subsistence are financially within reach for the unemployed, although standards of living are very low. Most of the novel takes place on Moss, a planet whose status has yet to be determined: a colony cannot be established until they ascertain whether there already is an indigenous sentient species. Dancing shapes who appear to be people have been observed, but all attempts at communication have failed. Jewel and several of the dogs she is cultivating – dogs who have been modified so that they can speak and have longer lives than other canines – go to Moss as part of an expedition to which Jewel is attached.

The dogs prove crucial to the success of human contact with Moss, whose intelligence is not found in any particular species but in the planet itself, able to communicate through smells with all the species who live upon it and serve 'a function' as part of its ecosystem. Through her close association with the dogs and their ways of perceiving the world, Jewel is able to conceive of a language communicated through smell and learns that the coloured entities that dance are not people but words, messages sent by the planet that ripen and then float free of their vegetative origin, emitting their meaning through a succession of smells. Jewel's capacity to perceive this and her openness to the differences that such a language implies for how the world is perceived and experienced make her an example of the sort of posthumanism that Braidotti associates with the embrace of *zoe*, a philosophy that 'displaces the primacy of the visual' and links becoming-animal to 'an expansion or creation of new sensorial and perceptive capacities or powers, which alter or stretch what a body can actually do' (103). Jewel is able to perceive things about Moss and its language to which the other humans are blind, and she has the requisite openness to alterity that enables communication to occur across the species barrier. What she values about the dogs, Jewel tells an alien, the Phaina, is that 'they were different. We need things to be different. If everyone is alike, it narrows our world down, it makes us narrow, too. It makes us think human things are the only things, human ideas the only ideas ...' (95, ellipses in original).

Her close connection to the dogs enables Jewel to be open to the Phain concept of dalongar, 'their respectful regard for others' (455). Moss proves to be a spatial anomaly in which various humans have been pulled into another plane, one controlled by a species called the Zhaar. Fifty thousand years ago, the Zhaar interfered in human evolution, changing us to enable better language skills and giving us what the Phain call 'Zhaar virtues, dog virtues: pride and packishness' (537). The Zhaar thus regard humans as their servants. The Phain hold that these Zhaar virtues are not flaws in 'dogs, who have no hands, who had no language, who needed pride of leadership and packish order in order to survive' (537), but are disastrous in technologically capable humans, cutting humanity off from an experience of 'living in mutual support, possessing the dalongar all those born into a world owe to all others born in that world as kindred creatures – creatures of that world' (536).

Another convoluted plot of various machinations to take over territory and wipe out competing species is thwarted by the joint capacity of Jewel and the dogs to demonstrate dalongar and thus earn the protection of the Phain. In the distant past, the Phain banned the Zhaar from the galaxy, but instead of leaving the Zhaar changed themselves to resemble dogs and called themselves a new species, the Simusi. The Simusi mirror the ideology of the human IGO-HFO humans, contending that 'any creature who needs any kind of accoutrement is considered inferior. Accoutrement includes shelter, clothing, devices, anything beyond one's own body and mind, because only vermin accumulate things' (433), and therefore that humans, a clearly inferior species, are made to serve them. The Simusi enslavement of humans is ended by the co-operation of Jewel and her dogs in overthrowing their regime, which requires that the dogs recant their initial seduction into a Simusi ideology that enabled them to feel superior, just as Jewel and humans like her distance themselves from anthropocentrism. The conclusion here is less harsh than in *The Family Tree*: both humans and dogs have the capacity for 'packishness' and pride and thus for a destructive relationship to other species; yet at the same time both humans and dogs have the capacity for dalongar and it is their mutual becoming-other, growing as companion species who are both changed by the encounter, that ensures that neither is the slave of the other or likely to enslave anyone. As Jewel explains at the novel's end, 'so long as we cared for one another, we kept one another from turning into Zhaar' (548).

Yet the novel is not free from the pull one finds in all of Tepper's work to sort subjects into 'good' and 'bad' categories, those who embrace a vision of multispecies community and the flourishing of life in general, and those who cling to notions of human exceptionalism and the ready-made morals of the human–animal boundary. This limitation of Tepper's work is a limitation more widely of the struggles we face in the twenty-first century regarding how to understand ourselves and our others if we are willing to abandon the certainties of the human–animal boundary and confront the gaze of the animal as the gaze of a subject. Derrida tells us that this gaze offers 'the abyssal limit of the human', a vulnerable place in which we are forced to recognise that we do not know how to address this other as a 'fellow, even less … [a] brother', nor do we know 'what happens to the fraternity of brothers when an animal appears on the scene' (12). This sense of passivity before the gaze of the other Derrida calls

> *the passion of the animal, my* passion *of* the animal, my passion of the animal other: seeing oneself seen naked under a gaze behind which there remains a bottomlessness, at the same time innocent and cruel perhaps, perhaps sensitive and impassive, good and bad, uninterpretable, unreadable, undecidable, abyssal and secret. (12)

Thinking seriously about animal subjectivity and human–animal interaction beyond the certainties of the human–animal boundary requires us to confront this void that keeps us from ever truly knowing the animal other, ever sorting it simply and finally into the category of fellow or brother. Little wonder, then, the temptation to fall back on the security of the old hierarchies, even if we want to change the contents of who counts as a subject (those who respect life, have dalongar) and who does not. Furthermore, Tepper's work, like the writing of many advocates for animal welfare, is fuelled by a strong sense of outrage at the many inequities perpetrated against animal being over the long history of human–animal interaction. Yet as the best sf shows us, the true accomplishment is to find a way to connect with and respect alterity without reducing it to an image of self.

As the texts discussed throughout this book have demonstrated, animals are at the core of many of the questions central to sf: what does it mean to be human? How can we communicate with another species, and how might we be changed by the experience? How might the world be otherwise were we to imagine sharing it with other beings? Correspondingly, the techniques and motifs of sf are instructive for thinking through many of the issues germane to HAS: how can we understand an animal's different experience of the world and seek to communicate with it? How do human ideologies of gender and race influence our reading of animal subjects? What is the relationship between the culture of science and our ways of understanding and relating to animal others? Certain patterns have emerged from looking at how the two discourses come together: animals have long served as a foil for how humans define themselves, a pattern that persists in sf; sf's interest in imagining the future or 'next stage' of human identity frequently turns to images of animals, figured both as what we might become were we to construe our subjectivity otherwise and as a warning that we can be displaced if we do not find ways to transcend our self-destructive qualities. In their many guises, the animals in sf offer possible lines of flight out of the problems confronting human life in the era of industrialised technoculture, the era of sf. They frequently offer the promise of other fashioning of life beyond the vicissitudes of alienated social relations,[8] environmental degradation and a world structured by vast inequities.

Berger argues that 'with their parallel lives, animals offer man a companionship which is different from any offered by human exchange. Different because it is a companionship offered to the loneliness of man as a species' (4). This is perhaps the most important connection between HAS and sf because the genre might be thought of as a kind of solution to the problem of 'the loneliness of man as a species'. Its aliens, robots, cyborgs and other posthumans are expressive of a longing to connect with a subjectivity radically different from our own, and perhaps more optimistically expressive of a presentiment that humanity would benefit from being 'transformed by an encounter with nonhuman perspectives' (Calarco 42). Terry Bisson's 'Bears Discover Fire' (1991) captures this sensibility. The story is humorous, told by a down-to-earth narrator who pragmatically takes in stride the bears' discovery of fire and simply goes about his business; yet an elegiac tone also permeates. The bears have discovered a new sort of community and group identity with the discovery of fire, sitting together by the fireside in evenings and striking back at the hunters who attack them, offering fellowship to the humans who approach them respectfully. Crucially, this is a fellowship that does not reduce the bears to mere talking humans, an image of the same, but rather one which respects that their radical alterity persists even in the moment of exchange. The story opens with the narrator's flashlight losing its batteries as he is changing a flat tyre. He suddenly discovers that he is being aided by two bears who stand at the edge of the woods holding torches, 'whether out of curiosity or helpfulness, there was no way of knowing' (181). Scientists offer a number of explanations for this cultural development, but no conclusion is reached.

The narrator's continued interactions with the bears are juxtaposed with the story of his mother's decline in a nursing home. The bears do not approach the humans or attempt to initiate communication, but there is a sense of living respectfully together in a shared space. The narrator explains to his nephew why it 'would be wrong' (184) to shoot one of the bears, but the story does not elaborate on what it seems to suggest is the very obvious truth of this insight. The narrator models another way of relating to an alien species when, exploring the bears' territory one afternoon, he 'cut a little firewood and stacked it to one side, just to be neighbourly' (184). Less respectful exchanges characterise human relations: the patients at the nursing home are left in front of televisions which the staff claim 'soothes them down' (182), and the narrator describes a nurse as coming to take away his mother's tobacco, 'which is the signal for bedtime' (182), without suggesting that there is any conversational exchange. When his mother goes missing from the nursing home, he rightly intuits that he will find her with the bears around their nightly fire, where he and his nephew join her, an experience he says is 'no different from visiting her at the Home, only more interesting, because of the bears' (187). The bears include the humans in their fellowship, allowing them to share the fire and offering them some of the 'newberries' (187), but they do not make any attempts to communicate. In the morning, the bears have banked the fire and gone, and the narrator finds that his mother has died peacefully in the night. The narrator returns to the bears' fire once more after his mother's funeral, but finds that he cannot fully participate in their fellowship, that the newberries remain unpalatable, 'unless you're a bear' (189). Nonetheless, the narrator retains his respectful attitude toward the bears' emerging culture, and the story suggests that his ability to commune with them is no less significant – or less effective – than his ability to connect with most other humans. His fascination with the new-ness of the bears suggests a wish that things might be otherwise, that he, like the bears, might eat the new fruit, transform his culture as the bears have transformed theirs by fire.

Animals in sf suggest many themes, but perhaps the most promising is this aspiration that humans might interact with an intelligence other than our own and be transformed by it, a recurrent dream of sf. Combining the sf imagination and its representation of animals with the field of HAS extends the hope that we might learn from the insights of both how to achieve this dream with the real 'alien' species with whom we share the planet, animals. Thinking about new ways to live with animals through the sf imagination can participate in the construction of 'future-oriented perspectives, which do not deny the traumas of the past but transform them into possibilities for the present' (Braidotti 268). And perhaps, as Neil Evernden suggests in *The Natural Alien*, a first step toward achieving this present is to transform our metaphors for understanding the human relationship with the rest of life. Evernden offers the metaphor of humanity as a 'natural alien' (122), a species that behaves like an exotic organism, misunderstanding the system in which all life is interconnected and unable to find a place in the community. Thinking about the animals in sf from the point of view of HAS is similarly productive. In sf, subjectivity is never certain and the more closely one looks at it, the more blurred becomes the line between human and animal, self and other, subject and alien. In sf, the animal is us and we are the animal, all continually involved in a never-ending process of becoming, of imagining new ways of conceiving humans and animals, new ways of organising our social relations, new futures to inhabit. This is sf's response to the question of the animal.

Notes

Introduction

1. This project focuses on animals in sf, excluding texts that are explicitly fantasy or children's literature from its scope. At the same time, however, I recognise that the boundary between sf and other speculative literatures is permeable and continually in flux. I follow Roger Luckhurst in defining sf as 'the literature of technologically saturated societies' (3) and thus dating its emergence to the late nineteenth century. Beyond finding this definition compelling, I also find it useful for positioning the relations between sf and HAS. The transformations wrought by the penetration of technological and scientific innovations into human lives during this period has been matched by equally radical transformation of both animal lives and the context in which human–animal social relations occur – or often no longer occur.

2. Regarding terminology, there is a considerable debate within the field of HAS regarding what language is appropriate to refer to humans collectively as distinct from non-human beings. Many people reject the terms 'human' and 'animal' as already ceding too much anthropocentrism and reinforcing a boundary whose deconstruction is precisely the point of much of this work. The distinction of human versus non-human is sometimes used, and occasionally I shall follow that usage when I am attempting to draw parallels between the discourse of speciesism and non-animal but similarly non-human others found in sf; although this terminology solves the problem of the conflation of widely disparate forms of life into the single category of 'animal', thereby obfuscating differences among them, it still retains a special and set-apart space for humans which remains problematic. For the most part, I will use the terms 'human' and 'animal' while recognising their limitations, as these terms connect to the history of human/animal separation in philosophy and history upon which I draw.

3. Interestingly, Gernsback felt it necessary to append an editorial note to this story which was published in the December 1928 issue of *Amazing Stories* suggesting that the author was having a bit of fun with speculations about a cat-race. Given Gernsback's insistence elsewhere – often in the absence of compelling evidence – of the plausibility of the 'scientific' premises of many of the stories he published, this anxiety about the non-centrality of *Homo sapiens* is intriguing.

4. See Calarco for an extensive overview and critique of this philosophical history.

5. For more on native ways of conceptualising human/animal relations and sf uses of these ideas, see Dillon.

6. The phrase is Teresa Mangum's, who argues: 'when empire and technology go terribly wrong, these dystopias unleash the truth about the violence and abuse animals often faced' (156–157). I agree with her analysis, but am also using the term in a broader way to encompass this and the other more positive ghostly presence of a desire to connect to being both like and unlike us.

7. James Serpell, building on Steven Mithen's argument that anthropomorphism is a defining characteristic of *Homo sapiens*, points out that it has defined the sorts of social relations that modern humans have with other species: 'By enabling our ancestors to attribute human thoughts, feelings, motivations, and beliefs to other species, [anthropomorphism] opened the door to the incorporation of some animals into the human social milieu, first as pets and ultimately as domestic dependents' (124).

8. A similar point can be made about genetic reasons for similar behaviour that can be traced back to a common shared ancestor. Eliot Sober argues that although cladistic parsimony does not provide 'a blanket justification for attributing human characteristics to nonhuman organisms' (95), nonetheless 'parsimony does favor anthropomorphism over anthropodenial. *If two derived behaviours are homologous, then the hypothesis that they are produced by the same proximate mechanisms is more parsimonious than the hypothesis that they are produced by different proximate mechanisms*' (95–96).

9. See Luc Ferry's *The New Ecological Order* (1995) for an impassioned defence of humanism and a resistance of animal rights based on his belief that the 'uniqueness' of humans must be protected to ensure the possibility of any ethics whatsoever. For an incisive critique of Ferry, see Cary Wolfe's *Animal Rites* (2003). For a more historical and less philosophical exploration of these issues, see Marjorie Spiegel's *The Dreaded Comparison* (1997). For a polemic from the opposite point of view from Ferry's, see Charles Patterson's *Eternal Treblinka* (2002).

10. For good overviews of some of the historically variable ways animals have figured in humans' material, intellectual and artistic lives, see Keith Thomas's *Man and the Natural World* (1984), Harriet Ritvo's *The Animal Estate* (1987), the collection *Companion Animals & Us* edited by Anthony Podberscek, Elizabeth Paul and James Serpell (2000), Erica Fudge's *Perceiving Animals* (2002), Linda Kalof's *Looking at Animals in Human History* (2007) and the Berg six-volume *Cultural History of Animals* series (2007).

11. See David Ulansey, 'The Current Mass Extinction', <www.well.com/user/davidu/extinction.html>, for updated coverage of new research findings and news stories on this topic. Accessed December 5, 2008.

12. See De Vos 183.

13. See Simmons and Armstrong 12.

Chapter 1

1. See Landström, Tiffin ('Bats') and Armstrong ('Farming Images') for a discussion of some of the complexities of these invader metaphors. At times the species migrations are the result of human intervention: either intentionally as in colonial efforts to remake 'new' environments in the image of familiar ones, or later in attempts to solve problems of over-populated introduced species by introducing a predator; at other times the human role is inadvertent as species become caught up in the movement of goods through imperialist and capitalist ventures. More recently climate change and the consequences of habitat change caused by industry have resulted in the self-directed migration of species into new areas (although, of course, this too might be regarded as an inadvertent consequence of human action). As these writers make clear, discursive constructions of who 'belongs' – and who does not – to a particular landscape, as well as human intervention in competition among species or consumption of one species (plant or animal) by another, always have more to so with human-constructed values and borders than with the 'nature' of the species and the 'authenticity' of their claims to indigeneity.

2. Organisations such as Heritage Foods USA also link the transformation of meat production to the erosion of economic independence for family farmers. They produce animals for meat outside of the factory farm system and restore a sense of interspecies relationships to modern meat-eating in allowing their customers to individually trace each meat purchase to a specific animal and thus to the conditions under which it is raised (see http://www.heritagefoodsusa.com/heritage/index.html#1; accessed December 4, 2008). Although the organisation's concern is not specifically with animal welfare (they continue to regard animals as food sources), at the same time the connection they draw between respect for worker autonomy and more 'natural' conditions for raising animals is another example of one of the points that I am making in this chapter; that is, the increased degree to which we ourselves become subject to dehumanising forces of industrial modernity the more we allow other living beings to be treated as objects.

3. See Martin Rowe's *The Way of Compassion* (1999) and Michael Fox's *Deep Vegetarianism* (1999) for a discussion of some of the connections among starvation, the cultivation of land for meat-producing animal feed and animal welfare.

4. Emel and Wolch state that meat production has quadrupled since 1950 (while population has doubled) and worldwide cheese consumption has doubled since 1970 (3).

5. Attempts to find alternatives to slaughter without giving up a meat-based diet are complex and at times contradictory. For example, animal tissue may be grown in a lab and harvested from a cell culture, not requiring an entire sentient animal in order to produce animal flesh (something imagined as commercially realised in Margaret Atwood's *Oryx and Crake* (2003)). Yet the bio-art collective Tissue Culture and Art reveals that it is not so simple to avoid animal exploitation. In their project *Disembodied Cuisine* they offered frog steaks grown in bioreactors to their audience. One of the things they learned

from this work, however, is that there is currently no such thing as victimless meat because 'current methods of tissue culture require the use of animal-derived products as a substantial part of the nutrients provided to the cells, as well as an essential part of various tissue culture procedures' (Catts and Zurr 132). In a bizarre displacement of issues of consumption, they must cultivate their non-sentient meat through feeding it animals: 'as a rough estimate (based on our experience with growing in vitro meat), growing around 10 grams of tissue will require serum from a whole calf (500 ml.), which is killed solely for the purpose of producing the serum' (133).

6. See Vint '*Who Goes There?*'.

7. I want to stress here that in drawing attention to these parallels, I am not advocating a conflation of the Holocaust with the treatment of animals in contemporary culture. Rather, with Matthew Calarco, I believe that 'the very difficult task for thought here is to bear the burden of thinking through both kinds of suffering in their respective singularity *and* to notice relevant similarities and parallel logics at work where they exist. To do so requires abandoning, or at least inhabiting in a hypercritical manner, the hierarchical humanist metaphysics that we have inherited from the ontotheological tradition' (112). The species boundary as a singular and indivisible boundary that sets 'human' life apart from all other life is at root in both examples of exploitation, but the solution is nothing so simple as rejecting this boundary. Instead, we need to pay attention mutually to the problem of a single boundary rather that the multiple sites of difference and relation discussed by Derrida and Haraway, and we need to beware, as Wolfe warns, of the way speciesist discourse remains appropriable for excluding some *Homo sapiens*.

8. See Vint 'Speciesism' for a more extended reading of the novel from this perspective.

9. See Rifkin for detailed analysis of conditions and statistics about number of animals slaughtered. See LePan for a sf tale which imagines the slaughter of humans under similar conditions, a trope also used by Faber. LePan's novel includes notations presented as non-fictional commentary on its narrative story, and these sections describe conditions consistent with practices of factory farming and mass slaughtering contemporary with the novel's publication.

10. See Ritvo 45–81 for an analysis of these agricultural interventions into animal breeding and their relationship to class politics in Britain. See Haraway *When Species Meet* 99–100 for a discussion of how colonial politics were implicated in the introduction and elimination of certain breeds as Western science forcibly replaced indigenous knowledge. Finally see Philip *Civilizing Natures* for a discussion of how indigenous knowledges embodied in plant and animal species bred over generations are appropriated by biotechnology companies, patented into new strains and commodified for profit in ways that exclude indigenous contributions.

11. See Marcus for a good overview. Torres also provides a number of examples of ways in which 'natural' animal behaviour has been manipulated or transformed in order to ensure maximum profit.

12. Research now confirms that a protein prion, incorporated into the body

via ingestion, injection or transplant, spreads the disease among individuals and between species (see Tiffin 'Foot in Mouth' 14).

13. A number of postcolonial studies such as Bergland, Hulme and Weaver-Hightower all explore the ways the discourse of cannibalism has been falsely attributed to non-Europeans (or ritual practices misread as a regular part of diet), revealing how species discourse is used to justify imperialist exploitation.

14. Some of those concerned with animal welfare approach the question from this perspective of animal rights, most commonly associated with the groundbreaking work of Tom Regan's *The Case for Animal Rights* and projects such as *The Great Ape Project*, which argues for extending 'human' rights, to primates who most closely resemble us. Derrida and those following in his tradition, such as Cary Wolfe and Matthew Calarco, find this approach limited in that it reinforces a philosophical tradition whose foundations are problematic, a position I share. Others such as Carol Adams and Josephine Donovan critique this perspective – and equally Peter Singer's utilitarian approach to animal rights in *Animal Liberation* – from a feminist point of view, emphasising the degree to which both traditions are rooted in masculine philosophical traditions that have been interrogated and revised by feminist philosophers. For a good overview of these issues see Ralph Acampora, 'Animal Philosophy'.

15. Swift's essay, critiquing the exploitation of the Irish by English landlords, satirically argued that the aristocracy should begin consuming Irish children, a proposal his speaker claims will solve the problem of 'excess' Irish population. Although the pretence that this is a serious proposal is maintained throughout the essay, it nonetheless makes clear that this literal consumption of children is a comment on the extent to which they are metaphorically consumed already by unjust social relations that condemn them to poverty.

16. Raccoona Sheldon is one of the pseudonyms of Alice Sheldon, who is more commonly known by her masculine pseudonym James T. Tiptree Jr.

17. Jim Mason suggests further links between capitalism and its exploitative social relations, and the shifting relations between humans and others species. In ancient societies, he argues, animal sacrifice was part of a redistributive feast that bound communities together as well as acknowledged their dependence upon – and hence social relation with – other species. With urbanisation and increasingly large societies, rulers could no longer provide enough meat for all and thus animal slaughter became detached from this notion of redistribution. Further, the rise of agriculture brought more fixed ideas about property and ownership into human cultures, both in terms of the animal bodies themselves becoming commodities owned by particular farmers, and also in designating a part of the land required for their provision as the property of the farmer occupying it (37–38).

18. The 'Dawn of Man' sequence in Kubrick's *2001: A Space Odyssey* depicts something very similar in the invention of the bone as weapon. See Vint 'Simians, Subjectivity and Sociality' for a more detailed reading.

19. Jane Goodall cites evidence of such violence between two primate species, chimpanzees and baboons, during her study of primate behaviour

in Gombe. As Armstrong points out, however, she further notes that her own intervention in provisioning bananas for the chimpanzees she was there to observe led to an increase in violence between the groups: 'Prior to this period, baboons and chimpanzees coexisted as an (admittedly ambivalent) interspecies community – their young playing together, adults from different species sometimes grooming each other – within which chimp predation of young baboons was the occasional exception to a more generally amenable relationship. Now, however, in the competitive atmosphere produced by Goodall's banana distribution, what Desmond calls "pure hunting" – that is, predation of another species for food, which Goodall observed amongst the Gombe chimps from the outset – became inflected with an exaggerated aggressive dimension' (212).

Chapter 2

1. The mirror test, of course, also presupposes a visual sensory perception that enables the animal in question to 'see' the reflected image as analogous to a three-dimensional object encountered in the world, and further that vision is the primary way of negotiating the world. It is thus not suitable for many species and, in any case, is anthropocentric in design, thereby already establishing in advance that the criterion for consciousness means consciousness as humans experience it.

2. Nim Chimpsky, a chimpanzee raised by humans in a family setting from infancy, was incapable of recognising self as a chimpanzee rather than a human. When asked to sort pictures into piles of chimpanzees and humans, he regularly put his own picture in the human pile (See Elizabeth Hess, *Nim Chimpsky* (2008)). 'Samaritan' refers to Nim although not by name.

3. Within the story, the pseudoparturition parties are preceded by symptoms of a pseudopregnancy, induced by drug injections. In our contemporary society, cross-species adoptions do occur. The documentary *The Disenchanted Forest* explores efforts to rehabilitate orang-utans raised as human back to a forest existence. Director Sarita Siegel notes that some 'have been removed from the breasts of women who were nursing them as their own. These orangutan infants are surrogate babies for women who cannot have children. These captives are acculturated to a human world rather than an orangutan world' (202).

4. Research in the social sciences has established the benefits to humans that result from a relationship with a pet, including improved health and facilitation of community interaction. For some examples, see: Wood, Gilles-Corti, Bulsara and Bosch; Brown; Staats, Wallace and Anderson; and Winefield, Black and Chur-Hansen. For an extended discussion of the ways in which pets are integrated into human families, see Greenebaum.

5. In fact, Deleuze and Guattari's lack of concern for animal being and experiences of human–animal interaction is very pronounced. They are interested in becoming-animal as a philosophical category, and in my analysis I try to extend their critique of subjectivity to a more politically engaged concern with animal lives that is absent in Deleuze and Guattari, but to

which I think their model can contribute through its bringing into question the individual and fixed categories of identity. For an incisive critique of their position which does not conclude it merits recuperation into HAS, see Haraway *When Species Meet* 27–30.

6. See Vint 'Becoming Other' for a more detailed reading of the series.

7. See Wallen and Marvin for a discussion of the currency of these myths in the material experience of fox-hunting which continues into the twenty-first century.

8. Ludwig is of course named for this castle's builder. The mad king was similarly imprisoned by a family who did not share his vision for a world made otherwise. He died under mysterious circumstances in his castle, just as all the dogs – save Ludwig and Lydia – die in Neuhundstein. The castle is also the model for those created by Disney in each of its theme parks, the original inspired by another man who also wanted to make the world over into an image of his imagination. The novel's Ludwig is not the creator of Neuhundstein and is in fact the only dog not to move into the castle. He seems to offer an alterative way to imagine a different world, not one based on abstract ideas and fantasies (and thus similar to Rank's fantasy of the dogs as perfectly faithful companions) but instead based on material and embodied connections with other beings, connections that are in flux and exceed the parameters of language, itself another system for fixing identities and categories.

Chapter 3

1. This story is published online at www.kijjohnson.com/evolution.html. All references are to this version of the story, accessed December 4, 2008.

2. See Hillix and Rumbaugh for a thorough overview of such research.

3. See chapter 4, 'Symbolic Exchange', of Alan Shapiro's *Star Trek: Technologies of Disappearance* for an insightful reading of how the fantasy of the universal translator negotiates some of the complications of language and alterity in sf.

4. This story is incorporated into the linked collection *City* (1952). The entire series will be discussed in more detail in my conclusion.

5. See my *Bodies of Tomorrow* (2007) for a more extended engagement with Hayles's ideas and the questions of posthumanism and embodiment in general.

6. See McNally for a critique of idealist linguistics from a Marxist point of view, and the development of a theory of materialist linguistics.

7. See Barad for a sustained analysis of this interaction which she calls the 'entanglement' of matter of meaning, and for a feminist analysis of how this understanding of physical reality can inform a transformative politics.

8. The phrase Schrödinger's Cat refers to a famous physics thought experiment described by Erwin Schrödinger that explores the problem of trying to apply quantum theory to the behaviour of everyday objects. In the thought experiment, we imagine a cat locked into a closed box with a vial of poison. The box also contains a Geiger counter containing a bit of radioactive

substance so small that it is randomly determined whether in the course of an hour one of the atoms decays. If it happens, the counter tube discharges, and provokes a hammer to shatter a flask of hydrocyanic acid, thereby killing the cat. Until one opens the box and observes the result, one does not know which outcome happened. Since the outcome depends on a single atomic participle – which quantum mechanics establishes can change its behaviour depending upon whether it is observed – in theory the cat exists in a smeared state of both alive and dead until the box is opened and the probability is collapsed into an observed actuality. The thought experiment is designed to pose the question of when the quantum system stops existing as a mixture of states, either of which resemble different classical states, and become a unique state described fully by classical mechanics. Ursula Le Guin's story 'Schrödinger's Cat' interrogates this famed experiment from the point of view of considering the difference between the cat as a 'parable-cat, a figment-cat, the amusing embodiment of a daring hypothesis' and the acknowledgement of the cat as 'an actual, biographical-historical cat' (187) she creates for her story. Le Guin's insistence that the animal has an equal role with the human in the constitution of reality through observation is consistent with Barad's *'ethico-onto-epistem-ology* – an appreciation for the intertwining of ethics, knowing and being – since each intra-action matters, since the possibilities for what the world may become call out in the pause that precedes each breath before a moment comes into being and the world is remade again, because the becoming of the world is a deeply ethical matter' (185). See Jackson for an insightful reading of this and other of the stories from *Buffalo Gals*.

9. Damon Knight's 'The Second-Class Citizen' (1963) emphatically makes the point that communication and other abilities are linked to a distinct *Umwelt* shaped by more than just intelligence or language use. In its early scenes, a visitor to researcher Craven's dolphin laboratory finds his demonstration of dolphin performance *'pathetic* …You talk about making them enter the human community. It's all wrong! He's a dolphin, not a man. He was trying so hard, but the best you could turn him into was something like a retarded, crippled child' (102). By the story's conclusion, some kind of massive explosion seems to have wiped out all human civilisation, Craven surviving only by having the foresight to enter the ocean with his diving gear the moment he realised television transmission was disrupted. Realising that it is not safe for him to return to land, he reminds himself *'I've got to learn … This is my element now, the sea – I've got to adapt'* (104). His own pathetic and unsuccessful attempts to catch fish are aided by a former laboratory dolphin, trained to speak, who 'kindly' catches a fish in its jaws and tells him 'this is the way to catch a fiss' (104). Even the primacy of tool use that humans take for granted as a sign of superiority must be questioned once anthropocentrism is dropped.

10. See Derrida 'Heidegger's Hand' for a more detailed analysis of the metaphysical implications of this distinction and of its inability to hold.

11. For a material-world example of research that attempts to assess communication between cetaceans and humans based on the idea of affordances and the two species' different perceptual experiences of the same material reality, see Warkentin.

Chapter 4

1. The title of this chapter is taken from Margaret Van de Pitte's essay of the same title, published in *Birding* 31.4: 367. The phrase, a common one in ornithology reference books, refers to the difference in plumage between male and female varieties of the species. Van de Pitte's essay interrogates the assumptions that lie behind this expression which is part of the gendering of animals in human discourse, the topic of this chapter.

2. See Vint *'Who Goes There? "Real" Men, Only'* for a further discussion of the way human subjectivity is construed as a specifically masculine subjectivity in John W. Campbell's novella.

3. In much of this chapter, I will be using 'man' in order to designate a position in discourse that is equivalent to that of 'human' but which is marked by the specifically gendered nature of its history, a history that has to a large degree excluded women from the category 'human'. At other times, when I want to refer to *Homo sapiens* collectively without drawing attention to this gendered history, I will use the term 'human' as I do elsewhere in this book.

4. The conclusions of sociobiology have been critiqued by many scientists and science studies scholars. Its limitations and the existence of other models to explain the behaviours of humans and other primates is one of the foci of Haraway's *Primate Visions*. Haraway notes the ways that the research itself is guided by assumptions about gender – such as caging primates in nuclear family units as the 'natural' grouping (78) or the expectation that female researchers would be better observers as they would be more 'sensitive' to mother–young interactions (151). Sociobiological assumptions – that scarcity, self-maximising strategic reasoning and constant adaptationism offer the best keys for understanding primate behavior – have been criticised, and new results emerged when founding assumptions were shifted. For example, Linda Fedigan found that 'females previously consigned to a category of resource or matrix emerged from [her] analysis as active generators of lives and meanings' (Haraway *Primate Visions* 320). For a specific critique of Wilson's work on ant society, see Deborah M. Gordon's *Ants at Work* (1999).

5. Wilson's major work on the species, *The Ants* (1990), co-authored with Bert Hölldobler, won a Pulitzer Prize.

6. I am here following Haraway, who argues in *Primate Visions* that 'scientific practice may be considered a kind of story-telling practice – a rule-governed, constrained historically changing craft of narrating the history of nature. Scientific practice and scientific theories produce and are embedded in particular kinds of stories ... Scientific practice is above all a story-telling practice in the sense of historically specific practices of interpretation and testimony' (4).

7. See also Chapter 5, where I develop this idea in more detail in relation to another Olsen story.

8. See Haraway *Primate Visions* 231–243 for a detailed analysis of these experiments in depriving infant monkeys of their mothers and offering a variety of surrogate mothers that repelled the infant in various ways.

9. It is important to note that issues of sexual orientation are also relevant

to this critique of carnophallogocentrism. Although space precludes a more extended consideration of such matters here, Derrida notes that males who fail sufficiently to occupy the masculine subject position, such as homosexuals, are excluded under this logic as well. Similarly, sociobiological discourses have been used to naturalise heterosexuality, attempts which have been plagued by the prevalence of non-heterosexual activity in many animal species that sociobiologists are at pains to discount. For a reading of *Who Goes There?*, a story I have analysed from the point of view of the human/animal boundary, which makes evident how discourses of sexual orientation are also implicated in these distinctions, see Wendy Pearson's 'Alien Cryptographies'. For a discussion of issues of sexuality, sexual orientation and biology, including analyses of much animal behaviour, see Joan Roughgarden's *Evolution's Rainbow*.

Chapter 5

1. See Francione for a more detailed argument about the various ways that the legal concept of 'standing' (which is related to property) hampers efforts for animal-welfare legal reform.

2. See Spiegel for an analysis of the complexities of these issues. Her work argues that the comparison is a useful one and not dismissive of the human suffering that occurred under slavery.

3. See Philip's 'Producing Transnational Knowledge' and *Civilizing Natures* for a discussion of sites of resistance to this appropriation of knowledge via the patent system.

4. Armstrong notes a similar dynamic at work in *Robinson Crusoe*, in which the protagonist's attitude toward the cats who come near his cabin shifts considerably. Some can be treated as pets, but when their numbers grow too great he begins to shoot them: 'As long as the animal belongs in the former category [pet] its apparent self-sufficiency can be accepted, and anthropo-morphically enjoyed, as a limited and trivialized form of agency. But once the animal becomes a pest – once its joins the category of those species competing with humans for resources, or threatening damage to human agriculture or domestic spatial arrangements – agency is reconfigured as ferity' (*What Animals Mean* 35).

5. Throughout the story, descriptions of the imagined labour among ants use the female pronoun for the worker ants. Whenever human labour is imagined and described, the male pronoun is used for the human workers.

6. See Vint 'Species and Species Being' for a detailed analysis of animals and Marx's theory of labour power. I argue for the inclusion of animals in the category of those who can be alienated from their labour.

7. See Sleigh *Ant* 189–191 for a discussion of other ways of theorising ant worker identity, especially for an argument that counters Wilson's view that worker ants are limited to a specific function. Researcher Deborah Gordon argues instead that ants can change function as the contingent conditions of the colony change and different types of work are needed. Sleigh points out that both ways of reading the ant have as much to do with the contemporary conditions of capitalism as with the actual behaviour of ants. When Wilson

developed his theory, a Fordist production line was the dominant labour paradigm. More recently, when Gordon's work appeared, worker flexibility as part of post-Fordist flexible accumulation is the norm.

8. Sleigh notes they are an image of contemporary fears about native resistance: 'Holroyd's concerns about the ants' anthropomorphic uprising echo the Belgians' anxiety about the behaviour of the Congolese, should they have taken it into their heads that they had been mistreated' ('Empire' 48).

9. See Rothfels and Hanson for a history of zoo development and descriptions of such animal deaths in the era before animals were protected from zoo visitors.

10. See Roediger for a detailed analysis of this history.

11. See Vint 'Speciesism and Species Being' for a more detailed treatment of this argument that engages more extensively with Marxist labour theory and its exclusion of animals.

12. Hominids in Smith's future are *Homo sapiens* whose bodies have been modified in order to survive in very different conditions from those of Earth on some of the planets that have been colonised. The hominids often look less like humans than do the underpeople, but their genetic relationship to human rather than animal 'stock' ensures their higher social status.

13. Torres also reports on research to develop Valkerase, an enzyme that breaks down keratin in feathers so that feathers from slaughtered birds can be used to feed other chickens; he further suggests that the appearance and spread of avian flu can be linked to factory farming methods (65). The desire to extract all possible profit and minimise 'waste' thus threatens animal and human health alike. Haraway ties the rapid spread of avian flu to 'that staple of global neoliberalism: illegal trade involving the world's poorest populations tied to the most economically entrepreneurial configurations' (*When Species Meet* 270). Her data suggests that 'worldwide, the illegal animal trade of all sorts is second in total value only to illegal drugs' (271).

Chapter 6

1. I have not found a citable published source for this quotation, but it has featured on a number of animal welfare posters and t-shirts, always attributed to Alice Walker.

2. See Niles Eldridge, 'The Sixth Extinction'. June 2001. <www.action-bioscience.org/newfrontiers/eldredge2.html#primer>. Accessed January 1, 2009.

3. See DeMello and Chapter 1.

4. See Vint 'The Animals in That Country' for specific examples.

5. See Kant's discussion of 'indirect duty' in *Groundwork of the Metaphysics of Morals*.

6. See Roberts.

7. See Vint and Bould for a more detailed argument of this point.

8. Barbara Gowdy's novel *The White Bone* (1998), not considered here as it is not sf, is a compelling example of fiction that adopts the elephants' point of view from a perspective of considerable knowledge of elephant ethology.

9. There are human antagonists as well whose characterisation reveals more of the book's ideology: examples include liberal journalists who do not place a high enough value on military secrets and African nations whose 'puppet governments ... *like* the way things are' (505) under the fithp.

10. This character is modelled on sf author C.J. Cherryh, according to an online FAQ last updated March 2007, one of whose contributors is Larry Niven. <http://pub38.bravenet.com/faq/show.php?usernum=3240227033&c atid=480#q8>. Accessed January 1, 2009. Although it is beyond the scope of this book's focus on animals to explore this argument in more detail, it is interesting to note that among Cherryh's publications is the *Foreigner* series (1994–2007), which focuses on the descendents of a human crew lost in alien space. Its major themes include the complexities of translation and multiculturalism. Cherryh's work thus effectively conveys that the thoughts, feelings and motivations of another species would not necessarily correspond to those of human culture and it is diametrically opposed to the anthropocentric (more accurately, American) jingoism of Niven and Pournelle's work.

11. During the 1980s, Pournelle formed the Citizen's Advisory Panel on National Space Policy, to which both he and Niven belonged. Their report *Mutual Assured Survival* (1984) was influential in the militarization of space under President Reagan and was instrumental in securing funding for the SDI ('Star Wars') project. Thus the authors might have some reason to believe that sf authors are a realistic source of public policy information in certain contingencies, but they mistake the neo-liberalism initiated by the Reagan era and its Cold War paranoia for an immutable human condition.

12. Natalie Jeremijenko's project Ooz attempts to achieve something similar through installation art. As her website explains, 'OOZ devices are species specific but designed for both nonhuman and human users, encouraging humans to mirror the actions of the animals: explore the unique capacities of each respective species: expose the tremendous incapacities of humans, and challenge the human centric view of intelligence, competence and management of natural systems'. The human/animal interactions made possible by Ooz are based on two principles: '1) an architecture of reciprocity, i.e. any action you can direct at the animal, they can direct at you and 2) an information architecture of collective observation and interpretation'. See <www.nyu.edu/projects/xdesign/ooz>. Accessed December 4, 2008.

13. See Chapter 2.

14. See Introduction and Chapter 3.

15. Deep ecology is most frequently associated with the work of Arne Naess. His popularising work *Life's Philosophy* provides an accessible introduction to his thought. See also *Ecology, Community and Lifestyle* for a thorough English overview of his work.

16. See Plumwood for a critique of Naess and deep ecology along these lines.

17. Inevitably, not all of Earth's citizens or governments agree on the wisdom of accepting eqbas help to solve their ecological crisis. The main action on Earth is set in Australia since the Australian government decides to accept the inevitable and invite the eqbas to land there. This means that

their continent experiences maximum benefit and minimum suffering in the necessary adjustment of population and climate. Yet it also shows the impossibility of complete and impartial application of the principles of deep ecology. As far as the eqbas are concerned, a certain number of humans have to go and it makes no difference to them from where; thus they are happy to privilege the Australians in exchange for co-operation. It should also be pointed out that the eqbas make their own decision to intervene for the good of the planet once they are aware of the crisis: they do not need an invitation. As well, their superior technology means that they can do as they please without co-operation: it merely makes things more convenient. Crucially, unlike the aliens in the recent ecologically themed remake of *The Day the Earth Stood Still* (2008), the eqbas never relent or decide that humans deserve another chance to change their ways. The series thus refuses a sentimentality characteristic of much sf, even that which at the same time critiques aspects of human behaviour.

Chapter 7

1. The allusion is to the characterisation of the Houyhnhnms in the fourth voyage of *Gulliver's Travels* (1726) in which Gulliver's preference for the horses and contempt for the Yahoos is used as a device to reflect on all the ways that humanity fails to live up to the image of itself it constructs via the human–animal boundary. Disch's satire is very clearly addressed to similar ends and modelled on a similar logic. Armstrong's analysis refers both to Swift and to images of animality in Defoe's *Robinson Crusoe* (1719).

2. This aspect of the story suggests a link with themes of Kafka's 'A Hunger Artist' (1922) and its vision of the artist dependent upon amusing the public as living a life similar to that of a circus animal.

3. Serpell notes that such dependency has been bred into dogs over centuries of domestication and thus is not merely a product of particular social relations with an individual dog in the present: 'A recent study in Hungary compared the problem-solving abilities of dogs and hand-reared wolves and found that when faced with an insoluble problem such as getting food out of a sealed container, wolves worked persistently at the task and ignored their human handlers. Dogs, on the contrary, struggled briefly with the problem and then looked at their handlers "for assistance" – exactly the same kind of behaviour we would expect from a person, especially a young person, in similar straits' (130). On the one hand, this suggests that dogs view humans as part of their social network and thus approach the relationship as true companion species; on the other, it also demonstrates the degree to which such animals are at risk when treated without respect by irresponsible human partners.

4. Sam is the Hoot collective noun for human males; Sue is the one for females.

5. See Chapter 1 for a fuller discussion of issues of meat consumption and animality.

Chapter 8

1. Brian Aldiss's argument that Mary Shelley's *Frankenstein* (1818) is the first sf novel has been influential in the field. Philip Armstrong finds a concern with technology and its invasion into animal life at the heart of this novel's conflict. He suggests the Creature 'emerges at the intersection of two forms of generation: one organic and one technological (or proto-industrial). Indeed his monstrosity derives from the conjunction of these two modes' (*What Animals Mean* 74). Armstrong further contends that 'the universally negative reactions the Creature faces within the narrative reflect a cultural concern during the early decades of the nineteenth century regarding the new wave of scientific, and especially agricultural, manipulation of nature: these included experimental stock breeding to accelerate meat production, the trialling of new crops, innovations in drainage and cultivation, and artificial alterations to chemistry of the soil' (*What Animals Mean* 74). Thus, a negative portrayal of the consequences of modern scientific culture for human and other life can be considered foundation to the genre even in theories that date its origin earlier than the nineteenth century.

2. Sf writer James Blish's *Dr Mirabilis* (1964), a fictional account of the life of Roger Bacon, shows Bacon engaged in similar experimentation. The novel depicts Bacon's struggles with a scientific culture in which authority rather than experience dominated theory. As the novel reveals, much of what was accepted as science in Bacon's time is no longer part of the field, and Bacon is celebrated because his work anticipated the experimental method of 'real' science popularised in the seventeenth century.

3. See Shapin and Schaffer, and Latour *We Have Never Been Modern*.

4. Richard Lewontin notes that recent research into strains of what have been labelled 'maze-bright' and 'maze-dull' laboratory rats revealed that those considered the most intelligent by human observers because they were able to most swiftly navigate mazes were in fact able to do so because their senses were less acute than the maze-dull rats, who were too easily distracted by visual and scent cues to which the maze-bright rats were oblivious (12).

5. See my Introduction for a more complete discussion of this aspect of Heidegger's work.

6. See Vint 'Animals and Animality' for a more thorough analysis of the novel along these lines, as well as a comparison to the created animals in David Brin's *Uplift* series (1980–1998). I argue that although Brin's series is more explicitly concerned with imagining animal sentience, its failure to critique the values of science crystallised in the 'unmarked' body of the 'scientist' (white, male, bourgeois, *Homo sapiens*) results in a more conservative treatment of subjectivity and ethics in this latter work.

7. Wells's novel is alluded to within the text as a fictionalised account of a Dr McMoreau who 'was probing the borderland between human and animal nature, where the springs of modern man's behaviour lie. Territorial imperatives, to name but one example I expect you're au fait with. Questions the scientific world tries to answer today by resort to piddling disciplines

like palaeontology and archaeology' (40). Dart sees himself as following in McMoreau's worthy footsteps.

8. It is important to recall that the thalidomide disaster was caused by a failure of homology between animal trials and human application. The drug did not cause birth defects in the animals upon whom it was tested because of differences between their physiology and that of the humans affected by the drug when it went on the market.

9. See Haraway *Modest_Witness@Second.Millennium*.

10. Animal advocate and veterinary scientist Andrew Knight has done much to develop such an alternative laboratory practice. His publications have challenged the efficacy of using animal models for biomedical testing, articulated alterative experimental designs that minimise the use of animal test subjects and argued for the limited and responsible use of animals in ways that reduce overall suffering. His publications on animal research are available on his website at www.aknight.info/pages/publications/publications.htm. Accessed October 12, 2009.

11. One of the distinctions Heidegger makes between the *Dasein* and other being, as I discussed in Chapter 3, is the capacity to use technology, a capacity he associated with having hands. He thus suggests that while the paws of certain species might morphologically resemble hands, they are not the same as hands because they do not imply the same relationship of potentiality with the material world that the human unconcealing of technology enables.

12. Sirius is, of course, a cyborg figure as well and thus fits into a pattern of sf's technological created others (androids, cyborgs and AIs), many of whom aspire to be human. See Veronica Hollinger's 'Retrofitting *Frankenstein*' for a discussion of how *Frankenstein* has become a precursor text for such figures. Hollinger argues that increasingly such stories are not about the relationship between creators and created, human subjects and created objects, but instead interrogate 'the possibilities of radically alternative subjectivities which may yet come to share the world with us'. Sirius is just such a subject, but part of my argument regarding his animal origin is that this novel and other sf representations of animals at the same time enable reflections upon possible social relations with the radically alternative subjectivities with whom we already share the world.

13. This name is the best-known pseudonym for author Alice Sheldon. She also published under the pseudonym Raccoona Sheldon and stories published under this name are discussed earlier in this book.

Conclusion

1. De Vos argues that the destructive relationship between humans and other beings dates even further back, basically to the emergence of human-like social organisation: 'Our current notions of extinction are shaped both by the knowledge that more than 99% of all known animal and plant species are now extinct, and that we are currently living in a time of mass extinction argued to have commenced with the spreading out of humans from the African continent 50,000 years ago' (183).

2. Unfortunately, this important insight is somewhat marred by the novel's insistence on associating it almost entirely with characters who represent the worst aspects of twenty-first-century American politics. These figures insist that America's national security interests are more important than the lives of everyone else on the planet, that God has created the world for humans and for American in particular, and that 'America *is* the world' (802). While such portraits are not inconsistent with aspects of the George W. Bush administration's environmental and foreign policy, this caricaturising ultimately undermines the novel's critique. Rather than enabling a focus on reconfiguring human subjectivity and social relations, it suggests the problem is that of a few megalomaniacal Americans and not a systemic reflection of capitalist social organisation and a metaphysics of subjectivity rooted in the human/animal boundary. Thus, much like *Swarm* fails to present the Yrr as aliens who do not think 'like humans', it similarly fails to convey the true problems of human exceptionalism in its too easy binary between 'ignorant Americans' and a sensible rest-of-humanity, without working through the ways all of Western culture is complicit in exploitative relations with nature and other humans. There is a real connection between bioparanoia and US politics in the post-9/11 era, as the Critical Art Ensemble points out. For example, much of the suffering caused by the inadequate response to Hurricane Katrina was related to the fact that the Federal Emergency Management Agency was placed under the authority of Homeland Security because the government could not conceive of a threat other than a military one (see 'Bioparanoia and the Culture of Control').

3. I address only the two books written by Norton, although three others, *Beast Master Ark* (2002), *Beast Master Circus* (2004) and *Beast Master Quest* (2006), have recently been 'co-written' with Lyn McConchie. These books introduce a new animal, Prauo, who is a sentient species from another planet although he appears to be a cat. They retain the original Beast Master team animals, but relegate them to the background of the action. They thus suggest a very different engagement with animal consciousness, human/animal social relations and empathy, although ironically they often seem dismissive of 'real' animals in favour of the talking cat, Prauo. The differences are in part a consequence of the more than forty years that separate Norton's work from this more recent series, but it is nonetheless curious that the novels written at a time when much more is known about the communicative capacities of 'real' animals do not explore their subjectivity as much as do the earlier novels. The fantasy of Prauo, another species who can fully communicate in human language, is more compelling to a twenty-first-century audience, it would seem.

4. In the third tale, 'Census', the Webster who originally created the dogs through surgical modification explains that these changes are being inherited by new generations of Webster dogs and so this transformation exists as 'fact' within the story, however implausible from a biological point of view.

5. Jennifer Wolch suggests one such model in her version of the transformed city she calls a *zoöpolis*: 'To allow for the emergence of an ethic, practice, and politics of caring for animals and nature, we need to renaturalize

cities and invite the animals back in, and in the process re-enchant the city. I call this renaturalized, re-enchanted city *zoöpolis*. The reintegration of people with animals and nature in zoöpolis can provide urban dwellers with the local, situated, everyday knowledge of animal life required to grasp animal standpoints or ways of being in the world, to interact with them accordingly in particular context, and to motivate political action necessary to protect their autonomy as subjects and their life spaces' (124).

6. This behaviour, not incidentally, was first described and theorised by a female geneticist, Barbara McClintock. Her work did not fit the dominant paradigm which understood the genome as a fixed code in which certain sequences universally expressed the same behaviours. McClintock's work was ignored for most of her lifetime, dismissed as not rigorous; after forty years of neglect, she received a Nobel Prize and her work transformed the study of genetics. Feminist science-studies scholar Evelyn Fox Keller uses McClintock's life and work to reflect on the ways in which gender ideology has shaped science practice, a critique she develops in *A Feeling for the Organism*. See also Jones in which the story of a fictional female scientist conveys similar ideas about the relationship among science, how we experience the world and gender ideology, and my paper 'Why Are There No Great Women Scientists'.

7. See Joan Gordon 'Gazing Across the Abyss' for her development of what she calls 'the amborg gaze' which has similarities to both Braidotti's transpositions and Simak's vision of the Juwain philosophy. Gordon uses the notion of the amborg gaze to critique Tepper's *Six Moon Dance*, and by extension much of Tepper's work, for reintroducing fixed binaries and a hierarchy between being and becoming; as Gordon's work makes clear, Tepper's embrace of becoming-animal is, ironically, used as a ground from which to condemn subjectivities that fail to do so.

8. See my 'Speciesism and Species Being' for a more extended discussion of the ways reconnecting with animals might transform alienated social relations among humans as well.

Works Cited

Acampora, Ralph R. 'Animal Philosophy: Bioethics and Zoontology'. *A Cultural History of Animals in the Modern Age*. Edited by Randy Malamud. Oxford: Berg, 2007. 139–161.

—. *Corporal Compassion: Animal Ethics and Philosophy of Body*. Pittsburgh, PA: University of Pittsburgh Press, 2006.

—. 'Nietzsche's Feral Philosophy: Thinking through an Animal Imaginary'. *A Nietzschean Bestiary: Becoming Animal beyond Docile and Brutal*. Edited by Christa Davis Acampora and Ralph R. Acampora. Boulder, CO: Rowman and Littlefield, 2004. 1–13.

Adams, Carol. *The Sexual Politics of Meat: A Feminist-Vegetarian Critical Theory*. New York: Continuum, 1990.

Adorno, Theodor. *Minima Moralia: Reflections on a Damaged Life*. London: Verso, 1984.

Agamben, Giorgio. *Homo Sacer: Sovereign Power and Bare Life*. Translated by Daniel Heller-Roazen. Stanford, CA: Stanford University Press, 1998.

—. *The Open: Man and Animal*. Translated by Kevin Attell. Stanford, CA: Stanford University Press, 2003.

Aldiss, Brian. *Billion Year Spree: The True History of Science Fiction*. New York: Schocken, 1974.

—. *Moreau's Other Island*. London: Jonathan Cape, 1980.

Alexander, W. 'The Dog's Sixth Sense'. *Amazing Stories* (September 1952): 540–543.

Armstrong, Philip. 'Farming Images: Animal Rights and Agribusiness in the Field of Vision'. *Knowing Animals*. Edited by Laurence Simmons and Philip Armstrong. Leiden: Brill, 2007. 105–128.

—. *What Animals Mean in the Fiction of Modernity*. New York: Routledge, 2008.

Ash, Paul. 'Big Sword'. *Spectrum V: A Fifth Science Fiction Anthology*. Edited by Kingsley Amis and Robert Conquest. New York: SFBC, 1967. 205–247.

Asimov, Isaac. 'No Connection' [1948]. *The Best Science Fiction Stories, 1949*. Edited by Everett F. Bleiler. Hollywood: Frederick Fell, 1949. 226–249.

Bakis, Kirsten. *Lives of the Monster Dogs*. New York: Warner, 1997.

Barad, Karen. *Meeting the Universe Halfway: Quantum Physics and the Entanglement of Matter and Meaning*. Durham, NC: Duke University Press, 2007.

Benton, Ted and Simon Redfearn. 'The Politics of Animal Rights – Where is the Left?' *New Left Review* 215 (1996): 43–58.

Berger, John. 'Why Look at Animals?' *About Looking*. New York: Pantheon, 1980. 1–26.

Bergland, Jeff. *Cannibal Fictions: American Explorations of Colonialism, Race, Gender and Sexuality*. Madison: University of Wisconsin Press, 2006.

Birke, Lynda. *Feminism, Animals and Science: The Naming of the Shrew*. Buckingham: Open University Press, 1994.

Bisson, Terry. 'Bears Discover Fire'. *Year's Best Science Fiction 8th Annual Collection*. Edited by Gardner Dozois. New York: St. Martin's, 1991. 180–189.

Blish, James. *Dr. Mirabilis* [1964]. New York: Avon, 1982.

Boehrer, Bruce. 'Introduction: The Animal Renaissance'. *A Cultural History of Animals in the Renaissance*. Edited by Bruce Boehrer. Oxford: Berg, 2007. 1–26.

Braidotti, Rosi. *Transpositions: On Nomadic Ethics*. Cambridge: Polity, 2006.

Breur, Miles. 'The Hungry Guinea Pig'. *Amazing Stories* (January 1930): 926–935.

Brown, Sue-Ellen. "The Human–Animal Bond and Self Understanding: Toward a New Understanding'. *Society and Animals* 12.1 (2004): 67–86.

Burkett, Paul. *Marx and Nature: A Red and Green Perspective*. Basingstoke: Palgrave Macmillan, 1999.

Butler, Octavia. *Clay's Ark*. New York: Warner, 1984.

Calarco, Matthew. *Zoographies: The Question of the Animal from Heidegger to Derrida*. New York: Columbia University Press, 2008.

Campbell, John W. *Who Goes There?* [1938]. New York: Rosetta, 2000.

Čapek, Karel. *War with the Newts* [1936]. North Haven, CT: Catbird, 1999.

Carr, Terry. 'The Dance of the Changer and the Three' [1968]. *Nebula Award Stories V*. Edited by Poul Anderson. New York: Doubleday, 1969. 39–54.

Catts, Oron and Ionat Zurr. 'The Ethics of Experiential Engagement with the Manipulation of Life'. *Tactical Biopolitics: Art, Activism, and Technoscience*. Edited by Beatriz da Costa and Kavita Philip. Cambridge, MA: MIT Press, 2008. 125–142.

Charnas, Suzy McKee. 'Scorched Supper on New Niger'. *Women of Wonder: The Contemporary Years: Science Fiction by Women from the 1970s to the 1990s*. Edited by Pamela Sargeant. New York: AB & Company, 1995. 47–80.

Coetzee, J.M. *Elizabeth Costello*. New York: Penguin, 2003.

Cooper, Melinda. *Life as Surplus: Biotechnology and Capitalism in the Neoliberal Era*. Seattle: University of Washington Press, 2008.

Critical Art Ensemble. 'Bioparanoia and the Culture of Control'. *Tactical Biopolitics: Art, Activism, and Technoscience*. Edited by Beatriz da Costa and Kavita Philip. Cambridge, MA: MIT Press, 2008. 413–427.

Crowley, John. *Beasts*. New York: Doubleday, 1976.

Daston, Lorraine and Gregg Mitman. 'Introduction'. *Thinking with Animals: New Perspectives on Anthropomorphism*. Edited by Lorraine Daston and Gregg Mitman. New York: Columbia University Press, 2005. 1–14.

De Lauretis, Teresa. 'Signs of W[a/o]nder'. *The Technological Imagination: Theories and Fictions*. Edited by Teresa de Lauretis, Andreas Huyssen and Kathleen Woodward. Madison, WI: Coda Press, 1980. 159–174.

De Leemans, Pieter and Matthew Klemm. 'Animals and Anthropology in Medieval Philosophy'. *A Cultural History of Animals in the Medieval Age*. Edited by Brigitte Resl. Oxford: Berg, 2007. 153–177.

Deleuze, Gilles and Felix Guattari. *A Thousand Plateaus: Capitalism and Schizophrenia*. Translation and foreword by Brian Massumi. Minneapolis: University of Minnesota Press, 1987.

DeMello, Margo. 'The Present and Future of Animal Domestication'. *A Cultural History of Animals in the Modern Age*. Edited by Randy Malamud. Oxford: Berg, 2007. 67–94.

Derrida, Jacques. *The Animal that Therefore I Am*. New York: Fordham University Press, 2008.

—. '"Eating Well," or the Calculation of the Subject: An Interview with Jacques Derrida'. *Who Comes after the Subject?* Edited by Eduardo Cadava, Peter Connor and Jean-Luc Nancy. New York: Routledge, 1991. 96–119.

—. 'Heidegger's Hand (Geschlecht II)'. *Psyche: Inventions of the Other*, Volume II. Edited by Peggy Kamuf and Elizabeth G. Rottenberg. Stanford, CA: Stanford University Press, 2008. 27–62.

De Vos, Ricardo. 'Extinction Stories: Performing Absence(s)'. *Knowing Animals*. Edited by Laurence Simmons and Philip Armstrong. Leiden: Brill, 2007. 183–195.

Dick, Philip K. *Do Androids Dream of Electric Sheep?* New York: Ballantine, 1968.

Dickson, George. 'Dolphin's Way' [1964]. *The Best Animal Stories of Science Fiction and Fantasy*. Edited by Donald J. Sobol. New York: Frederick Warne, 1979. 97–117.

Dillon, Grace. 'Totemic Human–Animal Relationships in Recent Sf'. *Extrapolation* 49.1 (2008): 70–96.

Disch, Thomas M. *The Puppies of Terra*. New York: Pocket, 1966.

Donovan, Josephine and Carol Adams. *The Feminist Care Tradition in Animal Ethics*. New York: Columbia University Press, 2007.

Ellison, Harlan 'A Boy and His Dog'. *Essential Ellison: A 35 Year Retrospective*. London: Nemo, 1987. 905–938.

Emel, Jody and Jennifer Wolch. 'Witnessing the Animal Moment'. *Animal Geographies: Place, Politics and Identity in the Nature–Culture Borderlands*. Edited by Jennifer Wolch and Jody Emel. London: Verso, 1998. 1–24.

Emshwiller, Carol. 'Animal'. *Joy in Our Cause: Short Stories* [1968]. New York: Harper & Row, 1974. 84–95.

—. *The Mount*. New York: Firebird, 2002.

—. 'Sanctuary'. *Lady Churchill's Rosebud Wristlet* 21 (2007): 59–60.

Evernden, Neil. *The Natural Alien: Humankind and Environment*. Toronto: University of Toronto Press, 1985.

Faber, Michel. *Under the Skin*. New York: Harcourt, 2000.

Fast, Howard. 'The Large Ant'. *Spectrum IV:* Edited by Kingsley Amis and Robert Conquest. New York: Harcourt, Brace and World, 1965. 124–133.

Ferry, Luc. *The New Ecological Order*. Translated by Carol Volk. Chicago, IL: University of Chicago Press, 1995.

Foucault, Michel. *The Birth of Biopolitics*. Translated by Graham Burchell. New York: Palgrave Macmillan, 2008.

—. *Security, Territory, Population*. Translated by Graham Burchell. New York: Palgrave Macmillan, 2007.

—. *Society Must Be Defended*. Translated by David Macey. New York: Picador, 2003.

Fox, Michael. *Deep Vegetarianism*. Philadelphia, PA: Temple University Press, 1999.

Francione, Gary. *Animals, Property and the Law*. Philadelphia, PA: Temple University Press, 1995.

Franklin, Adrian. *Animals and Modern Cultures: A Sociology of Human–Animal Relations in Modernity*. London: Sage, 1999.

Fudge, Erica. *Animal*. London: Reaktion, 2002.

—. *Perceiving Animals: Humans and Beasts in Early Modern English Culture*. Champaign: University of Illinois Press, 2002.

—. *Pets*. Stocksfield: Acumen, 2008.

Godwin, Tom. 'The Cold Equations'. *The Road to Science Fiction*, Volume III: *From Heinlein to Here*. Edited by James Gunn. Clarkston: White Wolf, 1996. 200–220.

Goodall, Jane. *In the Shadow of Man*. London: Collins, 1971.

Gordon, Deborah M. *Ants at Work: How Insect Society Is Organized*. New York: W.W. Norton, 2000.

Gordon, Joan. 'Gazing Across the Abyss: The Amborg Gaze in Sheri S. Tepper's *Six Moon Dance*'. *Science Fiction Studies* 35.2 (2008): 189–206.

Graham, Elaine L. *Representations of the Post/Human: Monsters, Aliens and Other in Popular Culture*. New Brunswick, NJ: Rutgers University Press, 2002.

Greenebaum, Jessica. 'It's a Dog's Life: Elevating Status from Pet to "Fur Baby" at Yappy Hour'. *Society and Animals* 12.2 (2004): 117–135.

Hanson, Elizabeth. *Animal Attractions: Nature on Display in American Zoos*. Princeton, NJ: Princeton University Press, 2002.

Haraway, Donna. *The Companion Species Manifesto: Dogs, People and Significant Otherness*. Chicago: Prickly Paradigm, 2003.

—. 'A Cyborg Manifesto: Science Technology, and Socialist-Feminism in the Late Twentieth Century'. *Simians, Cyborgs and Women: The Reinvention of Nature*. New York: Routledge, 1991. 149–181.

—. *Modest_Witness@Second_Millennium.FemaleMan_Meets_OncoMouse: Feminism and Technoscience*. London: Routledge, 1997.

—. *Primate Visions: Gender, Race and Nation in the World of Modern Science*. New York: Routledge, 1990.

—. *When Species Meet*. Minneapolis: University of Minnesota Press, 2007.

Harris, Clare Winger. 'The Ape Cycle'. *Science Wonder Quarterly* (Spring 1930): 380–405.

—. 'The Miracle of the Lily'. *Amazing Stories* (April 1928): 48–55.

Hayles, N. Katherine. *How We Became Posthuman: Virtual Bodies in Cybernetics, Literature and Informatics*. Chicago, IL: University of Chicago Press, 1999.

Hearne, Vicki. *Adam's Task: Calling Animals by Name*. New York: Knopf, 1986.

Heidegger, Martin. 'The Question Concerning Technology'. *The Question Concerning Technology and Other Essays*. Translated and with an introduction by William Lorett. New York: Harper Torchbooks, 1977. 3–35.

Herrnstein Smith, Barbara. *Scandalous Knowledge: Science, Truth and the Human*. Durham, NC: Duke University Press, 2005.

Hess, Elizabeth. *Nim Chimpsky: The Chimp Who Would Be Human*. New York: Bantam, 2008.

Hillix, William A. and Duane M. Rumbaugh. *Animal Bodies, Human Minds: Ape, Dolphin and Parrot Language Skills*. New York: Kluwer Academic/Plenum Publishers, 2004.

Hollinger, Veronica. 'Retrofitting *Frankenstein*'. *Beyond Cyberpunk: Cyberpunk in the New Millennium*. Edited by Graham J. Murphy and Sherryl Vint. New York: Routledge, 2010. 191–200.

Horkheimer, Max and Theodor Adorno. 'Man and Animal'. *The Dialectic of Enlightenment* [1944]. New York: Continuum, 2002. 245–255.

Hulme, Peter. *Colonial Encounters: Europe and the Native Caribbean 1492–1797*. New York: Routledge, 1992.

Jackson, Kasi. 'Feminism, Animals, and Science in Le Guin's Animal Stories'. *Paradoxa* 21 (2008): 206–231.

Jameson, Fredric. *Archaeologies of the Future: The Desire Called Utopia and Other Science Fictions*. London: Verso, 2005.

Johnson, Kij. 'The Evolution of Trickster Stories among the Dogs of North Park after the Change'. *Kij Johnson*. 2007. <www.kijjohnson.com/evolution.html>. Accessed December 4, 2008.

Jones, Gwyneth. *Life*. Seattle, WA: Aqueduct, 2004.

Kalof, Linda. 'Introduction: Ancient Animals'. *A Cultural History of Animals in Antiquity*. Edited by Linda Kalof. Oxford: Berg, 2007. 1–16.

—. *Looking at Animals in Human History*. London: Reaktion, 2007.

Kant, Immanuel. *Groundwork of the Metaphysics of Morals* [1785]. Edited and translated by Mary Gregor. Introduction by Christine M. Korsgaard. Cambridge: Cambridge University Press, 1997.

Kately, Walter. 'Remote Control'. *Amazing Stories* (April 1930): 22–30.

Keller, David H. 'The Steam Shovel'. *Amazing Stories* (September 1931): 510–513.

Keller, Evelyn Fox. *A Feeling for the Organism: The Life and Work of Barbara McClintock*. 10th anniversary edition. New York: W.H. Freeman, 1983.

Kennedy, Leigh. 'Her Furry Face' [1983]. *Alien Sex*. Edited by Ellen Datlow. New York: Dutton, 1990. 5–22.

Kessel, John. 'Animals'. *The Pure Project*. New York: TOR, 1997. 158–171.

Kete, Kathleen. 'Introduction: Animals and Human Empire'. *A Cultural History of Animals in the Age of Empire*. Oxford: Berg, 2007. 1–24.

Knight, Damon. 'The Second-Class Citizen' [1963]. *Apeman, Spaceman*. Edited by Leon E. Stover and Harry Harrison. New York: Berkley, 1968. 97–104.

Kotzwinkle, William. *Doctor Rat*. New York: Avon, 1971.

Landström, Catharina. 'Australia Imagined in Biological Control'. *Knowing Animals*. Edited by Laurence Simmons and Philip Armstrong. Leiden: Brill, 2007. 196–214.

Lansbury, Coral. *The Old Brown Dog: Women, Workers, and Vivisection in Edwardian England*. Madison: University of Wisconsin Press, 1985.

Latour, Bruno. *Pandora's Hope: Essays on the Reality of Science Studies*. Cambridge, MA: Harvard University Press, 1999.

—. *We Have Never Been Modern*. Translated by Catherine Porter. Cambridge, MA: Harvard University Press, 1993.

Le Guin, Ursula. '"The Author of the Acacia Seeds" and Other Extracts from the *Journal of the Association of Therolinguistics*' [1974]. *Buffalo Gals and Other Animal Presences*. New York: ROC, 1987. 200–210.

—. 'Buffalo Gals, Won't You Come Out Tonight?' *Buffalo Gals and Other Animal Presences*. New York: ROC, 1987. 17–60.

—. 'Introduction'. *Buffalo Gals and Other Animal Presences*. New York: ROC, 1987. 7–12.

—. 'Mazes' [1975]. *Buffalo Gals and Other Animal Presences*. New York: ROC, 1987. 69–76.

—. 'Schrödinger's Cat' [1974]. *Buffalo Gals and Other Animal Presences*. New York: ROC, 1987. 187–199.

—. 'She Unnames Them' [1985]. *Buffalo Gals and Other Animal Presences*. New York: ROC, 1987. 233–236.

Leinster, Murray. 'First Contact' [1945]. *Aliens from Analog*. Edited by Stanley Schmidt. New York: Dial, 1983. 13–36.

LePan, Don. *Animals*. Montreal: Véhicule, 2009.

Levinas, Emmanuel. 'The Name of a Dog, or, Natural Rights' [1976]. *Difficult Freedom: Essays on Judaism*. Translated by Seán Hand. London: Athlone, 1990. 151–153.

Lewontin, Richard. 'Living the Eleventh Thesis'. *Tactical Biopolitics: Art, Activism, and Technoscience*. Edited by Beatriz da Costa and Kavita Philip. Cambridge, MA: MIT Press, 2008. 25–33.

Lingis, Alphonso. 'Understanding Avian Intelligence'. *Knowing Animals*. Edited by Laurence Simmons and Philip Armstrong. Leiden: Brill, 2007. 43–56.

Lippit, Akira. *Electric Animal: Toward a Rhetoric of Wildlife*. Minneapolis: University of Minnesota Press, 2000.

London, Jack. *The Call of the Wild, White Fang and Other Stories*. Oxford: Oxford University Press, 1998.

Luckhurst, Roger. *Science Fiction*. Cambridge: Polity, 2005.

Mangum, Teresa. 'Narrative Dominion or The Animals Write Back? Animal Genres in Literature and the Arts'. *A Cultural History of Animals in the Age of Empire*. Edited by Kathleen Kete. Oxford: Berg, 2007. 153–173.

Manning, Laurence. 'The Call of the Mech Men'. *Wonder Stories* (November 1933): 366–385.

Marcus, Erik. *Meat Market: Animals, Ethics and Money*. Minneapolis, MN: Brio Press, 2005.

Marvin, Garry. 'Natural Instincts and Cultural Passions'. *Performance Research* 5.2 (2000): 108–115.

Mason, Jim. 'Animals: From Souls and the Sacred in Prehistoric Times to Symbols and Slaves in Antiquity'. *A Cultural History of Animals in Antiquity*. Edited by Linda Kalof. Oxford: Berg, 2007. 17–45.

McAllister, Bruce. 'The Girl Who Loved Animals' [1988]. *Vanishing Acts*. Edited by Ellen Datlow. New York: Tor, 2000. 74–97.

McAulay, Paul. *White Devils*. New York: TOR, 2004.

McCaffrey, Anne. *Decision at Doona*. New York: Ballantine, 1969.

McNally, David. *Bodies of Meaning: Studies on Language, Labor and Liberation*. New York: SUNY Press, 2000.

Miller, Walter. 'Conditionally Human'. *Conditionally Human*. New York: Ballantine, 1962. 7–66.

Mitman, Gregg. 'Pachyderm Personalities: The Media of Science, Politics, and Conservation'. *Thinking with Animals: New Perspectives on Anthropomorphism*. Edited by Lorraine Daston and Gregg Mitman. New York: Columbia University Press, 2005. 175–195.

Morgado, André Vilares. 'A Night on the Edge of Empire'. *Non-events on the Edge of Empire*. Edited by André Vilares Morgado. Lisbon: Simetria, 1996. 79–87.

Morgan, Jacque. 'The Feline Light and Power Company Is Organized'. *Amazing Stories* (July 1926): 319–321, 383.

Morrison, Grant and Frank Quitely. *We3*. New York: DC Comics, 2005.

Naess, Arne. *Ecology, Community and Lifestyle: Outline of an Ecosophy*. Cambridge: Cambridge University Press, 1993.

—. *Life's Philosophy: Reason and Feeling in a Deeper World*. Athens: University of Georgia Press, 2008.

Nagel, Thomas. 'What Is It Like to Be a Bat?' *Philosophical Review* 83.4 (1974): 435–450.

Nietzsche, Friedrich. *The Antichrist* [1888]. *The Portable Nietzsche*. Edited and translated by Walter Kaufmann. New York: Viking, 1968. 565–656.

—. *Thus Spoke Zarathustra* [1883–1885]. Edited by Adrian Del Caro and Robert Pippin. Cambridge: Cambridge University Press, 2006.

Niven, Larry and Jerry Pournelle. *Footfall*. New York: Ballantine, 1985.

Norton, Andre. *The Beast Master* [1959]. *Beast Master's Planet: A Beast Master Omnibus*. New York: TOR, 2005. 11–194.

—. *Lord of Thunder* [1962]. *Beast Master's Planet: A Beast Master Omnibus*. New York: TOR, 2005. 195–363.

Norton, Andre and Lyn McConchie. *Beast Master's Ark* [2002]. *Beast Master Team*. New York: SFBC, 2004. 1–195.

—. *Beast Master's Circus* [2004]. *Beast Master Team*. New York: SFBC, 2004. 197–388.

—. *Beast Master's Quest*. New York: TOR, 2006.

Noske, Barbara. *Beyond Boundaries: Humans and Animals*. Montreal: Black Rose, 1997.

Olsen, Bob. 'The Ant with a Human Soul'. *Amazing Stories Quarterly* (Spring/Summer 1932): 230–263, 279.

—. 'Peril among the Drivers'. *Amazing Stories* (March 1934): 36–83.

Patterson, Charles. *Eternal Treblinka: Our Treatment of Animals and the Holocaust*. New York: Lantern, 2002.

Pearson, Wendy. 'Alien Cryptographies: The View from Queer'. *Science Fiction Studies* 26.1 (1999): 1–22.

Philip, Kavita. *Civilizing Natures: Race, Resources and Modernity in Colonial South India*. Newark, DE: Rutgers University Press, 1993.

—. 'Producing Transnational Knowledge, Neoliberal Identities, and Techno-scientifc Practice in India'. *Tactical Biopolitics: Art, Activism, and Technoscience*.

Edited by Beatriz da Costa and Kavita Philip. Cambridge, MA: MIT Press, 2008. 243–267.

Phillips, Dana. 'Ecocriticism, Ecopoetics, and a Creed Outworn'. *New Formations* 64 (2008): 37–50.

Plumwood, Val. *Environmental Culture: The Ecological Crisis of Reason*. London: Routledge, 2002.

Podberscek, Anthony L., Elizabeth S. Paul and James A. Serpell. *Companion Animals & Us: Exploring the Relationships between People and Pets*. Cambridge: Cambridge University Press, 2000.

Pohl, Frederick. *Slave Ship*. New York: Ballantine, 1957.

Pragnell, F. 'The Essence of Life'. *Amazing Stories* (August/September 1933): 436–449, 455.

Raber, Karen. 'From Sheep to Meat, from Pets to People: Animal Domestication 1600–1800'. *A Cultural History of Animals in the Age of Enlightenment*. Edited by Matthew Senior. Oxford: Berg, 2007. 73–99.

Rader, Karen A. 'Scientific Animals: Reflections on the Laboratory and Its Human–Animal Relations, from *Dba* to Dolly and Beyond'. *A Cultural History of Animals in the Modern Age*. Edited by Randy Malamud. Oxford: Berg, 2007. 119–137.

Regan, Tom. *The Case for Animal Rights*. Berkeley: University of California Press, 1985.

Rementer, Edward. 'The Space Bender'. *Amazing Stories* (December 1928): 838–850.

Resl, Brigitte. 'Introduction: Animals in Culture, ca. 1000–ca. 1400'. *A Cultural History of Animals in the Medieval Age*. Edited by Brigitte Resl. Oxford: Berg, 2007. 1–26.

Reynolds, Mack. 'The Discord Makers' [1950]. *Invaders of Earth*. Edited by Groff Conklin. New York: Pocket, 1955. 134–145.

Rice, Louise and Tonjoroff-Roberts. 'The Astounding Enemy'. *Amazing Stories Quarterly* (Winter 1930): 78–103.

Rieder, John. *Colonialism and the Emergence of Science Fiction*. Middletown, CT: Wesleyan University Press, 2008.

Rifkin, Jeremy. *Beyond Beef: The Rise and Fall of the Cattle Culture*. New York: Plume, 1993.

Ritvo, Harriet. *The Animal Estate: The English and Other Creatures in the Victorian Age*. Cambridge, MA: Harvard University Press, 1987.

Roberts, Kim. 'Interlocking Oppressions: The Nature of Cruelty to Non-human Animals and its Relationship to Violence toward Humans'. *A Communion of Subjects: Animals in Religion, Science, and Ethics*. Edited by Paul Waldau and Kimberley Patton. New York: Columbia University Press, 2006. 605–615.

Roediger, David. *The Wages of Whiteness: Race and the Making of the American Working Class*. Revised and expanded edition. London: Verso, 1999.

Rothfels, Nigel. *Savages and Beasts: The Birth of the Modern Zoo*. Baltimore, MD: Johns Hopkins University Press, 2002.

Roughgarden, Joan. *Evolution's Rainbow: Diversity, Gender and Sexuality in Nature and People*. Berkeley: University of California Press, 2004.

Rowe, Martin (ed.). *The Way of Compassion*. Tulsa, OK: Stealth Management Institute, 2000.

Ryman, Geoff. *Air, or, Have Not Have*. New York: St. Martin's, 2004.

Schatzing, Frank. *The Swarm* [2004]. Translated by Sally-Ann Spencer. New York: HarperCollins, 2006.

Scholtmeijer, Marian. 'The Power of Otherness: Animals in Women's Fiction'. *Animals and Women: Feminist Theoretical Explorations*. Durham, NC: Duke University Press, 1995. 231–286.

Serpell, James A. 'People in Disguise: Anthropomorphism and the Human–Pet Relationship'. *Thinking with Animals: New Perspectives on Anthropomorphism*. Edited by Lorraine Daston and Gregg Mitman. New York: Columbia University Press, 2005. 121–136.

Shakespeare, William. *Timon of Athens*. Edited by John Jowett. Oxford: Oxford University Press, 2004.

Shapin, Steven and Simon Schaffer. *Leviathan and the Air-Pump: Hobbes, Boyle and the Experimental Life*. Princeton, NJ: Princeton University Press, 1989.

Shapiro, Alan N. *Star Trek: Technologies of Disappearance*. Berlin: Avinus, 2004.

Sheldon, Racoona. 'Morality Meat'. *Despatches from the Frontiers of the Female Mind*. London: The Women's Press, 1985. 209–234.

—. 'The Screwfly Solution' [1977]. *The Oxford Book of Science Fiction Stories*. Edited by Tom Shippey. Oxford: Oxford University Press, 1992. 435–453.

Siegel, Sarita. 'Reflections on Anthropomorphism in *The Disenchanted Forest*'. *Thinking with Animals: New Perspectives on Anthropomorphism*. Edited by Lorraine Daston and Gregg Mitman. New York: Columbia University Press, 2005. 196–222.

Simak, Clifford D. *City*. New York: Ace, 1952.

Simmons, Laurence and Philip Armstrong. 'Introduction'. *Knowing Animals*. Edited by Laurence Simmons and Philip Armstrong. Leiden: Brill, 2007. 1–26.

Singer, Peter. *Animal Liberation*. New York: HarperCollins, 1973.

Sleigh, Charlotte. *Ant*. London: Reaktion, 2003.

—. 'EMPIRE OF THE ANTS: H.G. Wells and Tropical Entomology'. *Science as Culture* 10.1 (2001): 33–71.

Smith, Cordwainer. 'The Ballad of Lost C'mell' [1962]. *The Rediscovery of Man*. Framingham, MA: NESFA, 1993. 401–418.

—. 'The Dead Lady of Clown Town' [1964]. *The Rediscovery of Man*. Framingham. MA: NESFA, 1993. 223–287.

— *Norstrilia*. New York: Ballantine, 1975.

—. 'Think Blue, Count Two' [1962]. *The Rediscovery of Man*. Framingham, MA: NESFA, 1993. 129–154.

Smith, Julie. 'Beyond Dominance and Affection: Living with Rabbits in Posthumanist Households'. *Society and Animals* 11.2 (2003): 181–197.

Sober, Elliot. 'Comparative Psychology Meets Evolutionary Biology: Morgan's Canon and Cladistic Parsimony'. *Thinking with Animals: New Perspectives on Anthropomorphism*. Edited by Lorraine Daston and Gregg Mitman. New York: Columbia University Press, 2005. 85–99.

Spiegel, Marjorie. *The Dreaded Comparison: Human and Animal Slavery*. 2nd revised edition. New York: Mirror, 1997.

Staats, Sara, Heidi Wallace and Tara Anderson. 'Reasons for Companion Animal Guardianship (Pet Ownership) from Two Populations'. *Society and Animals* 16.3 (2008): 279–291.

Stapledon, Olaf. *Sirius*. Harmondsworth: Penguin, 1944.

Stone, Leslie. 'The Human Pets of Mars' [1936]. *Before the Golden Age: A Science Fiction Anthology of the 1930s*. Edited by Isaac Asimov. New York: Doubleday, 1974. 729–775.

Tepper, Sheri S. *The Companions*. New York: Eos, 2003.

—. *The Family Tree*. New York: Eos, 1997.

Thomas, Keith. *Man and the Natural World: Changing Attitudes in England 1500–1800*. London: Allen Lane, 1983.

Tiffin, Helen. 'Bats in the Gardens'. *Mosaic* 38.4 (2005): 1–16.

—. 'Foot in Mouth: Animals, Disease and the Cannibal Complex'. *Mosaic* 40.1 (2007): 11–26.

—. 'Pigs, People and Pigoons'. *Knowing Animals*. Edited by Laurence Simmons and Philip Armstrong. Leiden: Brill, 2007. 244–265.

Tiptree. James T. 'The Psychologist Who Wouldn't Do Awful Things to Rats' [1976]. *The Ascent of Wonder: The Evolution of Hard SF*. Edited by David Hartwell and Kathryn Cramer. New York: TOR, 1994. 672–688.

Torres, Bob. *Making a Killing: The Political Economy of Animal Rights*. Oakland, CA: AK Press, 2007.

Traviss, Karen. *Ally*. New York: EOS, 2007.

—. *City of Pearl*. New York: EOS, 2004.

—. *Crossing the Line*. New York: EOS, 2004.

—. *Judge*. New York: EOS, 2008.

—. *Matriarch*. New York: EOS, 2006.

—. *The World Before*. New York: EOS, 2005.

Tuan, Yi-Fu. *Dominance and Affection: The Making of Pets*. New Haven, CT: Yale University Press, 1984.

Van de Pitte, Margaret. 'The Female Is Somewhat Duller'. *Birding* 31.4 (1998): 367.

Vint, Sherryl. 'Animals and Animality on the *Island of Moreau*'. *Science Fiction, Gender and Species* 37.2 (2007):85–102.

—. '"The Animals in That Country": Science Fiction and Animal Studies'. *Science Fiction Studies* 35.1 (2008): 177–188.

—. 'Becoming Other: Animals, Kinship and Butler's *Clay's Ark*'. *Science Fiction Studies* 32.2 (2005): 281–300.

—. *Bodies of Tomorrow: Technology, Subjectivity, Science Fiction*. Toronto: University of Toronto Press, 2007.

—. '"Simians, Subjectivity and Sociality: *2001: A Space Odyssey* and Two Versions of *Planet of the Apes*.' *Science Fiction Film and Television* 2.2 (2009): 225–250.

—. 'Species and Species Being: Alienated Subjectivity and the Commodification of Animals'. *Red Planets: Marxists on Science Fiction and Fantasy*. Edited by Mark Bould and China Miéville. London: Pluto, 2009. 118–136.

—. 'Speciesism and Species Being in *Do Androids Dream of Electric Sheep?*' *Mosaic* 40.1 (2007): 111–126.

—. '*Who Goes There?* "Real" Men, Only'. *Extrapolation* 46.4 (2005): 421–438.

—. 'Why Are There No Great Women Scientists?' *NYRSF* 254 (2009): 1, 8–13.

Vint, Sherryl and Mark Bould. 'There Is No Such Thing as Science Fiction'. *Reading Science Fiction*. Edited by James Gunn, Marleen Barr and Matthew Candelaria. Basingstoke: Palgrave, 2008. 43–51.

Wallen, Martin. *Fox*. London: Reaktion, 2006.

Warkentin, Traci. 'Animal Matters: Ethics, Embodied Agency and Sensory Experience in Whale–Human Interactions'. Paper presented at *Nature Matters* conference in Toronto, Canada, October 26, 2007.

Watson, Ian. *The Jonah Kit*. London: Gollanz, 1975.

Weaver-Hightower, Rebecca. *Empire Islands: Castaways, Cannibals and Fantasies of Conquest*. Minneapolis: University of Minnesota Press, 2007.

Weinbaum, Stanley. 'A Martian Odyssey' [1934]. *The Oxford Book of Science Fiction Stories*. Edited by Tom Shippey. Oxford: Oxford University Press, 1992. 70–94.

Wells, H.G. 'The Empire of the Ants' [1905]. *Earth Is the Strangest Planet*. Edited by Robert Silverberg. Nashville, TN: Thomas Nelson, 1977. 47–65.

—. *The Island of Doctor Moreau* [1896]. New York: Dover, 1996.

—. *The War of the Worlds* [1898]. New York: The Modern Library, 2002.

White, Paul S. 'The Experimental Animal in Victorian Britain'. *Thinking with Animals: New Perspectives on Anthropomorphism*. Edited by Lorraine Daston and Gregg Mitman. New York: Columbia University Press, 2005. 59–81.

Williams, Raymond. *The Country and the City*. London: Chatto & Windus, 1973.

Willis, Connie. 'Samaritan'. *Fire Watch*. New York: Spectra, 1998. 214–234.

Wilson, E.O. *Journey to the Ants: A Story of Scientific Exploration*. Cambridge, MA: Belknap, 1994.

Wilson, E.O. and Bert Hölldobler. *The Ants*. Cambridge, MA: Belknap, 1990.

Wilson, F. Paul. *Sims*. New York: TOR, 2003.

Winefield, Helen R., Anne Black and Anna Chur-Hansen. 'Health Effects of Ownership of and Attachment to Companion Animals in an Older Population'. *International Journal of Behavioral Medicine* 15.4 (2008): 303–310.

Wolch, Jennifer. 'Zoöpolis'. *Animal Geographies: Place, Politics and Identity in the Nature–Culture Borderlands*. Edited by Jennifer Wolch and Jody Emel. London: Verso, 1998. 119–138.

Wolfe, Cary. *Animal Rites: American Culture, the Discourse of Species, and Posthumanist Theory*. Chicago, IL: University of Chicago Press, 2003.

—. 'Introduction: Exposure'. *Philosophy & Animal Life*. Edited by Cary Wolfe. New York: Columbia University Press, 2008.

Wood, Lisa J., Billie Gilles-Corti, Max K. Bulsara and Darcy A. Bosch. 'More than a Furry Companion: The Ripple Effect of Companion Animals on Neighborhood Interactions and Sense of Community'. *Society and Animals* 15.1 (2007): 43–56.

Woolf, Virginia. *Flush: A Biography*. Orlando, FL: Harcourt, 1933.

Wylie, Dan. *Elephant*. London: Reaktion, 2008.

Zelazny, Roger. *Eye of Cat*. New York: Simon and Schuster, 1982.

—. *He Who Shapes*. New York: TOR, 1965.

—. "Kjwalll'kje'k'koothaïlll'kje'k'. *An Exaltation of Stars*. Edited by Terry Carr. New York: Simon and Schuster, 1973. 71–140.

Index